THEATRE LANGUAGE

THEATRE LANGUAGE

A DICTIONARY OF TERMS IN ENGLISH

OF THE DRAMA AND STAGE

FROM MEDIEVAL TO MODERN TIMES

BY

WALTER PARKER BOWMAN

AND

ROBERT HAMILTON BALL

THEATRE ARTS BOOKS   NEW YORK

© 1961 by Theatre Arts Books

Library of Congress Catalog Card Number: 60-10495

Second Printing, 1976

Designed by Owen Scott

Published by Theatre Arts Books
333 Sixth Avenue
New York 14, N. Y.

Printed in the United States of America

TO ERNA AND ESTHER
ASSOCIATE PRODUCERS

PREFACE

Theatre Language, within the limits to be noted, is an attempt to select and define the words and phrases which constitute the vocabulary of the "legitimate" drama and stage in the United States and Great Britain. The considerable and increasing attention given to this terminology in theatrical and linguistic publications during the last thirty years provides evidence of the need for the publication of a book comparable to the lexicons which have long existed in other languages.

In 1919 Brander Matthews, whose very small American glossary appeared in *The Principles of Playmaking* (New York), could observe, "It is a curious thing that these technicalities of the theatre are only a few of them to be found even in the largest and most comprehensive of the dictionaries of the English language, and it is even more curious that they have never been assiduously selected and set in order in a subordinate dictionary of their own." H. L. Mencken, making a similar comment, put a fair sprinkling of stage expressions in *The American Language* (New York, 1919) and stressed the significance of theatre vocabulary as a source of American slang. An Englishman, C. B. Purdom, noted in *Producing Plays* (London and New York, 1930), "There is no good modern dictionary of stage terms"; he described his glossary in that book, some 400 expressions, as "a first attempt at the preparation of such a dictionary." Thereafter, general or specialized glossaries, running to several hundred entries each, came into print, the most substantial of them being those by W. G. Fay (*A Short Glossary of Theatrical Terms,* London and New York, 1930), Edward W. Betts ("A Dictionary of Stage Terms," in *Theatre and Stage,* edited by Harold Downs, London, 1934), Ken Carrington (*Theatricana.* Privately published, Chicago, 1939), and A. O. Gibbons and others for the Strand Electrical Engineering Company (*A Completely New Glossary of Technical Theatrical*

Terms, London, 1947). Manuals and handbooks frequently incorporated explanations, more or less glossarial, of stage terminology; of these mention should be made of *Glossary of Stage Lighting* (New York, 1926) and *A Method of Lighting the Stage* (New York, 1932, revised and amended fourth edition 1958), both by Stanley McCandless; *The Theatre Handbook and Digest of Plays* by Bernard Sobel (New York, 1940, eighth edition revised, 1959), "The New Scene Technician's Handbook" by Philip Barber (in *Producing the Play* by John Gassner, New York, 1941; revised edition, 1953), *A Stage Crew Handbook* by Sol Cornberg and Emmanuel L. Gebauer (New York, 1941; revised edition, 1957), and *The Oxford Companion to the Theatre,* edited by Phyllis Hartnoll (London, 1951; revised edition, 1957). During this period the growth of interest in the subject was also marked by an increase in the number of short notices which appeared in theatrical and linguistic periodicals. Then in 1952, while *Theatre Language* was already well advanced in preparation, there was published the first substantial book specifically devoted to theatre vocabulary, Wilfred Granville's *Theatre Dictionary* (New York), published the same year in London as *A Dictionary of Theatrical Terms.*

These and other compilations have built up a corpus of great value, but *Theatre Language* attempts to carry the study still farther. Hundreds of publications dealing with all aspects of the stage and dramatic literature in the United States and Great Britain have been examined, not only to augment the list of terms but also to provide the authority which derives from repeated citation. Oral usage has of course been taken into account, but we have found it less dependable as a source than the best information in print. Although the expressions treated in the earlier glossaries, handbooks, and specialized literature mentioned above have often been included in the present volume —and we have consulted the major general dictionaries—the scope has been increased and the definitions reworked through independent investigation.

All glossaries run into certain dangers. We have tried to

make our definitions accurate, clear, concise, and fresh, but for
the sake of compression meanings may be oversimplified, fine
distinctions between synonyms ignored, historical changes
omitted, and the differences of opinion among experts insuffi-
ciently stressed. However the most serious and nagging problem
has been the judicious selection of terms within the limits set.
In the gathering of material for *Theatre Language* we have
accumulated twice as many expressions as we have now entered.
"Theatre" is a large term. Inclusion or exclusion has been
determined by our judgment, and that of numerous consultants,
of what will be most useful. The choice will not please every one,
perhaps not any one, of our readers. We shall be grateful for
approval, thankful for criticism and avid for suggestions for
improvement. Nevertheless we have followed certain principles
which readers may wish to know.

We have taken into account the usage of the past 500 years
in the English-speaking countries. By "theatre" is meant the
"legitimate" stage and the dramatic works written for it; and
by exception closely related forms of entertainment such as
musical comedy and to some extent vaudeville, because they
have contributed language to the legitimate theatre. It is im-
possible and in any case unwise to be absolutely rigid, and we
have included primary terms from other forms of theatrical
art: minstrelsy, burlesque, puppetry, ballet, opera, circus, etc.
Thus we have an entry for **grand opera** but not for **aria,** for
ballet but not for **pas de deux.** Nevertheless we have felt that
in some instances it would be absurd not to list entries which
a general reader might reasonably expect to find in a book
with this title: **end man, principal boy, top banana.**

The words and phrases selected for *Theatre Language* belong
to three principal but not always completely distinct classes:
technical terms (**lobsterscope, traveler**), standard non-
technical terms (**soliloquy, understudy**), and slang, jargon,
or cant (**Annie Oakley, the deck**). Foreign terms have been
admitted if there is good evidence that they have been more
or less absorbed into English (**deus ex machina, divertisse-**

ment, Jessner treppen). We generally exclude expressions originating in the theatre which have passed into non-theatrical use (*Wake me up when Kirby dies*); those, new or old, of extremely limited currency (*overfiddling*); and those which we take to be merely ephemeral slang (*pony*). We have avoided names which are copyrighted or trademarked unless they have become common parlance (**klieglight**), and proper names of persons, organizations, and places unless they have become theatre language (**ANTA,** so pronounced, but not the full American National Theatre and Academy).

Two other classes of expression cannot be handled with even so much consistency. One is a large group of combinations and compound words and phrases, either self-explanatory or explicable under one or another of their component words; these do not need principal entries of their own (*ensemble acting, pantomime-extravaganza, to miss a cue*). The other is the even larger group of technical words and phrases which do not really belong to the vocabulary of the theatre, though some specialized glossaries may mention them (*breathing, coefficient of reflection, distemper, mascara, muslin, pulley*). Expressions which fall within these two groups are nevertheless occasionally retained, if they seem to have some special significance (**act call, theatrical hardware**). As for the methods of presentation which we have used, the reader is referred to the "Note" which follows.

We hope this book will be helpful to many groups of people: to the general reader deep in a theatrical detective story, perhaps by Ngaio Marsh; to the theatre-going and play-reading public; to theatrical amateurs; to students, teachers and scholars concerned with the dramatic arts, dramatic literature, and linguistics; even on occasion to members of the theatrical profession. It has, at any rate, provided long hours of work, discussion, and enjoyment to two people whom Dr. Johnson might define as harmless drudges but who prefer to consider themselves devotees of the theatre and of language.

It is an additional pleasure to indicate our indebtedness to a great many individuals for encouragement and help. We cannot possibly thank them all here. Mr. George Freedley, (Curator, Theater Collection, New York Public Library) has long been our wise consultant; twenty years ago he began to collect information for a study of theatre terminology, and later gave us his notes. Mr. Joel E. Rubin (of Kliegl Brothers), has been particularly generous with advice. Dr. A. L. Davis, Mrs. Harry C. Thomson, and Professor William B. Hunter, Jr., have read the manuscript from particular viewpoints to our great profit. Mrs. Ruth R. Mayleas (of ANTA), Professor William G. McCollom, Dr. Philip B. Gove (of the G. and C. Merriam Company), Miss Rosemary Sprague (now Mrs. E. G. W. Bush), Mrs. Elizabeth Reynolds Hapgood, Mr. Norris Houghton, Mr. Walter P. Mazurek, Mr. Donald Oenslager, and Mr. R. Gillespie Williams have given special assistance. Miss Agnes D. Peters expertly prepared the difficult final copy for the printer. And the patience, understanding, and good sense of our publisher, Mr. Robert M. MacGregor, have been invaluable.

We have made use over a number of years of the New York Public Library, the Western Reserve University Libraries, the Queens College Library and the Library of Congress, and are grateful to their staffs for many courtesies.

Having drawn freely on hundreds of printed sources for our raw materials, we must express our gratitude to their authors collectively.

WALTER PARKER BOWMAN
The American University Language Center
ROBERT HAMILTON BALL
Queens College of the City of New York

NOTE

The terms defined in this dictionary, printed in bold face type, are arranged in strict alphabetical order; and this applies whether or not there are word or punctuation breaks and whether the term is one word, a series of words, hyphenated or separate, or an abbreviation. Thus **actors' agent** precedes **actor's Bible** and **layout** is followed by **L.C.**, then **L.C.E.**, **lead** and **lead block.**

When headings consist of more than one term, usually variations of form or spelling, a semicolon divides them and ends the alphabetical order. These variations are arbitrarily, though consistently, arranged, and their placement does not indicate the preference of the editors or of usage. When a term exists in longer and shorter form, the additional, often understood, words are given in parentheses to save repetition.

Small capital letters designate terms to which the reader is further referred. "Which see" is added where the cross reference to the new term and its definition will be particularly helpful for full understanding. Where there are several terms to which the reader might be directed, all of which include the same word used in the same sense, one cross reference is given. It is either to the first of the terms in alphabetical order or to the one where the primary sense of the word is defined.

Italics, aside from their usual uses for foreign words or the titles of works, indicate theatre terms referred to within definitions but not cross referenced and not separately defined in this book, either because their meaning is thought obvious from their context and the terms that are defined, or because they are illustrative variations.

National and period labels signify the places and historical times in which the most common usage occurs. They are not meant to suggest currency only in those places and periods.

A

abandon
In British terminology, an actor's absorption in the spirit of a part—19th century.

Abbot of Misrule (or **Unreason**)
See MISRULE.

above
1. On an UPPER STAGE or in a GALLERY—Elizabethan stage direction. 2. Upstage, upstage of—A stage direction.

abstract setting
A stage setting which is stylized rather than imitative or representational; that is, one which does not attempt to present a stage picture realistically.

academic (or **academical**) **drama**
Collectively, plays produced (and sometimes, written) at schools, colleges, universities—Especially Renaissance. Hence *academic play, academic theatre.* See also EDUCATIONAL THEATRE.

accent lighting
Lighting which stresses certain stage areas. Hence, an *accent light.*

acoustic
1. Usually in the plural, those qualities in the construction or furnishing of an auditorium which affect the transmission and hearing of sound. 2. Pertaining to sound. Also, *acoustical,* as *acoustical effect* (see EFFECT).

across
See GO (*across*).

1

act

1. One of the principal structural divisions of a dramatic work, usually, in a play, from one to five in number. 2. To perform, to represent a character in a dramatic production. Hence *acting* (noun and adjective). 3. In British terminology, said of a dramatic work which is actable, as, It *acts* well. (U.S.: to PLAY well). 4. An independent portion of a performance; a skit— Vaudeville. British (and sometimes U.S.): TURN. 5. An act intermission—Elizabethan. 6. In British terminology, now obsolete, short for ACT-MUSIC.

act call; short form, call

1. A stage manager's summons, relayed by a call boy, to bring actors onstage for the beginning of an act, or for an entrance. See also ACT WARNING. 2. A stage manager's signal, as by means of an *act call bell* or a lowering of lights, to summon patrons to their seats from the lobby or elsewhere.

act-change

A change in the stage setting at the end of an act.

act curtain

A term, used in the U.S. only, for a curtain behind the asbestos curtain, and behind the grand drapery if there is one, closing the proscenium opening, and raised, or less frequently drawn, to reveal the stage during an act or scene. British (and also U.S.): ACT DROP, FRONT CURTAIN, HOUSE CURTAIN.

act division; act-division

The separation of a dramatic composition into its major portions (*i.e.*, acts).

act drop

An ACT CURTAIN.

acted drama

See ACTING DRAMA.

Act for Regulating Theatres
See THEATRES ACT.

acting area
That part of the stage floor available for acting. Also, a specific portion of such an area actually used for acting during all or part of a performance, and hence combinations such as ACTING AREA LIGHT (which see). See also STAGE AREA, STAGE POSITION.

acting area lamp (or **lantern**)
In British terminology, a floodlight fitted with a restricting device and flied, used to illuminate a portion of the acting area from directly overhead.

acting area light (or **spotlight**)
A term, used in the U.S. only, for a spotlight flied, or mounted in the auditorium, on the bridge, or on the first pipe, to illuminate a portion of the acting area from the front or side.

acting clothes; short form, **clothes**
A stage costume—Restoration.

acting company
See COMPANY.

acting (or **acted**) **drama**
A dramatic composition written for stage production; also collectively.

acting edition
The published text of a dramatic composition, with alterations from the standard text to accord with the actualities of stage production, often including staging information.

acting fee
1. A fee payable to the Master of the Revels for licensing a play for performance—16th and 17th centuries. 2. In British terminology, a fee payable to the holder of the copyright for the production of a dramatic piece—19th century.

acting level
A platform or other area for acting, above the stage floor.

acting manager
A British term for a BUSINESS MANAGER.

acting play
1. A play of the ACTING DRAMA (which see). 2. An actable play, one offering considerable acting opportunity.

acting property
A property (a business, character, or hand property) used by an actor.

acting space
The ACTING AREA.

acting text
An ACTING EDITION.

acting time
The running time of a performance, act, or scene.

acting troupe
See TROUPE.

acting version
1. An ACTING EDITION (which see). 2. A production conforming to an acting edition.

act in one (or **two,** or **three**)
See IN ONE, IN TWO, IN THREE.

act intermission
An intermission between acts. British: *act interval.*

act interval
A British term for an ACT INTERMISSION.

action
1. The physical movement of an actor on the stage, or such movements, collectively; pantomime; sometimes, collectively,

not only such movements but also the speaking of the lines (and then sometimes called *stage action*). See also PARALLEL ACTION. 2. The movement or development of the plot of a dramatic composition, or an incident in that movement, as it is revealed or meant to be revealed by actors on the stage through dialogue, physical movement, etc. Short for *dramatic action*.

action cue
A cue calling for some specific action by the cast or crew.

activism
An expressionistic movement tending towards realism. See EXPRESSIONISM, REALISM, for the theatrical significance of these terms.

activity
Acrobatic performance—Elizabethan.

act-music; short forms, (the) **act,** (the) **music**
Formerly, music played between the acts.

actor; (feminine) **actress**
A person who acts, that is, who represents a character in a dramatic production.

actor folk
Collectively, actors.

actor list; actor-list
A roster showing the parts played by the actors in a dramatic production.

actor manager; actor-manager
An actor who has his own company, in which he himself is usually producer and star—Chiefly 19th century.

actor-proof
Said of a role or script which is practically certain to be effective even if badly acted.

actors' agent
A business representative of actors, who arranges jobs for them and handles negotiations and contracts.

actor's Bible, (the)
A publication currently in vogue with actors, such as *Variety* (British: *The Stage*). In U.S. called also *Broadway Bible*.

actors' call
An ACT CALL or an ACT WARNING.

actor-sharer
An actor who owned a share (or part of a share, or more than one share) in an acting company, receiving a proportionate part of the profits in lieu of salary—Elizabethan.

actor's script
A script for the use of an actor in learning his part, commonly made up of SIDES (which see).

actress
Feminine form of ACTOR.

act-tune; short form, (the) **act**
Formerly, music played between the acts.

act-wait
An intermission.

act warning
A stage manager's call to actors and crew to announce the time remaining before the beginning of an act or scene; usually synonymous with ACT CALL.

adaptation
1. A dramatization; a reworking, as of a novel, into dramatic form; or a reworking of an old dramatic entertainment into a new one, as by shortening it. 2. A non-literal translation of a dramatic entertainment into another language.—Hence, in both senses, *adapt, adapter*. 3. In the Stanislavski method, the inner

and outer human means that an actor can use to adjust himself
to other actors in the given circumstances of the play.

ad curtain
Short for ADVERTISEMENT CURTAIN.

additive lighting
The addition of light of one color to light of another color to
produce a final desired color.

adjustable proscenium
An inner proscenium (see FALSE PROSCENIUM) capable of variation in size and position.

adjustment
ADAPTATION (sense 3).

ad lib; ad-lib
To add lines or business not in the script, or songs or music not
in the score, especially as improvisation or extemporization.
Also, an extemporization. Hence, too, *ad-libbing* (noun). Short
for *ad libitum* (Latin, "as one wishes").

administration
Short for BUSINESS ADMINISTRATION. So also *administrative
offices*.

admission
The privilege of entering a theatre; the charge made for a
theatre ticket (also as *admission fee, admission price*). See also
GENERAL-ADMISSION FEE.

adult actor
A mature actor, in contradistinction to a child actor. Hence
adult company, etc.

advance; advances
Short for ADVANCE ROYALTIES, ADVANCE SALE.

advance agent
An ADVANCE MAN.

advance booking
A British term for an ADVANCE ORDER.

advance director
A director sent to a resident company to rehearse it for the appearance of the star and other actors in a *package show* (see under PACKAGE).

advance man
A representative in charge of business arrangements, who precedes a touring company.

advance manager
1. Short for ADVANCE STAGE MANAGER. 2. A British term for an ADVANCE MAN.

advance notice
Preliminary publicity announcing the theatre and time at which a production is to open.

advance order
A reservation forming part of an ADVANCE SALE.

advance representatve
An ADVANCE MAN.

advance royalties; short form, **advance(s)**
Money paid to an author by a producer before a production opens, and deducted from the author's royalties as earned.

advance sale; short form, **advance(s)**
The total ticket sales, either before the opening night or for any single future performance. British: also, *bookings*.

advance stage manager; short form, **advance manager**
A stage manager sent to work with a resident company prior to the arrival of a *package show* (see under PACKAGE).

adventurer
A backer of a theatrical production—Renaissance and Restoration.

advertisement curtain; short form, **ad curtain**
A front curtain, immediately behind the ASBESTOS or ACT DROP, raised just before the performance, and formerly (now rarely) bearing advertisements.

advice-sheet; short form, **advice**
A business contract drawn up by the ADVANCE MAN, the local MANAGER, and the COMPANY MANAGER, to cover the business arrangements for a tour.

aesthetic distance
In the theatre, the maintaining of artistic illusion by sufficient physical or other separation or detachment.

affective memory
In the Stanislavski method, the recollection of feelings that an actor himself has experienced and can use on the stage.

after-money; **aftermoney**
Money received from late patrons for the fourth and fifth acts and divided among patentees and actors—Restoration.

after-piece; **afterpiece**; **aftershow**
A play, dance, etc., especially a short one, performed after the principal offering.

agent
An intermediary who performs certain business services in the theatre world, such as helping actors obtain engagements and helping dramatists find producers for their compositions. Hence *agency*. See ACTORS' AGENT, ADVANCE AGENT, AUTHOR'S AGENT, BOOKING AGENCY, CASTING AGENT, PLAY AGENT, PRESS AGENT, TALENT AGENT, THEATRICAL (or DRAMATIC) AGENT, TICKET AGENCY, and DO THE AGENTS.

agit-prop; **agitprop**
Pertaining to a kind of drama and dramatic technique of social protest with a Marxist outlook—1930s. From "agitation" and "propaganda."

aisle
A passage between blocks of seats. British: GANGWAY. Hence *aisle seat* (a seat next to an aisle).

aisle-sitter
A spectator in an aisle seat, and especially a drama critic. Hence *aisle-sitting*.

alarum
A call to arms by drums or trumpets—Especially Elizabethan, a stage direction. Sometimes *alarums and excursions* (see EXCURSIONS).

alcove
The INNER STAGE (which see)—Elizabethan.

alive
See KEEP ALIVE, LIVE.

allegory
A dramatic work or a portion of one, expressing meaning metaphorically, as by means of personification and symbolism; for example, the medieval morality play. Hence *allegorical,* etc.

alley
See FOP'S ALLEY, SHUBERT ALLEY, TIN PAN ALLEY.

all-star
Said, especially in theatrical publicity, of a production in which star actors play all, or many, of the parts; as, an *all-star cast,* an *all-star revival.*

alternate
1. One of two actors who alternate in a specific role. 2. An understudy.

alternating cast
A cast which interchanges with another, usually the regular, cast.

10

aluminum powder
A silvery powder, used to give the appearance of gray hair.

amateur
A person who acts without pay; sometimes used in ridicule to mean "not of high caliber"; in full, *amateur actor.* Hence such combinations as *amateur company, amateur performance, amateur theatre,* etc.

amphitheatre
1. An auditorium, outdoors or indoors, circular, semicircular, or elliptical in shape, in which a central arena is more or less surrounded by rising banks of seats. 2. In British terminology, sometimes the first tier of seats in a gallery, or some other designated seating area in a theatre. Hence *amphitheatre stalls.*

anagnorisis
A recognition of identity leading to a denouement—A Greek word ("recognition") used in English.

and cakes
A supplementary allowance that may be part of an actor's contract, the words meaning that the manager supplies board or the money for it.

and Co.
And the rest of the company—A phrase, 19th and early 20th centuries, following the name of the star in the billing.

angel
A person who invests in a prospective production, a backer. Also, to make such an investment.

Annie Oakley
A free admission PASS. Named for the American markswoman, whose full name was Phoebe Anne Oakley Mozee Butler (1860–1926), presumably because the holes punched in tickets resemble the holes Annie Oakley shot through targets.

Annual, (the)
In British terminology, the yearly production of a CHRISTMAS PANTOMIME.

ANTA
Abbreviation of *American National Theatre and Academy,* a privately supported, Congressionally chartered organization founded in 1935 for the encouragement of "the best in the theatre, both professional and non-professional."

antagonist
A principal role, opposed to that of the PROTAGONIST (HERO).

antelude
A short dramatic piece played before the principal piece.

anti-climax
A point in a dramatic piece, after the climax, which may emphasize the meaning of the climax by some lesser tension, or may merely lessen the effect of the climax, sometimes to absurdity.

anti-masque; ante- (anti-, antic-, antick-)
   masque or **mask**
A grotesque element, usually a dance by professional performers, introduced before or during a masque—Chiefly first half of 17th century. Hence *antick-masquer.*

apart
At one side, at a distance; an aside—A stage direction.

ape
To steal lines or business belonging to another actor—Chiefly Vaudeville. Also, an actor who so steals.

appear
To act, as, to *appear* in a play or a part. Hence (*stage* or *theatrical*) *appearance*. See also IN ORDER OF THEIR APPEARANCE, *appear opposite* (under PLAY OPPOSITE).

12

applaud
To indicate approval, when one is a spectator, by hand-clapping or otherwise. So also *applause,* etc.

apprentice
A person who serves without pay in an acting company in order to learn about acting (or other aspects of theatrical work). Hence *apprentice actor.* In Elizabethan times, apprentices were usually assigned to women's roles.

approach
To move nearer another actor. Also, movement towards another actor.

apron
1. The forestage, the part of the stage floor in front of the curtain line. Called also *apron-piece, apron-stage.* 2. The trim under a sill. 3. A canvas to mask a fly gallery. 4. A U-shaped flap in a canvas scenic piece.

aquatic drama
A spectacular entertainment played on a stage equipped with water tanks in which mimic sea battles or other events at sea could be represented; also collectively—First half of 19th century. Called also NAUTICAL DRAMA, TANK SPECTACLE, etc.

arbor
See COUNTERWEIGHT SYSTEM.

arc; arc lamp; arc-lamp; arc spotlight
Short for CARBON ARC SPOTLIGHT. Hence *arc-lighting.* British: Also, *arc-lantern.*

arch
1. An opening in a piece of scenery, representing an arch or a space of some other shape intended to remain empty or to be filled with a door, a window, or the like. 2. A flat in the form of an arch. Called also *arch flat.* 3. See PROSCENIUM ARCH. 4. In combination, shaped like an arch, as, an *arch border.*

architectural setting
A setting composed of massive structures; a formal or sculptured setting (see FORMAL). Hence also *architectural stage.*

archway
A flat with an arch opening.

arena
1. A space more or less circular, in the center of a theatre.
2. Said of a theatre without a proscenium, and commonly without curtains, in which the spectators' seats, usually rising in tiers, wholly or partially surround the acting area, which may be the theatre floor, or a platform or platforms. Hence *arena production, arena stage,* etc.

arena floodlight; arena lantern
In British terminology, a hanging floodlight with an especially wide beam angle, used to illuminate large portions of the stage.

Are you decent?
"Are you dressed to receive visitors?"—Query made at a dressing-room door before entering.

argentine
A metal alloy, resembling silver, used in scene-building to simulate window glass.

Arlequin
Formerly, variant spelling of HARLEQUIN.

arm cyclorama
A folding cyclorama in three curtains hung from battens, one running across the stage at the back and the other two running from the back downstage at the sides.

Armenian bole; short form, bole
A reddish powder, used in making up for sunburn effects.

arrange
To adapt a score for orchestral use. See ARRANGER.

arranger
A person who helps a composer write and orchestrate a score for a musical comedy, a revue, or a play with music. See ARRANGE.

arras
1. A drape curtain loosely suspended across a stage. Hence *arras setting, arras stage,* etc. 2. A curtain (tapestry) used to screen the inner stage, or serving as a wall hanging or as a temporary traverse—Elizabethan.

artificial comedy
A comedy portraying sophisticated society; often synonymous with HIGH COMEDY or COMEDY OF MANNERS.

artist; artiste
An actor or performer of either sex.

artist-in-residence
A person from the professional theatre, employed full-time for a specified period to train university students in acting and other theatre arts.

art theatre
A type of non-commercial theatre emphasizing certain artistic purposes, such as theatricalism rather than naturalism, freedom for experimentation in design, presentation, and script; often, a LITTLE THEATRE (which see).

as
In the role of.

asbestos curtain; asbestos drop; short form,
    (the) **asbestos**
The FIREPROOF CURTAIN. British: FIRE(PROOF) CURTAIN, IRON CURTAIN, SAFETY CURTAIN.

Asbestos going up!
An act warning, five minutes before the rise of the curtain.

ascension
See MAKE AN ASCENSION.

ashcan
In British terminology, a footlight unit in a compartment.

aside
A speech, a monologue, usually fairly short, to convey a character's thoughts or other information to the audience, while in the presence of other characters some or all of whom are supposed not to overhear him—A stage convention, and frequently a stage direction.

A.S.M.; ASM
British abbreviation of ASSISTANT STAGE MANAGER.

Asphaleia stage
A stage of iron, with metal cables and a hydraulic lifting system, used to render a theatre fireproof; developed in Austria-Hungary—Late 19th century. Hence, the *Asphaleian system*, a mechanical system using such a stage.

assistant stage manager; British abbreviation, A.S.M.
A stage manager's general helper, who checks properties and equipment, assembles cast and crew, calls time for actors, supervises the curtain raising, etc. In British usage, he also helps direct the setting of the stage, calls actors, and usually prompts.

at back
See BACK.

at half check
See CHECK.

athletic droll
A British term for a knockabout comedian.

at leisure
See AT LIBERTY.

16

at liberty
Having no current acting engagement, out of work, available for casting. An actor is also said to be *available* (U.S.), *at leisure* (chiefly British), *resting*.

atmosphere
The mood, the general emotional quality, of all or part of a dramatic piece or of its representation. Hence (of lighting, scenery, etc., created to establish a mood) *atmospheric*, as *atmospheric lighting*. See also PLAY OF ATMOSPHERE.

atmospheric scenery
Scenery intended to produce a special emotional effect.

at rise
At the moment when the rising curtain first discloses a scene; said often of the relative positions of actors at such a moment.

attendant
A theatrical employee, as, an assistant to the box-office treasurer, or (in British usage) an usher.

attiring-
See TIRE, TIRING HOUSE, and TIRING-ROOM.

attraction
Any production, but especially one which has proved itself successful.

audience
Collectively, hearers; by extension, spectators. Also as *theatrical audience*, etc.

audience-proof
Said of a production that is thought to be certain of success.

audition
1. A try-out hearing, usually competitive, of an actor or other performer seeking employment. Hence, to *audition for*, to be *auditioned*. 2. A reading aloud of a dramatic work to prospective investors.

17

auditor
A member of an audience.

auditorium
A place for listeners, for spectators, as in a theatre building; a theatre building. Plural, *auditoriums* or *auditoria*.

auditory
A term, now rare, for the following: An auditorium, a place for auditors; an audience in an auditorium; of, pertaining to, or belonging to an auditorium or audience.

Augustan drama
The English neo-classic drama, and especially the tragedy, of the reign of Queen Anne, or of a somewhat longer period from the late 17th through the early 18th centuries. Named for a period of literary excellence in ancient Rome.

author
1. The writer of a dramatic composition, a dramatist, a playwright. 2. A call by the audience, after a successful opening performance, to summon the dramatist to the stage for applause.

author's agent
A PLAY AGENT.

author's night
A benefit night, traditionally the third night of a production, the proceeds of which were given to the dramatist—Restoration and 18th century.

author's scene sketch
A dramatist's instructions, giving the production information needed to stage a scene.

author's theatre
In British terminology, a theatre producing a play to which the public is attracted by the name of the author rather than by the names of the cast.

auto(matic) colour change; short form, **auto**
A British term for a COLOR BOOMERANG.

auto-transformer dimmer
A dimmer controlled by a lever which touches contact points and passes a magnetically induced current from a coil to a lighting circuit. British: *choke dimmer, plus and minus dimmer, tapped transformer dimmer, variable transformer* (or *load*) *dimmer* (which is also U.S.).

auxiliary
In British terminology, a visiting star playing with a provincial stock company—19th century.

available
See AT LIBERTY.

avant garde; avant-garde
Any fresh leadership in theatrical production, but more especially a realistic movement in England in the latter half of the 19th century and a movement towards greater freedom in France in the first half of the 20th century—A French expression ("advanced guard," "vanguard") used in English. Often italicized.

away
See GET-AWAY NIGHT; TAKE IT AWAY; THROW AWAY.

B

baby spotlight
A small spotlight used at a short distance to give sharp illumination to an actor's face or to a limited portion of the acting area.

back
1. To invest in a prospective production. 2. Short for BACK STAGE. 3. *At back:* Against the stage back wall. 4. See TRY BACK.

back batten
In British terminology, a strip light used to light a backdrop.

back cloth; back-cloth; backcloth
A term, chiefly British, for a BACK DROP.

back drop; back-drop; backdrop
A large curtain, usually painted to represent the sky, a landscape, or some other background, dropped upstage to form the back of a wing set and to mask the backstage space; now commonly supplanted by a cyclorama. British: Usually *back cloth*.

backer
A person who invests in a prospective production; an angel.

backflap (hinge)
A PIN HINGE capable of being turned back on itself, used to join flats.

back flat
A flat used at the back of the stage.

background scene
An expository scene in which the events and dialogue indicate the time, the place, or other information needed by the spectator.

backing
1. Financial support for a production. See BACK (sense 1).
2. A flat or scenic cloth visible through an opening such as a door, used to mask the offstage space and to complete the setting. More specifically, an *exterior backing*, a *housetop backing*, a *sky backing*, a *window backing*, etc. Hence also *backing cloth*, *backing flat*.

backing light
A low-wattage light, used to give diffused illumination to the space beyond openings such as doors, and placed behind, or less often in front of, a backing. Hence *backing strip light*.

back lighting; back-lighting; backlighting
The illumination of a scene from the back of the stage.

back of the house
The parts of the theatre behind the proscenium, or behind the stage setting.

back-piece
A wig for the back of the head only.

back scene
Scenery at the back of the stage, behind other scenery, as, a backdrop or (formerly) a back shutter.

back shutter; back-shutter; backshutter
A SHUTTER (which see) used at the back of the stage—17th century.

back stage; back-stage; backstage; short form, **back**
1. Collectively, the parts of the theatre which lie behind the proscenium arch (or behind the back wall of the stage setting),

including the stage, the workshops, the dressing rooms, and the areas and spaces beside, above, or under the stage, etc.; or some portion thereof, particularly the dressing rooms (see GO BACKSTAGE). Hence *backstage gossip*, etc. 2. UP STAGE (which see).

back wall
1. The rear wall of the stage. 2. The rear wall of a stage setting.

bad box office
Said of a production unsuccessful in its appeal to the public, having a poor run.

bad join
1. An unsatisfactory joining of two flats. 2. An unsatisfactory blending of make-up with the front of a wig.

bad laugh
An audience's laugh at the wrong moment.

baffle
1. A sheet of metal or other material used in a lighting unit, or in a setting, to limit light spill. 2. A board, or sheet of other material, used in sound equipment to limit echo. Short for *baffle board*.

bag
To CLEW (sense 2).

bail
Collectively, small brass balls set in sockets in the front edge of a stage door, to catch on the door frame and serve as latches to keep the door from swinging.

baize
See GREEN.

balance
The equalization of the stage picture, composition, and action, so that the position and movements of the actors, the archi-

tectural masses, the furniture, the color, the light, etc., are most effectively placed in unobtrusive well-proportioned relationship. Hence *balancing*.

balcony

1. A seating area above the orchestra section of the auditorium. Sometimes a part of this area, particularly its front, as a location for equipment (hence *balcony lighting*). British: DRESS or UPPER CIRCLE, GALLERY, and by exception BALCONY STALL. 2. An elevated platform with a railing, used in a stage setting. 3. A TARRAS (which see) with or without a CHAMBER (which see)— Elizabethan. 4. See PROSCENIUM BALCONY—Restoration and 18th century.

balcony box

A metal enclosure for a balcony spotlight. British: *cage*.

balcony front

The vertical front face of a BALCONY (sense 1); a compartment in or fastened to such a face to hold spotlights (*balcony front lights, balcony spotlights*).

balcony stage; balcony-stage

The balcony, when used for a playing area— Elizabethan.

balcony stall

In British terminology, a stall in the front rows of the DRESS CIRCLE.

balcony tray

A metal pan under a balcony spotlight.

bald-headed row

The front row of seats in the orchestra, formerly at girlie shows the most desirable seats for elderly playboys.

ballad

A song, usually simple, sentimental, short, and narrative— Musical comedy. But see also BALLAD OPERA.

ballad-farce
A BALLAD OPERA.

ballad opera; ballad-opera
A light satirical comedy, consisting of dialogue in verse or prose and songs set to popular and folk tunes, burlesquing Italian opera—18th and early 19th centuries. Often called *ballad-farce*.

ballerina
A female dancer, now especially in ballet and usually a star. Hence *prima ballerina*. Plural *ballerinas* or *ballerine*.

ballet
An artistic theatrical dance, especially a *ballet d'action* (French, "ballet of action") performed by a group and telling a story in pantomime with musical accompaniment, either as an entertainment by itself or as a *ballet divertissement* (French, "ballet interlude") introduced into some other entertainment; also, collectively, such dances. A troupe which dances in ballet. Also, to dance in or express by ballet. Hence *ballet dancer, ballet master* (or *maître de ballet*), *ballet stage*, etc.

balloon
In acting, to forget one's lines or business. British: *make an ascension*, etc.

banana
A burlesque comedian—Musical comedy, etc.

band
A British term for an ORCHESTRA (sense 2).

band room; band-room
In British terminology, a music room, a room, usually under the stage, for the relaxation of the musicians of the orchestra.

bank
1. A section of seats in a theatre, especially a sloping section.
2. A group of lighting units or dimmers arranged in rows.

Hence COLOR BANK, etc.—In both senses, to arrange or to be arranged in this manner.

banns, bans
Public announcements in advance of a performance—Medieval.

bar
In British terminology, short for BARREL.

bar bell
In British terminology, a bell used to summon members of the audience from a bar or other place for the rise of the curtain.

bare stage
A stage without any scenic decoration.

barker
A person who is employed (especially at an entrance) to attract patrons by loudly advertising a side-show or the like—Now chiefly Circus and Carnivals. Hence, to *bark*.

barn door shutter
A spotlight shutter consisting of two or more doors which may be adjusted to vary the size and shape of the beam opening horizontally and vertically.

barnstorm
To tour, playing in barns or other such simple auditoriums, not necessarily with advance arrangements. Hence *barnstormer, barnstorming* (noun). Formerly, in British terminology, to ham, to rant.

barn theatre
A barn converted into a theatre.

barrel; short form, **bar**
1. In British usage, a pipe batten (see BATTEN). 2. A perforated pipe used in producing stage effects, as, a RAIN BARREL, a STEAM BARREL.

barrel clamp (or **clip** or **grip**)
A British term for a PIPE CLAMP (which see).

barrel loft; barrel-loft
A space above the GRIDIRON for drums on which fly lines were coiled—19th century.

barrier
An entertainment in which dialogue accompanied a mock tournament—Renaissance.

basement
A CELLAR (which see). Called also *stage basement*.

basic situation
The central dramatic situation in a play.

basket (box)
Formerly, in British terminology, a private box separated from other seating areas by a lattice or screen.

bat
1. Short for BATTEN. 2. Harlequin's wand.

batten; short form, **bat**
A narrow strip of wood used to make or reinforce the frame of a flat, to fasten flats together, to stiffen a drop, to suspend a hanging piece of scenery or equipment, etc. A length of metal pipe is sometimes used for the latter purpose, called a *batten*, or (U.S.) *pipe batten*, or (British) BARREL; the four lighting battens are numbered from front to rear, FIRST PIPE (British: *number one batten*), etc. In British usage, *batten* can also mean a strip light or border light; see ELECTRIC BATTEN. Also, to fasten a batten to a scenic piece. British: *batten out* (and hence the noun *battening-out*).

batten clamp
Any clamp used to fasten a lighting unit or a scenic piece to a batten, or to fasten two battens together. See PIPE CLAMP.

batten floodlight
In British terminology, a floodlight mounted on a pipe batten
(see BATTEN).

battening batten
A batten used to stiffen a flat.

batten light
In British terminology, a border light or strip light.

batten ring
A ring with a set-screw to slip over a batten, used for fastening
a batten trimming chain.

batten trimming chain; short forms, trim
  (or trimming) chain
A chain with a batten ring and snap, used to fasten a batten to
a scenic piece.

bay
Chiefly in British usage, short for SCENERY BAY.

beam
1. A piece of timber used in theatre construction, as across the
top of the stage, or supporting a platform in a stage setting.
2. Said of scenic pieces that simulate the appearance of such a
timber, as, a *beam border*. 3. Collectively, light rays. 4. A recess
in the ceiling of an auditorium, often a hollowed timber, used
for concealment of front lighting. Hence *beam (front) light,*
beam spotlight.

bearer
A batten to which scenery may be tied, or on which it may rest,
during transportation by truck.

bedroom farce
A farce in which a risqué bedroom scene is exploited.

beginner
An actor who appears in the opening scene of a performance or act.

Beginners, please!
In British usage, a call to summon the actors to take their positions on the stage when the curtain is about to rise. U.S.: PLACES!

belaying pin
A peg of wood or metal used to belay (fasten) a line to a PIN RAIL.

bell
Any electric bell used to give a signal to spectators (as *lobby bell, lounge bell*) or to theatre personnel and actors (as *act call bell*, PROMPT-BELL). Hence *bell board*.

belly-laugh
A hearty laugh, as at broad comedy.

below
1. Downstage, downstage of—A stage direction. 2. Under the stage—Elizabethan stage direction.

ben
Formerly, short for BENEFIT.

bench
A long seat for several spectators with or without a back or separating arm rests.

bends
See DO THE BENDS.

benefit; short form (formerly), **ben**
A theatrical performance, the profits of which are given to some cause or person. Hence *benefit night, benefit performance, benefit show.*

bespeak (performance)
In British terminology, a performance spoken for (*i.e.*, supported by) a wealthy patron, a school, etc.—19th century. The individual or group thus subsidizing the performance could choose the play and could dispose of the tickets by sale or gift.

between-acts
A vaudeville specialty act between the acts of a dramatic piece.

between engagements
Unemployed as an actor.

between the acts
In an act intermission.

Bible-historics
A term of modern scholarship for MIRACLE and MYSTERY PLAYS and other Medieval drama based on Christian Scripture.

big-head
In British terminology, a large mask covering the head, sometimes to caricature a prominent politician—Pantomime (sense 2), especially 19th century.

big name
A performer who obtains star billing, whose name attracts the public, a headliner. Hence *big-name actor*, etc.

Big Stem; short form, (the) **Stem**
Broadway, the principal avenue in the New York theatre district.

big time, (the)
A circuit of theatres giving two performances daily—Vaudeville. By extension, that part of the theatre world which is especially successful with the public. Hence *big-time performer*, etc.

bill
1. A playbill, a theatrical advertisement, such as a handbill or poster; formerly, and now infrequently, a program distributed

bill board

in a theatre. Also, to advertise a theatrical production by means of such bills. 2. A program, in the sense of items to be performed—Especially, Vaudeville. 3. An ACT (sense 2).

bill board; billboard
A board on which a theatrical advertisement may be posted; the advertisement itself.

bill board pass; bill pass
A free admission pass given to a person who permits the display of theatrical advertising on his property.

billing
A notice, posted inside or outside a theatre or distributed by hand, advertising a production, as by title, author, cast, etc. Also, mention or placement in such a notice, as *star billing*, *top billing*.

bill inspector
In British terminology, a person charged with the distribution of theatrical BILLS (sense 1).

bird
See DICKY BIRD, GET THE BIRD.

bird's nest
Crepe wool formed to serve as a beard.

bit
1. A very minor speaking or silent role. Hence *bit actor*, *bit part*. 2. A small portion of dialogue. 3. A burlesque sketch.

bite cues
In acting, to interrupt another's speech or to deliver one's cues too unemphatically. Hence *cue biter*.

biz
Short for *business*, especially in the form SHOW BIZ.

black, (the)
A British term for the forestage, the apron.

black-face; blackface
A face covered by black make-up material (as, burnt cork); the material itself; an actor wearing it. Hence *black-faced acting*, etc.

black light
Ultra-violet light, used to illuminate fluorescent material.

black out; black-out; blackout
1. To darken a stage suddenly, enhancing the effect of stage action and permitting a swift change of scenery. Hence, the darkening of a stage as a result of such a blackout. 2. To loosen a lamp bulb so that it no longer gives light.

black-out skit
A skit building up to end in a blackout on the CURTAIN LINE (sense 2)—U.S. Revue and Vaudeville. British: *Variety turn*, etc.

black-out switch
A master switch for the simultaneous extinction of all stage lights.

black pencil
A pencil-shaped stick of grease paint.

black up
To put on blackface make-up.

black wax
A make-up material for concealing teeth.

bladder
An inflated bag used for low-comedy thwackings, etc.

blank
A flat without decoration, used as a wing in an exterior setting.

blend
1. To smooth out make-up. 2. To dry-brush freshly painted scenery, so that two colors are irregularly smoothed together, avoiding color monotony. 3. To adjust body movements to those of other actors for a more harmonious effect. Hence, to

blender (wig)

blend in. 4. To adjust stage lighting, so as to favor an even illumination as an actor passes from one stage area to another.

blender (wig)
A wig with a flesh-colored band in front which receives the same make-up as the forehead.

blending powder
A face powder used for blending make-up colors, and for a dry make-up foundation.

blinder
1. In a sense now uncommon: One of several lights outside the proscenium arch, shining into the faces of the audience, used to conceal the stage during scene-shifting while the curtain remains up. 2. A disc in a lighting unit used to eliminate rays which cannot be directed at a suitable angle.

blind seat
A seat from which a spectator can see only part of the stage.

block
1. A wood or steel frame, in which turn one or more pulleys to take fly lines. 2. A number of theatre seats, taken together.

block out
To work out the principal business, positions, and movements of actors, including their entrances and exits, during rehearsals. A planning of this kind; also as *blocking* (*-out*).

blood-and-thunder play
A play with a violent plot running to rant and bloodshed.

blood tub; blood-tub
Formerly, in British terminology, a theatre producing lurid and bloody dramas.

bloomer
An obsolete term for an utter failure, a FLOP.

blow

1. In acting, to forget one's lines or business, as, to *blow the scene*, to *blow up*. British: *make an ascension*, etc. 2. To leave the cast during the run of a show; especially, to break an acting engagement, as, to *blow the show*.

blower

A machine with a fan used for wind effects.

blue

1. Pertaining to indecent or risqué lines, situations, or business. 2. A British term for a plain sky border (see BORDER)—19th century.

blue law

A term, used in the U.S. only (usually in the plural), for a law, especially a state or municipal statute, severely restricting theatrical activity, as by prohibiting Sunday performances.

B.O.

Abbreviation of BOX OFFICE.

board

1. In the plural, a stage, as, to *walk* (or *tread*) *the boards* (to act on a stage). 2. Short for SWITCHBOARD. 3. A box-office ticket rack. 4. In British terminology, a placard carried onstage to convey a notice or a bit of dialogue, used to evade the LICENSING ACT (which see)—19th century. For an earlier use of such a device, with a different purpose, see TITLE BOARD. 5. Short for CALL BOARD. 6. A theatre advertisement, such as a poster. 7. Collectively, the administrative officials of a theatre.

(See also the combinations of SWITCHBOARD, with which the combinations of *board* are almost always interchangeable.)

Board of Green Cloth; short form, **Green Cloth**

Collectively, the officials charged with the responsibility for producing entertainments at court—Restoration.

boat-show

A showboat; a dramatic show on a showboat; formerly also a

boat truck

circus, vaudeville entertainment, etc., on a boat, in contradistinction to a dramatic show.

boat truck

In British terminology, a SCENERY WAGON. Originally used to support a stage boat behind a sea row, a type of GROUND ROW.

bobbinet(te)

Short for *theatrical bobbinet* (see THEATRICAL GAUZE).

body movement

The movement of an actor's body without a change in his stage position.

body position

The position of an actor's body, considered as a turning towards or away from the front of the stage.

boff

1. A box office; by extension, box-office appeal, drawing power, and hence (of a production, of theatre business) tremendously successful—Also in the forms *boffo* and *boffola*. 2. A hearty laugh, especially one even heartier than a belly-laugh, and usually in the form *boffo*.

bogie

A British term for a SCENERY WAGON.

bole

Short for ARMENIAN BOLE.

bones

Engraved metal tokens giving free admission to actors' guests —18th century.

bone yard; boneyard

A storage house for scenery.

boo

A word called out by audiences to show disapproval (as, of acting); a cry of "Boo." Also, to call out this word.

book

1. To engage, to contract for, a production, a theatre, the services of a company or an actor, etc. Hence *booking* (noun), *booked up* (having a full schedule of acting engagements). 2. In British terminology, to buy a theatre ticket or reserve a place, as, to *book* a seat. Hence *booked up* (of a theatre, sold out), *booking* (noun). 3. A play script or manuscript, especially one used as a prompt copy; also short for PLAY BOOK (a near equivalent of SCRIPT). See also HOLD THE BOOK, ON THE BOOK. 4. The libretto or text, without the lyrics, of a musical comedy, operetta, or the like. 5. To hinge two flats or the like so that they may be folded or used as one piece. Hence short for BOOK(ED) CEILING (or FLAT, or WING).

book ceiling

A ceiling in two pieces, booked (hinged) to fold lengthwise so as to make its handling in the flies easier.

book flat; book-flat; bookflat

A term, chiefly British, for a TWO-FOLD.

book holder; bookholder

A prompter—Elizabethan.

booking

1. See BOOK. 2. In the plural, in British terminology, the total advance sale of tickets.

booking agency

A business office where touring engagements are arranged. Hence *booking agent, booking clerk.*

booking office

A British term for a TICKET AGENCY. Hence *booking clerk.*

book-keeper; bookkeeper

1. A member of a theatrical company serving as librarian, and sometimes also as book holder (prompter)—Elizabethan. 2. A prompter; also, a stage manager—Restoration.

book number
A musical score or dance which advances the action of a show
—Musical comedy, etc.

book show
A musical show with a BOOK (sense 4), as, a musical comedy
in contradistinction to a revue.

book wing; book-wing; bookwing
A British term for the following: 1. A two-fold wing (see
TWO-FOLD. 2. A wing, usually one of four, mounted on a spindle
extending below the stage, where a system of wheels and ropes
permitted the rotation of wings for scene-changes—19th century.

boom
1. Short for BOOMERANG (sense 1). 2. A batten suspended horizontally across the stage. 3. A light suspended from a vertical
or horizontal batten. Hence *boom flood, boom spot.*

boom arm
A metal arm fastened horizontally to a BOOMERANG (sense 1)
to support a lighting unit.

boomerang; short form, **boom**
1. A pipe or other batten used to hold lighting units, especially
such a pipe placed vertically in the wings. 2. A mobile platform
for scene-painting. 3. Short for COLOR BOOMERANG.

boot
An alternative British term for a SLOAT.

booth
A place, usually enclosed and at the back of the auditorium,
from which an electrician can operate lighting and sound
equipment.

booth spotlight lighting
Illumination by means of a follow spotlight, normally from a
booth at the back of the theatre.

booth stage (or **theatre**)
A temporary outdoor stage, as in a market-place; a street stage.

Boots
A nickname for a tragedian. See COTHURNUS.

border
1. A strip of curtain stretched horizontally across the front top of the stage behind the proscenium arch, fastened to a batten, and flied, used to form the top of a setting and mask the flies and lights. When several are used, they are often numbered towards the upstage area (*first border*, *second border*, etc.) or named for the scenes painted on them (*foliage border*, *sky border*, etc.). 2. Short for BORDER LIGHT.

border batten
A batten to which a BORDER (in either sense) is fastened.

border light; borderlight; short form, **border**
A strip of lights used to give general illumination and color to the stage from above, mounted in a metal trough or compartments, and hung parallel to the proscenium arch behind a border. British: (*compartment* or *magazine* or ELECTRIC) BATTEN.

borderstrip
A BORDER LIGHT.

born in a dressing room (or **trunk**)
Born into an acting family. British: Also, *born in a property basket.*

borscht circuit
A theatre circuit of small hotels in the Catskill mountains in the state of New York—Named for a Russian soup (variously spelled) which is much liked by Jewish patrons. The initial letters are sometimes capitalized.

Boston version
A show produced after the deletion of risqué lines, in order to avoid censorship by municipal authorities such as those in Boston.

bosun's chair
A wooden seat hung by a rope, used by stagehands working aloft.

bottom lighting
In British terminology, the illumination of the lower part of a scene.

bourgeois
As applied to drama and more particularly to tragedy, characterized by middle-class dramatis personae; a development of domestic tragedy—18th and 19th centuries.

bow
To acknowledge, or invite, the applause of an audience, by bending forward at the waist. Also, the gesture involved in so doing. See also MAKE ONE'S BOW, and TAKE A CALL (or BOW).

box
1. An area for spectators, now typically one of several located at the sides of the mezzanine or balcony, more expensive than and railed off from other seating areas, and containing from four to six chairs rather than fixed seats. Hence *box ticket*, DRESS BOX, *upper box*, etc. 2. A ticket-taker's box; also, collectively, the stubs in such a container. 3. See also BALCONY BOX.

box holder; box-holder
1. Formerly, an attendant who collected admission fees, as, a GATHERER (which see). 2. A person who has tickets for the seats in a box.

box interior
A BOX SETTING (which see).

box-keeper; boxkeeper
An attendant in charge of theatre boxes.

box light; box-light
A hanging or standing lamp with reflector and color frame, but no lens, used for general lighting.

box lobby
See LOBBY.

box office; box-office; abbreviation, **B.O.**
An office in a theatre, commonly in the outer lobby, where tickets are sold. Hence *box-office assistant* or *attendant* (British, *box-office clerk*), *box-office treasurer* or *manager* (British, *box-office keeper* or *manager*), *box-office window*. Also, pertaining to the business aspects of theatrical production, as, a *box-office flop* (see FLOP), *box-office receipts* (also as *box office* only). See BAD (and GOOD) BOX OFFICE.

box-office appeal
Drawing power with the public, the power of an actor, author, etc., to attract audiences. Sometimes shortened to *box office*, for which see GOOD BOX OFFICE.

box-office draw
An actor, author, play, etc., able to attract audiences; also, the power to do so.

box-office plan; short form, **plan**
A diagram showing the location of theatre seats, on display at the box office.

box-office poison
An actor, author, play, etc., unable to attract audiences.

box-office statement
A report, usually rendered weekly and usually prepared by the box-office treasurer, informing the business manager, producer, and others of the number of tickets sold for each performance, with relevant data.

box scene; box-scene
A term, chiefly British, for a BOX SET.

box set; box setting
A term, used chiefly in the U.S., for an interior setting in which flats form the back and side walls, and often also the ceiling. British: Usually BOX SCENE.

box teaser
An L-shaped teaser made from a flat, the bottom of which is turned upstage at a right angle to support lights.

boy
1. In the plural, ticket brokers, collectively. 2. See PRINCIPAL BOY and SECOND BOY. 3. A young actor playing a female role—Elizabethan.

boy actor; boy-actor
A male child actor, in contradistinction to an adult actor. Hence *boy company*, which is Elizabethan.

brace
Short for CORNER BRACE, STAGE BRACE.

brace clamp
A clamp which regulates the length of a STAGE BRACE.

brace cleat
A metal cleat fastened to the back of the frame of a flat, with an eye into which a brace hook can be locked.

brace eye
A BRACE CLEAT. British: Also as *bracing eye*.

brace hook
A metal hook at the upper end of a stage brace; it locks into a brace cleat.

brace jack; short form, jack
A wooden triangle, fastened (usually by hinges) to the back of a piece of scenery, and at the lower end weighted or screwed into the stage floor, which is sometimes used in lieu of a STAGE BRACE. British: *French brace*.

brace rail
A British term for a CORNER BRACE.

brace-weight, braceweight
In British terminology, an iron weight which can be fitted over the lower leg of a stage brace as a replacement for a stage screw in a quick change.

bracing eye
A British term for a BRACE CLEAT.

bracket
Any arm-like device used to hold a block, a curtain track, a lamp, etc., to a wall.

bracket handle switchboard
In British terminology, a switchboard on which the dimmers, rotating on a color shaft, are controlled by a handle which can be screwed in and out.

Brady
A seat reserved for a friend of the management. Named for the American theatrical manager William A. Brady (1863–1950).

braggart soldier, braggart captain
The role of a cowardly, boastful soldier, derived from the classical MILES GLORIOSUS (which see)—Renaissance.

brail
In British terminology, to move and fasten a suspended piece of scenery in a new position by means of a special line (a *brail,* a *brail line;* U.S.: GUIDE LINE) running across the usual fly lines. Hence *brailing* (noun). See BREASTED.

brass
See DOUBLE IN BRASS.

bravo!
A shouted word of applause meaning "Excellent!" The Italian forms *brava* (for an actress) and *bravi* (for two or more actors) are also employed.

break
1. In acting, the accidental omission of lines or business. Hence, *make a break.* 2. The end of (or a temporary stopping point in) a performance or rehearsal. Also, to end or stop a performance or rehearsal. 3. See I HOPE YOU BREAK A LEG.

breakaway
Said of scenery, a scene, a property, or a costume which is designed to alter shape while the audience watches. Thus a *breakaway door* collapses when smashed, but is easily reassembled for another performance. British: *break-up, collapse.*

break-down; breakdown
A swift dance—Minstrel shows, and 19th century English Burlesque.

break-down scenery
A scenic piece, such as a practical window, which can be readily detached from other pieces to which it is fastened.

break-even
The point at which income and expenses balance, in the financial handling of a production. British: *get-out.*

breaking
The closing of a run.

breaking point
The moment in a run when the production costs are balanced by the receipts, and the backers begin to receive a return on their investment.

break up
1. To play a joke on a fellow actor so as to interrupt the delivery of his lines. Hence, an interruption from such a joke. 2. Hyphenated: A British term for BREAKAWAY.

breasted
Said of hanging scenery which is moved slightly to another position by means of an extra line. British: *brailed.*

breeches part
A male role (usually that of a young hero) played by an actress—especially 17th and 18th centuries.

bridge
1. Chiefly in British terminology, a section of the stage floor which can be raised or lowered. 2. A gallery, hung, fixed, or on tracks, of adjustable height, beside or above the stage, and especially in front, for the use of stagehands, light operators, scene painters. When temporary, a *fly* (or *flying*) *bridge*. Hence *bridge light, bridge spot,* etc.

bridge position
The position of the batten farthest downstage when used for lights.

bridging
In rehearsing, the director's insertion of explanatory words in an actor's lines so as to make the meaning clearer.

bridle
A line or chain used in flying scenery or equipment, fastened at both ends to a batten, as by means of clips, and with a ring or other device at the center to take a grid line. Hence *bridle chain, bridle ring,* etc. Also, to attach a bridle to a grid line and to scenery or a lighting unit.

brief
A British term for a free admission PASS.

bring the audience to their feet;
bring down the house
To gain the enthusiastic approval of the audience.

bring up the lights
To increase the illumination; antonym of *dim the lights.*

bristle trap
In British terminology, a trap through which an actor can rise and descend by pushing aside bristles or twigs projecting inwards from the edge.

broad
Said of a dramatic piece, an actor, etc.: Obvious in humor, unrestrained; sometimes, indelicate, risqué.

broadside
A term, now rare, for a theatrical advertisement printed on one side of a sheet of paper.

Broadway
The principal avenue running through the theatre district near Times Square in New York City, and so the district, and collectively the theatres on or near this avenue; by extension the commercial theatre of New York. Hence *Broadwayite*. British equivalent: *West End*.

Broadway Bible, (the)
See ACTOR'S BIBLE.

Brodie; Brody
See DO A BRODIE.

broken setting
A DIVIDED SETTING (which see).

broker
An intermediary who performs certain business services in the theatre world, such as helping dramatists find producers for their compositions, helping producers find theatres, selling tickets at a premium over box-office prices, etc. Short for PLAY BROKER, *theatre broker*, TICKET BROKER, etc. Now more frequently called an AGENT.

broker's men
A British term for a pair of comic roles—Pantomime.

Bronx cheer
A noisy jeer, a razzing (see GET THE RASPBERRY). Named for the county and borough in New York City where it originated in the theatre.

brutal
Said of a slow ticket sale.

buffo
Comic, hence a singer of comic roles (as, a *basso buffo*), a comic actor. Plural, *buffi*. Feminine, *buffa* (plural, *buffe*).

buffoon
A clown. Hence *buffoonery*.

build
1. In acting, to prepare for some climax, as by increasing the tempo of one's speech; thus, to *build an entrance*. Hence also a development towards some climax. 2. To develop a rich characterization. 3. To construct scenery. See BUILT.—Hence, for all three senses, *building* (noun).

builder
Short for *scene-builder* (see SCENE).

building
1. See THEATRE BUILDING. 2. See BUILD (all senses).

building crew
A crew comprising flymen, carpenters, painters, electricians, and persons in charge of properties and effects.

built
Said of a scenic piece which is constructed in relief (that is, which is three-dimensional), as, a *built rock*, a *built unit*. Formerly, *built-up*.

bull-dog; bulldog
An iron grip used to fasten one line or cable to another.

bull switch
A MASTER SWITCH.

bunch light; bunchlight; short form, **bunch**
A term, now uncommon, for a row of lamps in an open metal box with a reflector, used as floodlights, mounted on a standard in the wings.

burlesque

1. Originally, a play parodying drama (or other literature) and acting—17th and 18th centuries. Later, a lighter, less literary, more absurd satire, with song and dance—19th century. Now any comic entertainment or revue sketch sharply contrasting contents and presentation, commonly with song and dance, and often embodying satire on public personages and current events. Hence *burlesque play*, etc. See also BURLETTA and EXTRAVAGANZA. 2. A low comedy show featuring girls underdressed and rough, bawdy humor in songs, acts, dances, and sketches of set pattern; also collectively—19th and 20th centuries. Hence *burlesque queen, burlesquer*, etc. 3. A travesty or caricature. Also, to caricature humorously.

burletta

A type of musical entertainment, originally (18th century) a rhymed musical drama akin to comic opera; commonly later 19th century), to evade the LICENSING ACT (which see), any three-act play with at least five (sometimes six) songs, resembling burlesque and extravaganza.

burleycue

A popular variation of BURLESQUE (sense 2).

burner light

A light comprising clustered lamps on standards.

burnt cork

A make-up material for blackening the skin.

business; bus.

Short for SHOW BUSINESS, STAGE BUSINESS.

business administration; short form, administration

Collectively, the officials of a theatre.

business cue

See CUE.

46

business manager
A person charged with handling business matters for a company. British: *acting manager.*

business property
A property required by the script for use by an actor.

business rehearsal
A rehearsal emphasizing stage business.

busk
In British terminology (from BUSKIN), to journey about performing with simple theatrical equipment. Hence *busker, busking* (noun).

buskin
Tragedy, the tragic drama, tragic acting, or the art of acting— A term probably derived from Old French (*brousequin*) or Italian (*borzachino*), meaning a high boot (see COTHURNUS). See also SOCK AND BUSKIN.

butt hinge
See PIN HINGE.

buy
To purchase (theatre tickets). British: to *book* (*a seat*). Hence, a purchase of seats, usually in blocks, by a ticket agency, as, to *make a buy.*

by
A preposition used in programs and advertisements to give credit for participation in a production, as, *Costumes by. . . , Conducted by. . . .*

by-play, byplay
Action on the stage, carried on apart while the main action continues, as by two characters engaging in stage business in dumbshow.

C

C.; C
1. Abbreviation of CENTER (sense 1). 2. The designation, followed by a number, of a flat used to form a rear wall, as, C2. Numbers begin at stage right.

cabaret
A night club, restaurant, or the like, where performers dance and sing; the entertainment so provided (also as *cabaret entertainment*). Hence *cabaret style,* etc.

cable
1. Short for STAGE CABLE. 2. Any heavy rope or wire line.

cable clamp
A clamp used to secure a cable; for example, to attach a borderlight cable to a batten.

cable connector
Short for STAGE CABLE CONNECTOR.

cabtyre
In British terminology, a heavy-duty rubber-covered stage cable.

cackle
In British terminology, dialogue, especially meaningless patter spoken by an actor who forgets his lines. Hence *cackle-chucker* (or *-thrower;* a prompter). *Cackler* is sometimes U.S. for ACTOR.

cage
In British terminology, a metal enclosure for a balcony spotlight. U.S.: *balcony box.*

Cain's (Warehouse)
See GO TO CAIN'S.

cake
See AND CAKES; COFFEE AND CAKE.

calcium (light)
A LIME-LIGHT.

call
1. A notice to actors, etc. Also, to issue a notice. Short for ACT CALL, MATINEE CALL, PHOTOGRAPH CALL, etc. 2. Short for CURTAIN CALL. See also TAKE A CALL.

Call beginners!
A stage manager's order to a call boy to give an ACT CALL (sense 1) before a performance begins.

call board; call-board, short form, board
A backstage bulletin board near the stage door for the posting of notices to the staff and cast.

call boy; call-boy; callboy
A person employed to warn actors, at the stage manager's signal, to be ready to come on stage; now usually replaced in the U.S. by the assistant stage manager.

call door
In British terminology, a proscenium door, used for the entrance and exit of an actor taking a bow—19th century.

call over
In British terminology, a box-office treasurer's telephone call to a booking agency to identify seats sold and unsold.

call the act
To give an act call; also the stage manager's order to a call boy or to the assistant stage manager to do so.

cameo part
A minor role with particularly attractive acting possibilities.

49

camera angle
The angle formed by the deviation of the main lines of a set or of a stage picture from the audience's straight line of vision.

camera performance
A rehearsal at which photographs are taken for publicity purposes. See PHOTO(GRAPH) CALL.

canopy
1. The HEAVENS (which see)— Elizabethan. 2. A curtained recess—Elizabethan.

cantilevered structure
A concealed support behind an overhanging scenic piece onstage, such as a balcony.

canvas
Linen or duck canvas used to cover a flat, a drop, etc. Also to cover a flat with canvas. Hence *canvassing*.

capacity
The total number of seats available for the audience; also as *seating capacity*. Hence *capacity audience* (an audience which fills a theatre), *capacity house* (a theatre which is sold out for a particular performance), etc.

cape-and-sword play
A CLOAK-AND-SWORD PLAY.

capsule
Said of a condensation of a piece of dramatic writing, as, a *capsule play*.

car
A pageant wagon (see PAGEANT).

carbon arc spotlight; short forms, arc (lamp spotlight), carbon spot(light)
A spotlight with two carbon electrodes, giving a brilliant light; formerly used for flooding; now used for effects or for following.

50

carbon dimmer
Formerly, a dimmer operated by pressure on electrodes resting in a mixture of carbon powder and sand.

carbon holder
In a carbon arc spotlight, a device for gripping the carbon electrodes.

carbon spot(light)
Short for CARBON ARC SPOTLIGHT.

card
See ON ONE'S CARD.

career
Short for STAGE CAREER or THEATRICAL CAREER.

caricature
An exaggeration, distortion, or burlesque of characteristics, as in acting or dramatic composition, which is intentionally or unintentionally ludicrous. Also, to exaggerate ridiculously in this way.

Caroline (or Carolan) drama
The English drama of the reign of Charles I (1625–1642).

Carp
A nickname, used in the U.S., for a carpenter.

carpenter
1. The stage carpenter, or one of his assistants. 2. To perform the functions of a PLAY CARPENTER (which see).

carpenter's room (or shop)
A workshop for the making or repairing of scenery, etc.

carpenter's (or carpenter) scene
A front scene or incident to minimize the audience's awareness of preparations (often noisy) for the next scene behind it.

51

carpet cut
In British terminology, a STAGE CUT into which a floor covering, especially the front edge of a ground cloth, may be fastened tightly by means of hinged flaps.

carpet hoist
In the COUNTERWEIGHT SYSTEM of stage rigging, a way of separately counterbalancing a scenic piece, or a property such as a carpet, so that it can be lowered and detached from its lines for use during a performance without the removal of the weights; an extra cradle holding the weights is held aloft by an overhaul line which is tied off while the scenery or property is in use.

carpet pin
A nail which can be driven into the stage floor to hold a grommet fastened to a ground cloth or other floor covering.

Carps
A nickname, used in the U.S., for a carpenter.

carriage
1. See COUNTERWEIGHT SYSTEM, also CHARIOT-AND-POLE SYSTEM.
2. Sometimes, a WAGON STAGE—Medieval.

carriage-and-frame system
See CHARIOT-AND-POLE SYSTEM.

carriage trade
Collectively, theatregoers who are wealthy and fashionable. Hence, a *carriage-trade theatre*, etc.

carrier
A wheel which carries a curtain in a curtain track.

carry
To act so that the audience may see and hear clearly.

carry a scene
To be the acting mainstay of a SCENE (sense 1).

carry-off
An extension of a platform, with steps offstage.

cascade
In British terminology, the grouping of the characters of the harlequinade for the final tableau—Pantomime (sense 2).

cast
1. To assign, or to be assigned, an acting role or acting roles. Hence *casting* (noun). 2. Short for CAST OF CHARACTERS, CAST LIST.

cast-case
Formerly, a box on the wall of the GREEN ROOM, for the posting of a list of actors with the roles assigned them.

casting agent
A person who engages to find actors for a production; he may also be an ACTORS' AGENT (which see).

casting call
A director's announcement of a time and place for the selection of actors for a production.

casting director
A casting agent in charge of subordinate casting agents.

casting office
A bureau which makes available suitable actors for a producer.

cast list; cast-list; short form, **cast**
A list of actors with their roles.

cast of characters; short form, **cast**
Collectively, the actors to whom roles have been assigned; a CAST LIST.

cast to type
See TYPE.

catastasis
The climax of a dramatic work. Plural, *catastases.*

catastrophe
The action which terminates the conflict in a dramatic composition; especially, the final disaster in a tragedy. See DENOUEMENT.

cat call; cat-call; catcall
A noise, originally one like the cry of a cat, uttered, or produced by an instrument, to show disapproval; an instrument for making this sound; a person who uses such an instrument. Also, to make this noise; to indicate disapproval by this noise.

catch
To see (all or part of a performance), especially when one arrives at the theatre just in time to do so, and has a professional purpose; as, to *catch an act.*

catch flies
To pantomime, while acting, so as to divert the attention of the audience inappropriately from other actors.

catch scene
An alternative British term for CAT SCENE (which see)—Pantomime.

catharsis
The emotional purgation or purification in a spectator induced by tragedy—A term formulated by Aristotle, and variously interpreted.

cat (or catch) scene
In British terminology, the next to the last scene in the harlequinade, in which the backcloth opens to change the setting from a dark cavern to a fairy or woodland place—Pantomime (sense 2).

cat-walk; catwalk
A narrow bridge above the auditorium or stage, providing access to stage scenery or lighting units.

cauldron trap
A trap, commonly upstage center and square, through which actors or objects can be made to appear and disappear. Named from its use in the witch scenes in *Macbeth*.

caution notice
A notice printed on the copyright page of a published dramatic work, which warns the public that all rights are subject to permission, and indicates from whom the permission may be secured.

Cavalier drama
Collectively, plays less realistic, more sentimental and genteel, than other plays of the period, appealing to an aristocratic audience—17th century.

C.D.
Abbreviation of CENTER DOOR.

C.E.
Abbreviation of CENTER ENTRANCE.

ceiling
A flat, in one leaf or hinged in two or more leaves, or a cloth, hung horizontally to form the top of an interior set, concealing the flies. Short for CEILING CLOTH, *ceiling piece*.

ceiling border
A border simulating a ceiling, used in lieu of a ceiling cloth or a flat.

ceiling cloth; short form, ceiling
A CLOTH (sense 1) used for a ceiling.

ceiling flipper
A flipper fastened to the front of a ceiling frame to conceal the edge and the gridiron.

ceiling light
A beam light (see BEAM, sense 4).

ceiling piece
See CEILING.

ceiling plate
A piece of metal fastened to the back of a ceiling frame, with a ring to which a line from the gridiron may be attached.

ceiling spotlight
A beam light (see BEAM, sense 4).

cellar
A room or other space under the stage, a basement, used for the operation of equipment (for example, traps), for storage, and formerly for dressing rooms.

censor
To cause a dramatic piece or production to be suppressed or altered by governmental action, when it does not conform to legal requirements (now chiefly bearing on obscenity). A government official charged with this responsibility—although commonly not so titled. Hence also *censorship*, etc.

centage
In British terminology, a local theatre's share in the gross receipts of a touring production, expressed as a percentage.

center; (chiefly British) **centre**
1. A stage position, the middle area of the stage (*center stage* or *center-stage*), or the middle section extended also downstage and upstage—Sometimes, a stage direction. Abbreviation: C. 2. The center of a row of seats, as *fourth row center*. 3. To fix the mind on significant words while reading lines. 4. Short for CENTER LINE.

center door; abbreviation, **C.D.**
An entrance upstage center—Formerly a stage direction.

center door fancy
A decorative entrance, upstage center, for an interior setting.

center entrance; abbreviation, **C.E.**
An entrance upstage center—Sometimes, a stage direction.

center line; center-line; short form, **center;**
 abbreviation, **C.L.**
1. A dividing mark, actual or imaginary, across the middle of the stage from front to rear, to indicate stage positions. British: *centre mark* (or *line*). 2. The middle line or lines (LONG CENTER, SHORT CENTER) in a set of lines used to fly scenery.

center of interest
The point in a stage picture upon which the attention of the audience is meant to rest, shifting with the movements of the actors or for other reasons.

center opening
A CENTER ENTRANCE.

center stage; center-stage
See short form, CENTER (sense 1).

central character (or **figure**)
The protagonist, the hero.

central staging
Staging in the arena style (see ARENA, sense 2).

chairman
A British term for a MASTER OF CEREMONIES—Music hall, chiefly 19th century.

chair warmer
In British terminology, an unresponsive member of the audience.

chamber
1. A recessed part of the upper stage or gallery—Elizabethan.
2. In British terminology, said of a scene or a set: An interior setting, representing a room.

chamber batten
A British term for the FIRST PIPE (which see).

chamber border
A border painted to simulate a room ceiling and cornice.

chambermaid
The role of a female servant, of any soubrette; an actress playing such a role. Hence *singing chambermaid*.

chamois stump; short form, stump
A lining stick (see LINE) tipped with chamois.

channel
A gridiron beam shaped like the letter I.

character
1. One of the dramatis personae, or his name; an actor in such a role. 2. A type of personality portrayed on the stage. See also STAY IN CHARACTER. 3. Short for CHARACTER ACTOR. Thus also *character juvenile, character man, character old woman*, etc.

character actor
An actor who specializes in one or more striking roles which call for characteristics quite different from his own, as the roles of old men.

character-comedy
See COMEDY OF CHARACTER.

characterize
To develop character portrayal. Hence *characterization*.

character part
An acting role calling for emphasis on the characteristic peculiarities of a type (as, the amorous old man, the shrewish woman, the foreigner with an accent).

character property
A property used to emphasize an actor's portrayal of character.

character role
A CHARACTER PART.

chariot-and-pole system
A method of changing scenery—19th century and possibly earlier. Below the stage, on rails, ran a wheeled *chariot* (or *carriage*), above which projected, through a slot in the stage floor, either a *pole* or a *frame*, on which was mounted a wing piece (a flat). Two chariots at each wing position were pulled back and forth by ropes, which were wound on a common shaft, so that one group of wings moved onstage as the other was drawn offstage to be replaced. Called also *carriage-and-frame system*.

chaser
1. A BABY SPOTLIGHT—Early 20th century. 2. Music played at the end of a performance during the audience's departure.

check
1. Command form: Dim the lights (*check your light, check your house*), dim to a blackout (*check out*). Also, dimming. Hence *at half check*. 2. That portion of a ticket which is returned to a patron by a ticket-taker.

checker
A British term for a TICKET TAKER.

checkroom
A CLOAK ROOM.

check taker
A British term for a TICKET TAKER.

chew the scenery
To overact, especially in emotional scenes. Hence also *scene-chewer*.

chief electrician; short form, **electrician**
The person in charge of all the electrical preparations and operations in a production. British: Also, *chief engineer*.

chief engineer
In British terminology, a CHIEF ELECTRICIAN.

child actor; child-actor
A boy or girl actor. More specifically, the feminine form is *child actress*.

children's company
A company of child actors.

children's (or child's) theatre
1. A theatre specializing in entertainments for children. 2. A theatre using only child actors, usually also a children's theatre in the preceding sense.

chimney
1. That part of a magic-lantern housing which provides for the cooling and escape of the hot air currents generated by the lamp. 2. A recess for moving counterweights in the wall at the side of the stage.

china crash
A crash effect, obtained by dropping or pouring pieces of china to simulate the sound of breaking dishes.

chin piece; chinpiece
That portion of an artificial beard which simulates the beard on a man's chin.

Chips
A nickname for a carpenter.

chiseler
An actor who selfishly interferes with the performance of another actor in order to get more attention for himself.

choke dimmer
A British term for an AUTO-TRANSFORMER DIMMER.

choreography; (infrequently) **choregraphy**
The creation and preparation of stage dances, especially ballets.
Hence *choreographer*, to *choreograph*, etc.

chorine
A term used in the U.S. for a chorus girl—Musical comedy.

chorister
A British term for a member of a chorus—Musical comedy.

chorus
1. A group of singers or dancers performing as a unit; group
singing or dancing; a song or part of a song (especially a
refrain) to be sung by more than one person. Hence *choral*,
chorus girl, etc. Also, to sing together in a group. 2. A single
actor providing a commentary on the action of a play—Especially, Elizabethan. A group of actors providing such a commentary. 3. An ENTR'ACTE (sense 2), an *intermedio*—Restoration.

Christmas pantomime; short forms, **panto,**
   pantomime
In British terminology, a PANTOMIME (sense 2) produced annually in the Christmas season; by long-established tradition
the usual name attached to this kind of pantomime, which, however, has flourished in other seasons. Called also the (CHRIST-
MAS) ANNUAL.

Christmas play
A NATIVITY PLAY.

chronicle history play; short forms, **chronicle**
   history (or **play**), **history** (**play**)
A play with a plot based on stirring events in English history
in some period such as a king's reign—Especially, late 16th
century.

61

church theatre
A theatrical company, usually of amateurs, performing in a church building.

cinema
A British term (occasionally U.S. also) for the following: A MOTION PICTURE; a motion picture theatre.

circle
A term, now chiefly British, for a seating area above the orchestra, commonly the DRESS CIRCLE and above it the UPPER CIRCLE. U.S.: MEZZANINE and BALCONY.

circle front spotlight
In British terminology, a spotlight mounted in a compartment at the front of the dress circle. See BALCONY FRONT.

circle stock
Circuit stock (see CIRCUIT).

circuit
1. Collectively, theatres in various towns where a road company regularly plays by prearrangement. Hence *circuit booking*, *circuit stock*, etc. 2. Short for STAGE ELECTRICAL CIRCUIT.

circus
1. An entertainment which has grown from equestrian acts (18th century) to an elaborate combination of animal, clown, freak, and other shows. See also EQUESTRIAN DRAMA. 2. A place for a circus. 3. To reverse a scene or certain pieces of scenery so that the audience will see the other side. Hence also *circusing a scene*. 4. Said of a style of production or a theatre: as, a *circus style*, a *circus theatre*; see ARENA.

circus job
An extravagant publicity effort to promote a show, especially a show which is likely to flop.

citronella circuit
A circuit of summer theatres, so called from the name of an insect repellant. The initial letters are sometimes capitalized.

civic theatre
A permanent theatre or resident theatrical company, fostered and usually subsidized by a municipality for social and cultural rather than commercial reasons; sometimes, any theatre broadly serving a city, a COMMUNITY THEATRE (which see); such theatres, collectively.

C.L.
Abbreviation of CENTER LINE.

clamp
A fastening device of metal, used to hold lines, to hold lights on a pipe batten, etc., and often named for its shape (as, *bridge clamp, C-clamp*).

clap
To show approval by striking the hands together. Hence *clapper, clapping* (noun).

clapper
An effects device, consisting of two leather straps sewn together at one end, which are first pushed apart and then sharply pulled together to simulate the sound of crackling fire.

clap-trap; claptrap
1. An exaggerated and meretricious means used to draw applause, such as a rhetorical delivery of lines, artificial gestures, a sentimental portion of dialogue. Also as *theatrical claptrap*. Hence *clap-trap sentiment*, etc. 2. Formerly, a noise-making device used to stimulate applause.

claque
Collectively, persons employed to applaud. Hence *claqueur*.

classic acting
classic acting
An acting style marked by restraint and formality in the depiction of passion, by polished, stately movement, gesture, and delivery.

classic(al) drama
Greek and Roman drama; drama which imitates Greek or Roman models (see NEO-CLASSIC DRAMA, PSEUDO-CLASSIC DRAMA); drama which has become well established over the years (see STANDARD DRAMA), which possesses literary or other distinction. Hence also a *classic, classic play, classicism,* the *classic theatre,* etc.

class show
A play likely to draw only wealthy spectators, or the intelligentsia.

clean
See GO CLEAN.

clean house
A performance for which all tickets have been sold.

Clear!
A command by the stage manager before the curtain rises, to get stagehands and unneeded actors off the stage. Also as *Clear stage!*

clearance
See EDGE CLEARANCE.

clearer
A property man's assistant who carries properties on and off the stage.

clearing pole
A length of wood with a cross-piece, used to untangle fouled scenery and lines. British: CLEARING STICK.

clearing stick
A British term for a CLEARING POLE.

cleat
A wood or metal device to which a line can be tied, as, a BRACE CLEAT, a STOP CLEAT. Also, to fasten flats together by lines over cleats.

cleat-bar
An amateur's term for a FLY RAIL.

cleat line
A British term for a LASH LINE.

clew
1. A metal device, to which lines can be led from one or more pieces of scenery, and which is controlled by a single line dropped to a counterweight or sandbag, as, a *curtain clew*, a *five-line clew*, etc. Also, to fasten lines with such a device. 2. To maneuver a cloth by drawing it up so that it is folded to half its length and removed from view.

click
Said of a performer, a play, etc.: To gain approval, to be a success. A HIT (which see).

clicker
A term used in the U.S. for a free admission PASS.

climax
A culmination, the point in a dramatic work or one of its parts at which the interest or emotional effect is most intense. In acting, a *rising climax* is marked by quicker movement and a higher pitch of the voice, a *falling climax* by no less suspense but by a seemingly calmer demonstration of intensity.

clinching iron (or **plate**)
A metal plate on which a flat is placed for nailing so that the nail ends are turned back into the wood for strength and safety.

clip

1. A clamp or grip of various types, as, a *hanging clip*. See also BULL-DOG, PIPE CLAMP (*barrel clip*), WIRE ROPE. 2. In the expression, to *clip cues:* To interrupt another actor, intentionally or in forgetfulness, before he has given a speech cue.

cloak-and-sword play

A romantic play, filled with such excitement as duels, intrigue, and near escapes.

cloak room

A room in a theatre where patrons may leave coats and other belongings in the care of an attendant.

close

Short for CLOSE IN (sense 1) or CLOSE THE SHOW.

close in

1. To draw curtains together. Short form, *close*. 2. To turn the body from a full front position towards center stage. 3. Hyphenated: Formerly, a flat used at the side of a setting to piece out the central flats.

closet drama; closet-drama

A play intended or suited for reading rather than for performance; also collectively. Hence *closet dramatist, closet-play*, etc.

close the show

1. To end the run of a show. Short form, *close*. 2. To perform in the last number on a program.

closing notice

A call-board notice to staff and cast of the approaching end of a run.

cloth

1. A material such as canvas or muslin, used in making a curtain, a flat, etc.; a piece of such material, as, a *ceiling cloth*. 2. Chiefly in British usage, a DROP CURTAIN, as, a *mountain cloth*, a *sky cloth*. See also BACK DROP.

cloth border
A BORDER (sense 1) made of canvas.

clothes
See COSTUME.

cloud(ing)
Formerly, a cloud border (see BORDER). Hence SIDE-CLOUD.

cloud machine
A machine for creating a cloud effect by means of the projection of photographic or painted slides. U.S.: Also as *cloud projector*.

clown
The role of a jester, fool, buffoon, knave, or the like; an actor who plays such a role. Also, to behave as a clown, or to act the part of a clown. Hence *clownade, clownage, clowning* (noun), *clownish*, etc.

clown white
A make-up material (with a base formerly of white lead, now of zinc oxide) used by clowns and other performers who must appear pale or white-faced.

clue
Variant spelling of CLEW.

clutch-type switchboard
In British terminology, a switchboard with dimmers, operated magnetically from a remote control panel.

Co.
See AND Co.

coach
A person who instructs others in the dramatic arts, as, a *dramatic coach*, a *voice coach*, etc. Also, to provide such instruction.

coat room
A CLOAK ROOM.

cock-pit; cockpit
An obsolete British term for the PIT (sense 2).

coffee and cake(s)
A very small acting salary.

coherence
A principle applied to playwriting, production design, etc.: The unification of various elements.

cold cream
See THEATRICAL COLD CREAM.

collaborate
To join another playwright, librettist, or composer in preparing a dramatic piece for production or publication. Hence *collaboration, collaborator.*

collapse
A British equivalent for BREAKAWAY; also as verb and noun.

college play
A play produced at a college. Hence *collegiate drama.* See ACADEMIC DRAMA.

college theatre
A theatre in, and usually maintained by, a college; also collectively.

collodion paper
A paper chemically treated to give a FLASH EFFECT.

color bank
A grouping of dimmers or other controls, usually in horizontal rows, one for each lamp color.

color boomerang; short form, **boomerang**
A device for the remote control of a color frame in front of a light unit. British: AUTO(MATIC) COLOUR CHANGE or REMOTELY-OPERATED COLOUR CHANGE.

color box
A device with color frames for close or remote control of spotlight color changes; sometimes, a COLOR BOOMERANG.

color cap
A lens of colored glass that can be snapped on a projector or other lamp.

color change
See AUTO(MATIC) COLOUR CHANGE and REMOTELY-OPERATED COLOUR CHANGE.

color circuit
An electrical circuit connecting lights of a given color.

color filter
A COLOR MEDIUM.

color frame
A frame of wood or metal to hold a color medium in front of a lighting unit.

color master control
See COLOUR MASTER CONTROL.

color medium; short form, **medium**
A sheet of a translucent substance such as glass or gelatin, used to transform white into colored light, etc.

color section
A COLOR BANK.

color slide
A GELATIN SLIDE.

color wheel
A revolving frame, which brings windows fitted with colored discs in front of the lens of a spotlight to which it is attached, permitting rapid changes in the color of the beam.

colour master control
A British term for a master control system, consisting of a switch, a control wheel, and shafting, used to operate dimmers interlocked according to the color of the lamps they affect.

Columbine
Originally, a maid-servant (Colombina) in the *commedia dell' arte*. Later, and now—especially in British usage—Harlequin's sweetheart in a harlequinade. .

combination
A touring company—Latter half of the 19th century. Hence also a *combination house*, the *combination system* (a replacement of resident stock companies by such troupes).

comeback
An actor's return to the stage from retirement, or his achievement of success after failure.

Come back Tuesday
An allusion to a casting agent's stereotyped advice to an actor, when no engagement is available, to "inquire again another day."

comedian
1. A person who acts in comic roles; sometimes, any actor. Feminine form, *comedienne*. 2. A writer of comedies.

comedienne
Feminine form of COMEDIAN (sense 1).

comedietta
A brief comedy.

come down
To move downstage—Sometimes, a stage direction.

comedy
1. DRAMA (sense 1). 2. A play, varying over the centuries in its characteristics, but generally light and humorous, with a happy

ending; comedy is more thoughtful than farce, more realistic in character and situation; also collectively. Hence, too, the comic element in drama.

comedy act
A comic specialty act (see SPECIALTY)—Vaudeville, etc.

comedy drama; comedy-drama
A play somewhat heavier than comedy, but with a happy ending; also collectively.

comedy of character
A comedy which relies on character study for its chief interest; also collectively. Called also *character-comedy.*

comedy of humors (British spelling, **humours**)
A realistic, satiric comedy in which the dramatic action evolves from a single dominant trait in the character of each person satirized; also collectively—Especially, 17th and 18th centuries.

comedy of intrigue
A comedy which is primarily concerned with the amusements of amorous intrigue; also collectively—Especially, 18th century.

comedy of manners
A comedy which is gay, witty, sophisticated, and usually set against a background of aristocratic or well-to-do society. The terms *comedy of manners, drawing-room comedy* (under DRAWING-ROOM DRAMA), and HIGH COMEDY are commonly interchangeable. See OLD COMEDY (for Restoration *comedy of manners*).

comedy of morals
A comedy which takes a moralistic attitude towards deviations from a social code; also collectively.

comedy of sensibility
Sentimental comedy (see SENTIMENTAL DRAMA).

comedy team
A pair of actors whose comic effects are obtained by close dependence on each other; one is a comedian, the other a straight man.

come on
To make an entrance—Sometimes, a stage direction.

comic
1. A comedian. 2. Amusing, or of the nature of comedy, as *comic business*, the *comic drama*, a *comic interlude*, a *comic romance*, etc.

comic epilogue
A witty speech, used as an epilogue, commenting on contemporary society and politics—Restoration and 18th century.

comicer
A comedian in a comedy team.

Comic Muse
Thalia; the spirit of comedy.

comic opera
A musical dramatic entertainment, consisting of dialogue both spoken and sung, with comic incidents and characters and a happy ending; sometimes synonymous with musical comedy, etc.; also collectively.

comic relief; comic-relief
A comic or farcical scene or incident introduced into tragedy or any serious play to give the audience a momentary respite from emotional tension before further tension is required, or to intensify serious action.

command performance
In British terminology, a performance given at the royal family's request. The initial letters are sometimes capitalized.

commedia dell' arte

A kind of popular comedy of stock characters with masks, in which the actors improvised on a prearranged scenario; developed in Italy, 16th to 18th centuries, but influential on acting and dramatic form, as in pantomime, in the English-speaking countries—An Italian expression ("professional comedy") commonly used in English. Often italicized. In English called also *improvised comedy, masked comedy.*

commentator

1. An actor cast in the role of master of ceremonies, expositor, chorus, or narrator. 2. Formerly, a Master of the Revels, a Lord of Misrule, etc.

commercial

Said of the theatre in so far as it is concerned with profit; often pejoratively, implying a disinterest in art.

commissionaire

A British term for a DOORMAN (sense 1).

common flat

An ordinary flat, not a special type such as a WINDOW FLAT.

commonwealth (system)

A system of paying actors agreed-upon shares of the receipts, after the deduction of the expenses of production.

community theatre

A permanent theatre or resident theatrical company, operated expressly for local recreation, education, etc., commonly seeking to obtain the patronage and the production participation of the community as a whole; also collectively. Hence *community drama.* See CIVIC THEATRE.

company

A group of actors appearing together in one or more dramatic performances; usually understood to include also the business officials, stagehands, and others associated with the actors in production. Also as *acting* (or *dramatic* or *theatrical*) *company.*

company crew
The crew members who travel with a theatrical company on tour.

company list
A list of the actors belonging to a theatrical company.

company manager
A business manager, especially when a theatrical company is on tour. British: *acting manager*.

company rehearsal
A rehearsal scheduled during a long run, to keep a theatrical company in form.

company switch
A switch used to provide current for a portable switchboard, typically when a board is brought to a theatre by a touring company.

company treasurer; short form, **treasurer**
The paymaster of an acting company.

compartment
Applied to rows of lamps when each lamp, with its accessories, is mounted in its own box. Hence *compartment strip*, etc. British: Commonly *magazine*, as *magazine footlight, magazine batten* (see ELECTRIC BATTEN), etc.

compère
In British terminology, a commentator, master of ceremonies— Revue, etc. Also, to serve as a commentator.

complication
In a dramatic plot, a twist whereby some new development is added; the rising action or growth.

complimentary
Said of a seat or ticket which is free.

composition
1. An over-all principle or technique in design, direction, etc., based on a regard for emphasis, balance, and other considerations which enter into any production. 2. See DRAMATIC COMPOSITION.

compound parabolic-spherical-parabolic reflector
A reflector in three sections (a parabolic, a spherical, and another parabolic section) designed to combine efficiency and small size.

con
In British terminology, to memorize a role.

concert batten
In British terminology, the FIRST PIPE (which see).

concert border
1. The border light nearest the act curtain. 2. A strip curtain, concealing the FIRST PIPE (which see).

concert party
In British terminology, a type of summer entertainment at the seaside, featuring song and dance and various specialty acts, sometimes with pierrots and pierrettes.

concessionaire
A person who buys the right to operate a cloak room, a refreshment stand, or a similar business supported by the tips or purchases of theatre patrons.

condensation
A shortened form of a dramatic work. Hence also *condensed play, condensed version.*

condenser (or **condensing**) **lens**; short form, **condenser**
A lens, such as a plano-convex lens, for concentrating light rays into a single beam, especially in a spotlight.

conductor
An ORCHESTRA LEADER.

confidant; (feminine) **confidante**
The role of a close friend of a principal character, used dramatically for purposes of exposition, characterization, or development of dramatic action.

conflict
Short for DRAMATIC CONFLICT.

connector
Short for STAGE CABLE CONNECTOR.

connector box
A British term for a PLUGGING BOX.

connector strip
A row of stage cable connectors attached to a PLUGGING STRIP (which see).

conservation
In acting, the gradual rather than the outright revelation of certain character facets.

console
Short for LIGHT CONSOLE.

construction
1. The building of scenery, properties, stage, etc. 2. The building of the plot of a play. Also as *dramatic construction*. 3. A production technique emphasizing the use of various stage levels. Hence, a *construction play*, one using such levels.

constructivism
A technique in spatial scenic design, stressing skeletal structures, abstract and stylized, rather than the realistic reproduction of the world outside the theatre. Hence *constructivist*.

contact arm
A dimmer lever which moves over contact buttons.

contact button
A button on a dimmer, on which a dimmer arm rests to close an electrical circuit.

contactor switchboard
A switchboard on which the switches (contactors) are operated by remote electromagnetic control.

continuity
In dramatic composition or production, the cohesive sequence of events.

continuous
Said of a show which runs continuously through many hours, repeating itself, as, of vaudeville, a *continuous performance.* British: *continuous* (or *non-stop*) *variety*, etc.

continuously rated dimmer
Any dimmer which, when its maximum rated load is continuously applied, will sustain that load without exceeding a given temperature rise and without suffering any damage.

contour curtain
A curtain which can be drawn up into folds of various shapes by means of lines attached to its component sections.

contour piece
A piece of profile board or other material cut out in some appropriate shape and fastened to a frame to make a GROUND ROW.

contrast
Diversity, variation, used to heighten interest, as in dramatic construction, acting, etc.

contrived
Said of a character, an ending, etc., which is arranged by a dramatist, perhaps artfully, without carrying the conviction of complete plausibility.

control board
A stage SWITCHBOARD.

control console
A LIGHT CONSOLE (which see).

convention; conventionalism
1. A method or style of production which seeks to stress to advantage the artificiality of the stage, rather than to reproduce the conditions of actual life outside the theatre. Hence *conventional*. 2. Short for STAGE (or *dramatic* or *theatrical*) CONVENTION.

conversation piece; conversation-piece
A play which emphasizes dialogue rather than action or movement.

convertible (unit) set
A unit setting with no permanently arranged features.

cookie
Short for CUCKALORIS.

copyright
A legal privilege enabling the owner of a dramatic piece to control its performance and publication during a fixed period of time, now for a maximum term, generally speaking, of 56 years in the United States and 50 years from the death of the author in Great Britain. Also, to register a dramatic work for copyright. Hence, a *copyright play*. See also RIGHTS, ROYALTY.

copyright performance
In British terminology, a performance, usually without scenery or costumes, given to secure stage copyright under the Dramatic Copyright Act of 1833—19th century.

corker
In British terminology, an actor who spoils a performance.

cork opera
A nickname for a minstrel show.

cork up
To put on blackface.

corner
1. Short for CORNER BLOCK. 2. See TAKE THE CORNER.

corner block; short form, **corner**
A small triangle of plywood or profile board used to reinforce
a joint on a flat.

corner brace
A diagonal wooden supporting piece for a flat or parallel.
British: Also, *brace rail.*

corner iron
An L-shaped iron plate used to strengthen a corner joint of
a flat.

corner man
A British term for an END MAN (which see).

corner plate
A CORNER IRON.

corner trap
A trap towards the front of the stage floor, commonly one of
a pair about two feet square, through which actors can rise
and descend.

corps de ballet
A company or team of ballet dancers—A French term used in
English. Often italicized.

corpse
In acting, to forget one's lines or business; to spoil another
actor's lines or business by badly timing one's own.

corridor
1. A hallway or passage in a theatre, especially backstage. 2. A curtain painted to simulate a hallway, formerly much used to permit stage action to continue at the front of the stage during scene-shifting.

Corsican trap
A GHOST GLIDE (which see). Named for the piece in which it was first used (*The Corsican Brothers*).

coryphee
A female (formerly, also a male) ballet dancer—A French word used in English. Sometimes the first *e* bears an acute accent.

co-star
To share star billing with another actor. Hence *co-starring* (noun and adjective). Also, one who shares star billing.

costume
An actor's stage clothing. Also in the form *stage* (or *theatrical*) *costume*. Formerly called *clothes* or *habit*. To design, make, or wear such clothing. Hence *costume designer*, *costuming* (noun), etc.

costume drama
A dramatic piece which requires clothing not now current and especially of a much earlier period. Hence *costume comedy*, *costume part*, etc.

costume fitting; short form, **fitting**
The trying on of a costume for fit and appearance.

costume parade
A try-out of costumes by the entire cast, without a rehearsal.

costume plot
A list of characters, showing the costumes to be worn in a production.

costumer; costumier (feminine, **costumière**)
1. A costume designer. 2. A commercial supplier of costumes.
Also as *theatrical costumer*, etc.

costume rehearsal; costume-rehearsal
A try-out of costumes by the entire cast, either a full rehearsal
or an abbreviated one.

coterie theatre
A theatre for a private or special audience; also collectively.

cothurnus
Tragedy, the tragic drama, tragic acting, a lofty, stilted tragic
style—A word taken from the Latin, meaning the high, laced,
heavy, thick-soled boot worn in ancient Greek and Roman
tragic acting. Plural, *cothurni*. See also BUSKIN.

coulisse
1. A WING FLAT. 2. The space between wing flats. 3. Any backstage space.

counter
In acting, to maintain stage balance by moving across the stage
in a direction opposite to that in which another actor is moving.
Hence *countering* (noun).

counter-balance system
A COUNTERWEIGHT SYSTEM.

counterfoil
A British term for a TICKET STUB.

counterplot
A subplot which emphasizes the principal dramatic plot through
contrast.

counter weight; counter-weight; counterweight
1. A weight, now commonly of iron, used to balance scenery
and equipment, as in the COUNTERWEIGHT SYSTEM (which see).
2. A BRACE-WEIGHT.

counterweight system
A permanent rigging system to facilitate the handling of heavy pieces of scenery or equipment. Cables from a suspension batten attached to such pieces pass over pulleys to an iron frame, called an *arbor* (or *carriage* or *cradle*), which slides in two vertical grooved rails (*tracks*) at the side of the stage and holds the counterweights. Hence, a *counterweight house* (in contradistinction to a ROPE HOUSE), etc.

count the box
To count the ticket stubs in a collection box.

count the house
1. To COUNT UP (which see). 2. To stare at the audience while acting.

count the rack
To count the tickets remaining unsold in the box-office ticket rack.

count up; count-up
A box-office statement for each performance. Also, to prepare such a statement.

coup de théâtre
1. A theatrical success. 2. A showy or sensational device in stagecraft. 3. A sudden unforeseen but not necessarily illogical turn of events in the course of a play.—A French expression ("a theatrical stroke or thrust") used in English in all three senses. Often italicized.

coupon
A CHECK (sense 2).

court
Said of drama, a stage, a theatre, etc., which is financially supported by royalty or nobility.

courtesy
1. In the plural (a usage now rare): complimentary tickets.
2. *Courtesy of the profession:* the free admission to a theatre of a member of the theatrical profession, especially an actor. British: ON ONE'S CARD.

courtroom drama
A drama with a courtroom setting; sometimes the members of the audience represent the spectators in the courtroom, from among whom the actors emerge.

cover
1. In acting, to take a position so as to conceal another actor or an object from the clear view of the audience. 2. To canvas. Hence *covering*. 3. A property man stationed in the wings to fire a COVER GUN. 4. The HEAVENS (sense 2)—Elizabethan.

cover gun
A gun used backstage, for use when a stage gun fails to fire.

cradle
1. Short for *counterweight cradle* (see COUNTERWEIGHT SYSTEM). 2. Rocking equipment for wave and other effects. 3. A hoist platform for stagehands. 4. A wood and rope sling for the overhead storage of battens and drops. 5. Short for SPOTLIGHT CRADLE. 6. In British usage, a TRUCK (sense 2).

cradle support
A device to hold a stage cable so that it will not strain itself or the lights to which it is attached.

crane
A hoisting device used to lift or lower actors, heavy objects, etc.

crash effect; short form, **crash**
A device for simulating the noise of thunder, breaking glass, etc. Hence CHINA CRASH, GLASS CRASH, THUNDER CRASH, etc. Also, the resulting noise.

crash the gate
To enter a theatre without a ticket.

creak
Said of a play: To manifest signs of being outmoded.

create a role
To play in an acting role in the first production of a dramatic piece.

credit list
A list in a theatre program giving the names of firms which have provided costumes, equipment, etc., to dress the stage.

credits
1. Short for CREDIT LIST. 2. A note in a theatre program giving information about an actor's previous roles.

crepe hair; crepe wool
An artificial plaited hair (commonly made of wool or vegetable fiber, in various colors) used in making up for the stage. It can be cut, combed, and glued bit by bit to the face to form a beard, a mustache, sideburns, and eyebrows. Sometimes the first *e* bears a circumflex accent.

crew
The stage crew, or one of its component groups such as the electrician's crew.

crew head
1. The chief of the stage staff, in charge of building and shifting scenery. 2. Any department head.

crisis
A decisive moment, a turning point, in the dramatic action.

critic
A dramatic critic; or any person passing judgment upon dramatic composition or presentation, but usually someone qualified to do so by profession or scholarship. Hence *criticism*, etc.

cross; abbreviation, **X**

To move across the stage from one place to another, especially when passing in front of another actor—Sometimes, a stage direction. Such a movement; also as *crossing* and *stage cross*.

cross control

See GRAND MASTER CONTROL.

cross interlocking control

The control of a group of dimmers by a slow-motion wheel so that some lamps come up while others go down.

cross-light; crosslight

To illuminate the stage with two crossing beams of light. Hence the nouns *cross-light* and *crosslighting*. See also SIDE LIGHT.

crowd scene

A scene in which many actors, especially extras, participate.

cuckaloris; short form, **cookie**

A pattern for a spotlight, fitted into the optical system or attached to the front of the unit (depending upon the type of spotlight), and causing the resultant beam of light to be similarly patterned. Often confused with GOBO (which see).

cue

1. A signal (such as the last few words of a speech) to notify an actor, a stagehand, etc., that it is time to begin some prearranged speech, etc. Hence *business cue*, CUE SHEET, etc. Also, to give such a signal. See also BITE CUES. 2. A queue. 3. A part to be played— Rare.

cue bound

See CUE STRUCK.

cue light

Any of several off-stage lights, paired red and green, used by the stage manager to give a cue.

cue sheet
A list of cues, or a prompt copy marked with cues, for the use of the stage manager and other technicians.

cue struck
To be *cue struck:* To delay words or action by pausing for the precise cue in full. Also as *cue bound.*

cup-and-saucer drama
A DRAWING-ROOM DRAMA (which see), typically marked by the serving of tea and consequently by very little bustling stage movement; also collectively. Usually derogatorily, as originally of Robertson's plays of the 1860s. Hence *cup-and-saucer comedy, cup-and-saucer role,* etc.

curb
A single step in a STAGE STEP unit.

curse, (the)
The splintery edge of a flat.

curtain
A movable (commonly, suspended) barrier or screen of cloth or other material, used to conceal all or part of the stage, and commonly also (or instead) to provide scenic effect. Sometimes, the main curtain, which rises at the beginning of a performance and falls at the end, in contradistinction to an act or scene curtain. By extension, the end of a scene, an act, or a performance, marked by the fall or closing of a curtain; the rise or opening of the curtain at the beginning of a performance, as, an eight o'clock *curtain;* a warning call, announcing the rise of the curtain (British: *Curtain up!*) ; a theatrical effect, solution, or line at the end of an act or performance, as a *strong curtain,* etc.

curtain border
A border matching a curtain seen with it, in color and folds.

curtain call; short form, **call**
The appearance of an actor, or actors, at the end of a perform-ance or an act, in response to applause after the fall of the curtain, which is usually raised again. See also TAKE A CALL (or BOW).

curtain clamp
A clamp that fastens a partly rolled up curtain to a batten to shorten it.

curtain control
An electric motor controlling the operation of a curtain.

curtain cue
A signal given to a curtain operator by the stage manager to raise, lower, or draw a curtain; lines or business serving the same purpose.

Curtain going up!
A warning call to cast and crews for the rise of the curtain.

curtain guide; curtain-guide
A ring or spool fastened to the side of a curtain; a guide wire passes through it to prevent sway.

curtain lifter
A CURTAIN RAISER (which see).

curtain line
1. A mark, usually imaginary, where the act curtain will touch the stage floor. 2. In stage dialogue, the last line of a scene. 3. A rope or wire line for moving a curtain.

curtain man
A stagehand responsible for the operation of a curtain.

curtain music; curtain-music; short form, (the) **music**
Music played just before the beginning or resumption of a performance.

curtain operator
A British term for a CURTAIN MAN.

curtain plot
A list of the times when curtains are to be raised and lowered, with cues.

curtain pole
1. A pole used to shift scenery. See CURTAIN POLE HANGER. 2. A curtain rod, a horizontal rod from which a curtain can be hung by means of curtain rings.

curtain pole hanger
A metal device consisting of a *curtain pole socket,* attached to a flat, and a *curtain pole hook,* which slips into the socket and which in turn receives the end of a CURTAIN POLE (sense 1).

curtain raiser; curtain-raiser
A one-act play or other short dramatic piece performed before a longer play and having no connection with it.

curtain rope
A CURTAIN LINE (sense 3).

curtain runner
1. A stagehand stationed at the side of the stage to help open and close a draw curtain. 2. A curtain track.

curtain set(ting)
A stage setting hung with unpainted curtains and borders.

curtain speech
A speech at the end of a performance, commonly a short acknowledgment of applause delivered before the dropped curtain by the author, the manager, or an actor.

curtain time
The time when a performance is scheduled to begin.

curtain track; short form, **track**
A hanging wood or metal track, in which slide balls to which a draw curtain is fastened.

curtain track bracket; short form, **track bracket**
A bracket fastened to the theatre wall, at the bottom of the counterweight track when the track does not rest on the stage floor, to stop falling weights.

curtain tune; curtain-tune
Music played just before the beginning or resumption of a performance.

Curtain up!
In British terminology, a warning call at dressing room doors after the rise of the curtain.

custard-pie comedy
A farce dependent on such slap-stick elements as pie-throwing.

cut
1. Short for STAGE CUT or *slider cut* (see SLIDER). 2. To omit lines or business provided in the script, usually intentionally. Also, such an omission. Hence, *cutting* (noun). 3. To close or open an electric lighting circuit. 4. Said of a foliage border, drop, etc., when it includes a cut-out.

cut-and-parry (or **cut-and-thrust**) **dialogue**
STICHOMYTHIA (which see).

cut border
Short for CUT FOLIAGE BORDER.

cut cloth; cut-cloth
A British term for a CUT DROP.

cut-down scenery
Scenery less than 8 feet high, commonly used in front of drapes.

cut drop
A drop, painted and then cut out so that the spectator sees a scene formed not only by this drop but also by whatever is placed behind it.

cut flat scene
One of a pair of painted flats used as a back scene, cut out to display scenery behind—Restoration to mid-19th century.

cut foliage border; short form, **cut border**
A border simulating foliage, cut out here and there so that netting can replace the canvas to give the effect of space between branches and leaves.

cut line
A rope line which can be cut if fire breaks out, so that the asbestos curtain will fall or the smoke doors will open.

cut-off; cutoff
Any device, such as a funnel, an iris, a mat, or a shutter, used to confine and shape the beam from a lighting unit.

cut out; cut-out; cutout
A small flat, usually of profile board, cut to simulate trees, rocks, etc. Sometimes, a ground row. Hence *cut-out scenery*.

cut-out setting
A stage setting divided by a wall which is partially removed so that the spectators can better see the action.

cut stage version
A cut version for stage performance.

cut version
A playscript, with certain deletions.

cyc
Short for CYCLORAMA.
   (See also the combinations of CYCLORAMA, with which the combinations of *cyc* are almost always interchangeable.)

cycle
A sequence of plays on related themes—Especially, Medieval religions. Hence *cyclical drama,* etc.

cyclorama; short forms, cyc, cyke
A curving (sometimes U-shaped) drop curtain for an exterior stage setting, used to represent the sky or open space, to mask the rear and all or part of the sides of the stage, and to aid in certain lighting effects, and typically of canvas, colored white or pale blue, suspended from the grid, and reaching to the floor; or a permanent wall serving the same purposes, typically of plaster, semicircular, often also curving inwards at top and sides or dome-shaped (and then called a *dome horizon,* KUPPEL-HORIZONT, etc.); or any set of curtains (a backdrop with side pieces) enclosing a stage setting at back and sides, and usually raised or lowered as a unit. Hence *cycloramic, drapery cyclo-rama,* etc.

cyclorama arm
One of two battens running downstage at the sides of the stage to help hang a cyclorama.

cyclorama border
A strip of border lights used to light the cyclorama from above.

cyclorama footlight
A light illuminating a cyclorama from below.

cyclorama horizon light; short form, horizon light
A cyclorama footlight.

cyclorama knuckle
A joint of metal tubing, by means of which a cyclorama arm is fastened to the main cyclorama batten at any desired angle.

cyclorama light
Any floodlight or strip light used to illuminate a cyclorama.

cyclorama overhead
A light illuminating a cyclorama from above.

cyclorama strip
Any strip light used to light a cyclorama.

cyclorama trough
A trough for cyclorama lights near the base of a cyclorama.

cyke
A CYCLORAMA.

D

Daddy
A nickname for a stage manager.

dame
1. In British terminology, the role (a *dame part*) of a comic old woman; the actor (usually a man) who plays such a role—Pantomime (sense 2). 2. See GRANDE DAME.

dance
An art form consisting of rhythmic body movements, often introduced into stage representations as a solo or ensemble performance. Also, to perform such movements. Hence *dance director, dance drama, dance interlude, dance theatre,* etc.

dancing place
The space between the stage and the modern orchestra seating area—17th century.

danseur; (feminine) **danseuse**
A stage dancer, especially a professional ballet dancer—A French word used in English.

dark
Said of a theatre which is closed, as, a *dark house.*

dark scene
In British terminology, a scene in the harlequinade, when Harlequin and Columbine run away together—Pantomime (sense 2).

darling
A common form of professional greeting, used by or in speaking to an actress.

date

1. A sheet issued by a touring company for pasting to posters, stating the time and place of a local performance. 2. An engagement for a performance.

day bill

A poster advertisement of a play, to be placed in a store window.

day man; dayman

In British terminology, a stagehand employed for day work.

day-set

The setting for the first scene of a performance, usually prepared during the daytime.

D.B.O.

Abbreviation of DEAD BLACK-OUT.

D.C.; DC

Abbreviation of DOWN CENTER.

dead

1. Said of a property, a scenic piece, etc., which has been used but is no longer needed until the next performance. 2. In British terminology, said of a flat or a curtain which hangs trimmed in its proper place, usually with the bottom edge level on the stage floor; to *dead* (U.S.: to *trim*). Hence *on its dead, on the dead.* U.S.: ON SPIKE. 3. Said of a production which has been having a poor run.

dead area

A portion of the stage which is not, or is not to be, illuminated.

dead black-out; abbreviation, **D.B.O.**

A complete blackout.

dead-faced (or **dead-front**) **board**

A stage switchboard which allows no uninsulated wires or controls to appear on the front panel.

dead head; dead-head; deadhead
A person who uses a free admission PASS.

Dead it
1. An order, usually to a stagehand, to remove scenery, a property, etc., from the stage. 2. An order, usually to a stagehand, to fasten scenery or equipment at a given height or length; usually in the form *Dead it at that.*

dead-line
An imaginary line, indicating the limit of a seating area as determined by a SIGHT LINE.

dead pack (or **stack**)
A pile of scenic pieces which have been used in one performance and are not needed again until the next.

dead pan; dead-pan; deadpan
Said of an actor who is making no facial display of emotion; also, such an actor.

dead share
In the sharing system (see SHARE, sense 2), one of four shares paid to the manager to cover his outlay for the wardrobe, etc.— 18th century.

dead stack
A DEAD PACK (which see).

dead stick
In British terminology, an actor who spoils a performance.

dead wood; deadwood
Collectively, the tickets for a given performance which have not been sold, when the box-office sale stops.

death at the box office
Said of a dramatic piece which seems likely not to succeed with the public. But see also MURDER (*at the box office*).

Death Trail
Midwestern tank towns visited by touring companies.

debut
An actor's first appearance, whether (a *stage debut*) at the beginning of his theatrical career, in the opening of a new production, or in a new place. Hence *make one's debut*.

decent
See ARE YOU DECENT?

deck
The stage. Hence *deck hand* (a STAGEHAND), the *guy who runs the deck* (a STAGE MANAGER).

declaim
In acting, to deliver one's lines formally, pompously, artificially, bombastically; to rant. Hence *declamation, declamatory*.

décor
A French word used in English for STAGE DECORATION (which see). Often italicized. Also used in the phrases *stage* (or *theatre*) *décor*.

decoration
Short for *scenic* or *theatrical* or STAGE DECORATION. Hence *decorate*.

decorative property
A property which renders a set more complete and attractive, but which is not necessary.

décor simultané
A French term used in English for a MULTIPLE SETTING. Usually italicized.

decorum
A critical principle; as applied to drama, the observance of classical or neo-classical rules and standards of taste in language, characterization, and action, particularly in tragedy.

deep
Said of an acting area, apron, setting, stage, etc., which is wide from front to back.

degree
One of several levels in a gallery floor on which benches for spectators were placed—Elizabethan and Restoration.

delivery
The manner in which an actor utters his lines.

denouement
In a dramatic composition, the falling action after the climax, the unknotting of the complications of the plot; often, when applied to tragedy, the CATASTROPHE (which see). Sometimes considered to be still a French word, and then often italicized and given an acute accent on the first *e*.

department
One of the principal divisions of the stage staff, headed by a company official: wardrobe, scenery, lighting, etc. Hence *department head*.

depth
The distance from the front to the rear of the stage, or less commonly from the top of the proscenium arch to the stage.

depth-stage
A stage utilizing almost exclusively the space behind the proscenium.

design
1. A plan, such as a drawing, for the construction or manufacture of a theatre, scenery, costumes, etc., as, a *scene design*, a *stage design*, etc. Also, to create such a plan. Hence *designer*, *scenic designer*, *theatre designer*, *designing* (noun). 2. Any stage arrangement aiming at a pattern such as balance.

detective drama (or **play**)
A MYSTERY PLAY (sense 2).

deuce (flat)
A flat 2 feet wide.

deus ex machina
In the ancient Greek and Roman theatres, the introduction of a god to provide the denouement; in modern drama, any unlikely resolution of the problem posed in a play—A stage convention; a Latin term ("a god from a machine") used in English.

development
1. In dramatic construction, the events after the exposition which complicate the plot; a logical series in cause and effect. 2. In characterization, a change and expansion in character traits within a dramatic piece.

diagonal brace; short form, **diagonal**
A brace placed diagonally across a corner of a flat.

diagonal wall
A wall at the back of an interior set, not placed at a right angle to the center line of the stage.

dialect play
A play relying heavily on character parts requiring the simulation of local or foreign accents (*dialect parts*).

dialogue; dialog
1. Lines in a stage entertainment or dramatic work, usually those in which at least two persons take part. Hence *dramatic* (or *stage*) *dialogue*. 2. To break a song into alternating parts to be sung by different performers. Hence a *dialoged song*.

diamanté
Powdered glass used to give sparkle to scenery, costumes, etc.— A French term ("diamonded") used in English. Often italicized.

diaphragm
Short for *iris diaphragm* (see IRIS).

dicky bird
In British terminology, an actor who can sing.

diction
The style or manner in which an actor speaks his lines.

die
Of a production, to fail, to come to an end, as, to *die on the road*.

die standing up
To act without getting applause, as, *He died standing up.*

diffuse
To spread light softly, as by means of a DIFFUSING MEDIUM (which see). Hence *diffused, diffusion,* etc.

diffusing medium (or screen); diffusor
A translucent sheet of ground glass, spun glass, frosted gelatin, or the like, used to give a soft light.

digger
A speculator who buys theatre tickets illegally or improperly and resells them at a profit, usually in sidewalk transactions.

dim
To decrease the stage illumination; but also sometimes to increase it, to *dim down,* to *dim up.* Hence *dimming* (noun).

dimmer
Any electrical or mechanical device used to regulate the intensity of a lighting unit.

dimmer bank
A row of dimmers mounted horizontally. Often, a color bank. Sometimes used interchangeably with DIMMER BOARD (which see).

dimmer board
A stage switchboard on which dimmers are mounted.

diorama
A scenic device, an elaboration of the panorama, used to present a distant view, commonly on a painted canvas which rolls from one cylinder to another at the back of the stage, or which remains still, and which, by means of changes in the direction and intensity of the stage lighting and by means of cut-outs, translucencies, and transparencies, gives a three-dimensional (and commonly a moving or changing) effect. Hence *dioramic*, etc.

dip
1. To lacquer a lamp with coloring matter, as, a *dipped lamp*. Also, the lacquer so used (see THEATRICAL LAMP DIP). 2. A British term for a STAGE POCKET in the stage floor.

direct
To carry out the functions of a STAGE DIRECTOR.

direct control (or **direct operated**) **switchboard**
A stage switchboard which passes the full electric current through its switches and does not use pilot switches and relays.

direction
1. The work of a director. 2. See STAGE DIRECTION.

directional lighting
Illumination aimed at a limited portion of the acting area. Hence *directional lighting unit*. Also, lighting from a primary direction, as front lighting, side lighting, back lighting.

direct operated switchboard
See DIRECT CONTROL SWITCHBOARD.

director
Short for STAGE DIRECTOR.

director's holiday
A play lively enough to stimulate the director to unusually imaginative effort.

100

direct-profile position
The position of two actors face-to-face, with their profiles turned towards the audience.

direct staging
Presentational staging (see PRESENTATIONAL).

disappearing footlight
In the plural, a footlight strip which can be made to disappear into a trap.

disc
An optical effects device bearing pictures, which can be turned in front of a light source.

discover
To reveal a scene, a person, etc., to the audience, as by the raising of a curtain. Hence *discovery*.

discussion play
A play which emphasizes dialogue at the expense of stage movement.

diseur; (feminine) **diseuse**
An actor who gives dramatic recitals, usually with musical accompaniment—A French term used in English. Often italicized.

disguise
1. To conceal one's identity as a character in a stage entertainment, or to assume the identity of some other character, by altering one's appearance. Hence *disguised* (adjective). Also, a costume or other means of making such a change. 2. In an obsolete sense: A DISGUISING (which see).

disguising
Especially in the plural, court pageantry with music and masking, related to the masque—15th and 16th centuries. Also *disguiser* (masquer, mummer). See MUMMERS' PLAY.

dissolve
In stage lighting, to alter color tones slowly.

distortion
In stage lighting, an apparent alteration of some dimension onstage as the result of an accidental or deliberate lighting arrangement.

distribution
1. The assignment of roles in a production to the members of an acting company. 2. See LIGHT DISTRIBUTION.

diva
A PRIMA DONNA (which see). An Italian word used in English. Plural, *divas* or *dive*.

divertisement; divertissement
A short entertainment, usually between the acts of a play—An English derivative of a French word and, as *divertissement* ("diversion"), the French word itself used in English. (The latter is often italicized.) See *ballet divertissement* (under BALLET).

divided setting
A stage setting portions of which are revealed by the complete or partial removal of barriers (as, the front walls of rooms).

D.L.; DL
Abbreviation of DOWN LEFT.

D.L.C.; DLC
Abbreviation of *door left center*, DOWN LEFT CENTER.

do a Brodie
In acting, to fail, to flop, especially after exaggerated publicity. Also as *take a Brodie*. Named for Steve Brodie, who, it is said, as a publicity stunt jumped (or at least announced a jump) from Brooklyn Bridge in New York City.

dock
1. Short for SCENE DOCK. Hence *dock-doors,* etc. 2. The theatre basement, formerly used as a scene dock.

doctor
1. An expositor. 2. To revise and improve a script, especially by exercising the functions of a play doctor, as, to *doctor a script.*

documentary theatre
A British term for a LIVING NEWSPAPER (which see).

dodger
A small theatrical handbill or throwaway.

dog
1. A screw used to fasten a brace to the stage. 2. In a sense now rare: A stage manager. 3. See TRY IT ON THE DOG.

dog town; dog-town
See TRY IT ON THE DOG.

dome
1. Short for *dome horizon, plaster dome.* See CYCLORAMA. 2. Said of various lighting units which are placed in the auditorium ceiling.

dome horizon; short form, **dome**
A kind of CYCLORAMA (which see). Also, after the German, in the spelling *dome-horizont.*

domestic drama
Dramas, collectively or individually, which are concerned with middle or lower class persons, especially in their domestic relationships. Hence *domestic tragedy,* which tends also to be didactic—Especially, Elizabethan and 18th century.

dominate a scene
In acting, to occupy an outstanding position on the stage, as the position farthest upstage or on the highest plane of several levels.

door button
An ordinary household door thumbscrew, used on the stage not only to keep doors closed but also to keep flats in line.

door flat; door-flat
A flat with an opening for a door unit.

door frame unit
A removable door framework of wood, used in a door flat.

door keeper; door-keeper; doorkeeper
A DOORMAN (senses 1–3).

door list
A list of persons entitled to free admission passes.

doorman
1. An attendant at a theatre entrance who helps the patrons to alight from vehicles, etc. British: *commissionaire, link man*. 2. A TICKET TAKER. See also GATHERER. 3. A STAGE DOORMAN (which see).

door opening
A doorway through which spectators can see, and which therefore requires a backing or other scenery.

door shutter; short form, **shutter**
The swinging part of a door unit.

dope
1. In British usage, THEATRICAL LAMP DIP. 2. A paste of whiting, glue, and water, used to fasten canvas to the frame of a flat before tacking.

do the agents
A British equivalent for GO THE ROUNDS (which see).

do the bends
To take a bow.

double
To play two parts in one production; an actor who does so. Hence *doubling*. See DOUBLE IN BRASS.

double bill
A theatre program consisting of two separate dramatic pieces.

double-cast
To cast two actors in each part, either to provide an understudy or to permit their appearance in alternate performances. Hence *double-casting* (noun).

double in brass
Formerly, to play an instrument in a band or orchestra at a performance, as well as to take an acting part; later and now, to play two parts in one production. Hence *doubling in brass.*

double stage
A stage on two levels, so that one setting may be made ready while another is in view.

double take; double-take
An actor's comic response to a jest; one expression, followed after a pause by another, as he pretends to recognize the significance belatedly.

down
1. Short for DOWN STAGE. 2. See also COME DOWN, GO DOWN, RING DOWN.

down center; abbreviation, **D.C.; DC**
A stage position or area, center, downstage—Sometimes, a stage direction.

down left; abbreviation, **D.L., DL**
A stage position or area, left (audience's right), downstage—Sometimes, a stage direction.

down left center; abbreviation, **D.L.C., DLC**
A stage position, downstage of left center position—Sometimes,
a stage direction.

down right; abbreviation, **D.R., DR**
A stage position or area, right (audience's left), downstage—
Sometimes, a stage direction.

down right center; abbreviation, **D.R.C., DRC**
A stage position, downstage of right center position—Sometimes, a stage direction.

down stage; downstage; short form, **down**
1. The entire front half of the stage. Hence *downstage wall*, etc.
2. Any part of the stage considered as a position in relation
to something or someone farther back. 3. Friendly (see, in contrast, UP STAGE, sense 4).

Do you recognize the profession?
Asked at a theatre by a visiting theatrical person: May I attend
this performance without paying an admission charge?

D.R.; DR
Abbreviation of DOWN RIGHT.

drag cues
To fail to give clearly spoken cues when they are expected.

drama
1. A representation on a stage by actors before an audience;
such representations, collectively. Also, the ensemble of whatever is connected with theatrical representation. Hence *drama
critic, drama school.* 2. A piece of writing, particularly one of
marked emotional intensity, intended, or appearing to be intended, for stage representation; also collectively. 3. A play,
between comedy and tragedy, possessing some of the characteristics of both, serious but not catastrophic; also collectively.
4. Conflict, tension, emotional intensity, the quality of being
dramatic.

106

drama club
An organization of amateurs for the production of dramatic pieces.

drama columnist
A person who writes a newspaper column on theatrical matters. Hence *drama column.*

drama critic
A person who passes judgment in print on the quality of dramatic compositions and productions; especially, a professional person, as a reviewer on the staff of a newspaper or magazine. Also, chiefly in British usage, as *dramatic critic.*

drama editor
A newspaper staff member in charge of the preparation of a drama section.

drama festival; short form, **festival**
1. A special (often an annual) series of plays, to celebrate some anniversary, or given for some other reason. 2. A series of competitive performances by amateur companies.

drama league
An organization for the encouragement of dramatic activity.

dramalogue
A dramatic reading (see DRAMATIC READER).

drama of ideas
Individually or collectively, plays providing not only emotional entertainment, but also a thoughtful discussion of ideas, often concerning modern social conditions; the dramatis personae advance conflicting views. (Distinctions between *drama of ideas, thesis play,* and *problem play* are rarely sharp. One may say that a problem play poses a problem, a thesis play answers it.)

drama of sensibility
Individually or collectively, plays which demonstrate that human nature is perfectible by an appeal to the emotions; sentimental drama—18th century.

drama page
A newspaper page devoted to theatrical matters.

drama school
A school, often attached to some professional theatre or university, where instruction in the dramatic arts is provided. British: *dramatic school* (which is sometimes U.S. also). Also as *school of dramatic art*, etc.

dramatic
1. Pertaining to or connected with stage representation or compositions intended for the stage, as, *dramatic action*, a DRAMATIC AUTHOR, *dramatic criticism*, a *dramatic performance*. Hence also *dramatical(ly)*. 2. Emotionally intense, as DRAMATIC LIGHTING, a DRAMATIC ROMANCE. 3. Intended for or connected with the production of straight plays, in contradistinction to musical comedies, television shows, etc., as, a *dramatic actor*, a DRAMATIC PLAY. 4. See DRAMATICS. 5. In an obsolete sense: A dramatist.

dramatic action
See ACTION (sense 2).

dramatic agent
A THEATRICAL AGENT (which see). Hence *dramatic agency*.

dramatic art
The arts or skills involved in dramatic representation (sometimes, more particularly, in playwriting or acting), collectively. Also in the plural.

dramatic author; short form, **author**
A writer of dramatic compositions. Hence *dramatic authorship*.

dramatic club
An amateur organization for stage productions.

dramatic column
A newspaper column devoted to theatrical matters.

dramatic company
See COMPANY.

dramatic composition
1. A drama, a play or other piece of writing of a theatrical nature. 2. Playwriting, the writing of a dramatic work.

dramatic conflict; short form, conflict
A struggle from which the dramatic action grows.

dramatic convention; short form, convention
A STAGE CONVENTION (which see).

dramatic critic
A term, chiefly British, for a DRAMA CRITIC. Hence, both British and U.S.: *dramatic criticism*.

dramatic editor
A DRAMA EDITOR (which see).

dramatic festival; short form, festival
A DRAMA FESTIVAL (which see).

dramatic foreshadowing
See FORESHADOW.

dramatic history
The history of the drama.

dramatic irony
1. The use of actions or words carrying a hidden meaning for the audience in the development of a plot. 2. A character's failure to realize a truth evident to the audience.

dramaticism
The quality or character of being dramatic.

dramatic lighting
Stage lighting which is meant to intensify dramatic effects rather than to be realistic.

dramatic literature
Collectively, plays and similar dramatic works.

dramatic metaphor
The central theme, idea, or image to be considered by the actor, scenic designer, etc., in bringing drama to the stage.

dramatic opera
A spectacular entertainment, all the lines of which were spoken rather than sung, although song and musical accompaniment were part of the performance—Restoration and sometimes later.

dramatic play
A play for the stage rather than for other uses such as the motion pictures; a legitimate play rather than the book of a musical show.

dramatic poem
A poem in dramatic form; a play in verse. Hence also *dramatic poetry*.

dramatic preparation; short form, **preparation**
Any means used by a dramatist, as, foreshadowing, to prepare the spectator for something which will later be introduced in the play.

dramatic reader
A person who, alone or with others, reads a play aloud, usually with some characterization, in a public performance. Hence, a *dramatic reading*.

dramatic recital
A public performance given by one or more actors who recite excerpts from plays or their own dramatic sketches, usually without scenery, costume, or music.

110

dramatic reversal; short form, reversal
A point in a plot at which some development is introduced which leads a character or the spectator to alter his expectation of the outcome of the action; thus a sudden change from joy to grief might be occasioned.

dramatic rights
The privilege retained by a copyright-holder of granting or refusing permission to produce a dramatic work, or to make a dramatic adaptation of a non-dramatic composition.

dramatic romance
A romantic play with serious overtones, swiftly changing emotions, adventurous narrative, sometimes fantasy; allied to tragicomedy—Especially, early 17th century.

dramatics
1. Usually as a plural noun: Dramatic activities of all kinds, especially those of amateurs. 2. Usually as a singular noun: Dramatic skill, especially in amateur performance.

dramatic school
A term, chiefly British, for a DRAMA SCHOOL.

dramatics editor
A DRAMA EDITOR.

dramatic situation; short form, situation
1. The essence of a dramatic work, reduced to character relationships and the forces operating on them under a given set of conditions. 2. Any point at which the action of a plot crystallizes significantly. 3. In British terminology, the physical position of actors relative to each other, especially at some significant moment; usually shortened to *situation*.

dramatic society
An amateur organization for stage productions.

dramatic structure; short form, **structure**
In a dramatic composition, the arrangement of plot materials in a unified, effective form, including exposition, complication, climax, denouement.

dramatic suspense; short form, **suspense**
Uncertainty provided in a dramatic piece as to the outcome of a principal crisis or the subsidiary crises. See also DRAMATIC TENSION.

dramatic technique
The means by which a dramatist achieves the ends at which he aims.

dramatic tension; short form, **tension**
In dramatic composition and production, heightened emotional intensity.

dramatic theatre
A theatre for dramatic productions rather than for motion pictures, radio performances, etc.

dramatic unity; short form, **unity**
The principle of "oneness," applicable to every aspect of dramatic writing and production, each element contributing to a single over-all effect. For the neo-classic "Aristotelian" unities, see UNITY OF ACTION, UNITY OF PLACE, UNITY OF TIME.

dramatic version
A dramatic script derived from a non-dramatic piece of writing.

dramatic workshop
A DRAMA WORKSHOP (which see).

dramatic writer
A DRAMATIST.

dramatism
Dramatization; dramatic style or structure.

dramatis personae
The CHARACTERS (sense 1) or actors in a dramatic composition, especially a list of them—A Latin expression ("persons of the drama") used in English, and treated in English as either singular or plural.

dramatist
The writer of a dramatic work.

dramatize
To make into or express as drama, by converting a non-dramatic work into dramatic form, by realizing a script in stage action, etc. Hence *dramatization, dramatizer*, etc.

drama tournament
A DRAMA FESTIVAL (sense 2).

dramaturgy
The art or technique of dramatic composition or representation. Hence *dramaturge* (or *dramaturgist;* a dramatist), *dramaturgic(al)*.

drama workshop; short form, workshop
A course given by a drama school, a theatre, or a university, providing training in actual production work as well as in theory.

drame
A French word used in English for a DRAMA (sense 3). Often italicized.

drame à clef
A play for which a key exists or can be guessed at, so that the characters may be identified with actual persons—A French expression occasionally used in English. Usually italicized.

drapery; short form, drape
Any soft curtain material, hung, usually loosely, as part of the scenic decoration. Hence *drapery border, drape-curtain, drapery cyclorama*, etc.

drapery hanger
A CURTAIN POLE HANGER.

drapery rake
An instrument used to push a drapery about on its track, on its batten, etc.

drape scenery
Scenery made of curtains.

drapery setting
A term, used in the U.S. only, for an ARRAS *setting.*

draw
Said of a production or an actor: To attract the public. See also BOX-OFFICE DRAW.

draw curtain; draw-curtain
A curtain that divides in the middle so that it can be pulled to the sides of the stage.

drawing card
An actor, production, etc., able to attract the public.

drawing-room drama
Dramas, collectively or individually, which depict the social life of well-to-do persons in a drawing-room or similar setting. Hence *drawing-room comedy,* etc. See COMEDY OF MANNERS.

draw tab
A term, chiefly British, for a single curtain pulled across the stage rather than raised and lowered.

drayma
A misspelling and mispronunciation of DRAMA, used humorously.

D.R.C.; DRC
Abbreviation of *door right center,* DOWN RIGHT CENTER.

drencher (pipe)
In British terminology, a RAIN PIPE placed above the safety curtain for fire protection. U.S.: *sprinkler*.

dress
To costume a stage production. Hence *dressing* (noun), *over-dress*, etc.

dress box
A box for spectators in evening dress—19th century.

dress circle; dress-circle
In British terminology, a seating area just above the PIT (sense 2, which see), also known as the *grand circle*, the *royal circle*, etc. (U.S.: MEZZANINE, *first balcony*, rarely *dress circle*.)

dress double
To wear one costume over another for quick changing.

dresser
A person who helps actors get into and out of costume.

dressing room; dressing-room
A room backstage where an actor can dress and make up. Hence *star dressing room*, etc.

dressing-room actor
An actor whose success in the theatre is limited to his self-satisfied dressing-room posturing. Hence *dressing-room comedian*, etc.

dressing-room list
A list of rooms with the actor and dresser assigned to each.

dress parade
A COSTUME PARADE (which see) or a COSTUME REHEARSAL.

dress plot
A COSTUME PLOT.

dress rehearsal
A complete rehearsal, in costume, usually the last one before the opening night.

dress stall
An alternative British term for an ORCHESTRA STALL (which see).

dress the house
1. To paper the house (see under PAPER). 2. To assign seats to an audience with artful spacing so that the theatre appears to be more crowded than it really is.

dress the stage
To place the actors, and often such objects as the furniture, so as to give the spectator a pleasing effect of balance. Hence *dressing the stage.*

droll
1. Formerly, a farce, puppet show, or similarly amusing production, especially (17th and 18th centuries) a short farce based upon a popular full-length play. 2. A clown or comedian.

drop
1. Short for DROP CURTAIN. 2. To lower a curtain. 3. To slow down action too much.

drop clamp
A special stage brace in the form of a bar which at one end is clamped to the lower batten of a drop curtain and at the other is screwed to the stage floor.

drop cloth; drop-cloth
A term, chiefly British, for a DROP CURTAIN.

drop (curtain)
Any curtain of canvas or other cloth material hung so as to fall from and rise to the flies; usually large, reaching to the floor,

116

and painted or dyed to add to the scenic effect. British: Usually *drop cloth.*

drop hanger (or holder)
A BATTEN CLAMP.

drop scene; drop-scene
1. A curtain, formerly made of canvas and painted, before which a scene is played while the setting behind it is being changed; an olio drop (see OLIO, sense 2); sometimes, a drop, an act drop. 2. The final scene of a performance. 3. A scene which is played in a lower emotional key than the previous scene.

drop stage
A DOUBLE STAGE.

drum and shaft
See SHAFT AND DRUM.

Drury Lane melodrama
In British terminology, an especially sensational melodrama— 19th century. So called after the London theatre of that name.

dry
DRY UP (sense 1).

dry brush
To paint scenery, usually with a second color, by drawing a brush which is nearly dry across it.

dry rouge
A powder rouge for coloring the cheeks.

dry up
1. In acting, to forget one's lines or business. Also, forgetfulness while acting. 2. To cause another actor to forget his lines or business, by giving him the wrong cue.

dual rated dimmer
A type of resistance dimmer which can handle varying loads.

dual role
Two parts in a production, played by a single actor.

ducat
1. A theatre ticket. 2. A free admission pass.

dud
A term, especially in British usage, for a FLOP (which see).

dumb
Said of a dramatic presentation or part of one in which the story is acted in pantomime, that is, with gesture and movement but without dialogue, as, a *dumb act*, a *dumb show*. Hence *in dumbshow*. See also PANTOMIME.

dump
1. To return to the box office the tickets which an agency cannot sell. 2. To sell at a discount the tickets which an agency has on hand as a performance is about to start.

duodrama
A dramatic piece for two speaking characters.

duologue
1. A scene or part of a scene in which two actors converse in the presence of other actors who, by stage convention, do not overhear. 2. Part of a scene, a whole scene, or even an entire dramatic piece or performance in which only two actors participate.

dutchman
1. A cloth strip used to conceal a crack or joint; especially a strip of muslin glued to the front or back of two flats. To cover a joint with such a strip. 2. Formerly, a wooden wedge used to level a flat on a raked stage. 3. A wood batten, or some other device, used to support folding flats from behind. 4. A second condensing lens on an effect machine.

118

E

E.
Abbreviation of ENTRANCE.

Ease your long
An order to a flyman to let down a LONG LINE (which see), while fixing flied scenery.

eccentric (comedian); (feminine) eccentric comedienne
An actor playing a CHARACTER PART (which see) calling for emphasis on humorous peculiarities. Hence *eccentric part.*

edge
See SHARP-EDGED, SOFT-EDGED.

edge clearance
The distance of a corner block or keystone from the edge of a flat, which is allowed for the placing of stage hardware so that it will not impede the later handling of the flat.

edition
A version of a production (or part of one) which differs from the original version—Revue.

educational theatre
A term used in the U.S. for an amateur theatre maintained by an educational institution for the entertainment and cultural profit of the student body and for the training of students in dramatics; also collectively. Hence *educational dramatics,* etc. See ACADEMIC DRAMA for *academic theatre,* which is both British and U.S.

effect
Short for *special* (or *stage*) *effect:* A device or apparatus (mechanical, electrical, or chemical) by means of which a sight, a sound, or (very rarely) a smell can be simulated, usually to

119

effect lantern

give a realistic impression. With the exception of the equipment used to produce light changes (but not LIGHTNING or FLAME EFFECTS or the like), such devices and apparatuses are considered to be STAGE PROPERTIES (which see). Also, the simulation achieved by such means. Effects are commonly classified in two categories: *acoustical* (or *sound*), such as a CRASH EFFECT, a *thunder effect;* and *visual* (or *optical*), such as a *moon effect,* a *smoke effect,* a *star effect.* See also FLYING EFFECT.

effect lantern; effects lantern
In British terminology, a visual effect machine. See EFFECT.

effect machine
A mechanical, electric, or chemical apparatus for creating a visual or audible effect (see EFFECT). See also SCENIC EFFECT MACHINE.

effect projector
A term, chiefly British, for a projector used for visual effects. U.S.: PROJECTION MACHINE.

effects man
A person who conceives and executes stage effects (see EFFECT).

egg
See LAY AN EGG.

Eidophusikon
A scenic entertainment—devised and first presented by Philippe Jacques de Loutherbourg in London in 1781, and influential thereafter on scenic design—making use of concealed overhead lighting, varied in color and intensity to give an appearance of change and movement in the scenic background.

electrical circuit
Short for STAGE ELECTRICAL CIRCUIT.

electric batten; short form, **batten**
In British terminology, a pipe batten (see BATTEN) supporting a row of lights in a metal trough; the trough with the lamps and their accessories. U.S.: BORDER LIGHT, STRIP LIGHT, etc.

electrician
An electrician who works in the theatre; sometimes short for CHIEF ELECTRICIAN. Also as *theatrical electrician.*

Electrics!
A call sometimes used to summon the electrician.

elevator
A machine to move part or all of the stage floor vertically. Also as *stage elevator.* British: BRIDGE, STAGE CUT.

elevator stage
A stage which can be moved vertically on an elevator, usually so that one set can quickly replace another; such a stage may consist of a single unit or of sections. British: *lift stage.*

Elizabethan drama
The English drama of the period when Elizabeth I occupied the British throne (1558–1603), although these dates are sometimes adjusted (for example, to the closing of the theatres in 1642) to conform to stage rather than to political significance.

ellipsoidal (or **elliptical**) **reflector**
A reflector with a curved surface based on an ellipse. Hence *ellipsoidal(-reflector) floodlight, ellipsoidal reflector spotlight.*

emcee
A master of ceremonies. The initial letter is usually capitalized. Also, to perform the functions of a master of ceremonies.

emergency door
A British term for a FIRE EXIT (which see) or ESCAPE DOOR (which see).

emergency light
A light for emergency use, either on or off the stage.

emergency rope
A line, which can be cut in an emergency, to lower the asbestos curtain.

emphasis
In the designing of stage productions, the stressing of important elements. See also *emphatic*.

emphasized void
An empty space which is given emotional significance by means of light and shadow.

emphatic
Said of stage business, a property, etc., which is necessary or important in a production. Also in related forms, as, an *emphasized property*.

emphatic curtain (or **ending**)
An ending with an especially significant piece of business or curtain line.

enact
To perform, to act.

encore
A call or summons by an audience, by shouting, applause, etc., for the reappearance of performers, for the re-enactment of a portion of the performance, etc.; the word *encore* itself (meaning "again!") so used. Also, to call in this way; or to repeat for the audience in response to such a call.

endless line
An OPERATING LINE (sense 2).

endless runner
A treadmill, a portion of the stage moving on an endless belt.

end man; end-man
One of the comic performers (Mr. Bones and Mr. Tambo) at either end of the seated semicircle—Minstrel shows. British: *corner man.*

engagement
1. An actor's period of employment in a part. 2. An arrangement for a company to play in some theatre for a stipulated period of time.

engineer
See CHIEF ENGINEER.

English
See STAGE ENGLISH.

English trap
A term, chiefly British, for a kind of BRISTLE TRAP, in the stage floor or in a wall, consisting of twigs, or steel teeth, covered with painted canvas—19th century.

ensemble
1. A cast of characters, except for the principals. 2. The grouping of the whole stage picture, including actors and set. 3. Said of acting, a scene, etc., which emphasizes group rather than individual performance.

ensemble theatre
A theatre using actors by the year rather than for a single play; also collectively.

enter
To come onstage—Sometimes, a stage direction.

entertainment
A stage performance or production. Also as *stage* (or *theatrical*) *entertainment,* etc. Hence *entertain, entertainer.*

entertainment tax
A tax on theatre tickets.

123

entr'acte
1. An intermission. 2. A brief entertainment provided during an intermission. Hence *entr'acte music*, etc.

entrance
1. A door or other access to the stage. Abbreviation, especially as a stage direction: E. 2. A door through which patrons may come into the theatre or some portion thereof. Also as *entrance door*. 3. An actor's entry onstage. Hence, *make an entrance*, especially when an actor enters in an effective or spectacular manner.

entrance backing
A backing used at a door leading offstage.

entrance cue
A cue for an actor to come onstage.

entrance fee
The charge made for admission to a theatre.

entrance flat
A flat on a platform, sliding in a track.

entrance-hall
A British term for a foyer, a lobby.

entrance light
A light placed where an actor comes onstage or goes offstage, to light him and the entranceway. Hence *entrance lighting*.

entrance unit
An entrance flat with a backing, a plug, or similar additions.

epic
1. Said of a drama, a setting, a type of theatre, acting, etc., using an anti-naturalistic technique, concerned with social documentation for purposes of propaganda—20th century, and especially the period 1919–1932. See LIVING NEWSPAPER. 2. Said of a drama which takes a vast historical sweep.

epilogue; epilog
A scene or speech following a performance.

episode
An incident.

episodic play
A play consisting of linked incidents, rather than of developed scenes and acts.

epitasis
The part of a dramatic work in which the main dramatic action is worked out, between the protasis and the catastrophe.

equally divided scene
A scene written for two actors to share with equal prominence.

equestrian drama
A type of spectacular entertainment in which horses (or by extension other animals) were used—19th century. Also as *equestrian spectacle,* etc.

Equity
Short for *Actors' Equity Association,* the professional guild for actors in the U.S. (1913   ). The British equivalent is *British Actors' Equity Association* (1930   ).

escape door
A door leading offstage, through which actors (or others) may escape in the event of fire. British: *emergency door.*

escape play
A play offering escape from the conditions of actual life; obviously a subjective and relative term. Hence *escapist.*

establish
In playwriting or production, to make clear to an audience such matters as character, locale, etc.

esthetic distance
See AESTHETIC DISTANCE.

Ethiopian minstrelsy
Negro minstrelsy (see MINSTREL SHOW). Hence *Ethiopian entertainer*, etc.

Examiner of Plays
In British terminology, an official serving under the Lord Chamberlain, charged with the licensing of stage productions within the London area; sometimes incorrectly called *Censor, Licenser*—19th century.

exchange courtesy
An arrangement whereby free tickets are given to shopkeepers and others who will display theatrical advertisements.

exciting force
The factor in a dramatic story from which all the dramatic action springs; it may or may not precede the play itself.

excursions
Running about by groups of soldiers, as in *alarums and excursions* (see ALARUM)—Especially, an Elizabethan stage direction.

Exeunt
"They go out"—A Latin word used in English as a stage direction. Hence *Exeunt omnes* ("They all go out"); in this form, often italicized. See also EXIT.

exhibition room
A term sometimes used in the U.S. instead of "theatre" in order to avoid possible censorship—18th and 19th centuries.

exit
1. A going offstage. To go offstage; "he goes out" (a stage direction). Hence also *exit speech*, etc. 2. A door or other place at which an actor goes offstage. 3. A door through which patrons may leave the theatre or some portion thereof. Hence *emergency exit door, exit light, exit sign*, etc.

126

exit line
A line of dialogue spoken by an actor just before, or just as, he goes offstage.

exit without lines
To go offstage silently.

expense money
The money paid to an actor during the rehearsal period.

experimental
Said of drama, staging, a type of theatre, etc., which seeks freshness in the writing and production of plays rather than the traditional formulas for commercial or conventional success; often non-realistic; imaginative, and sometimes exaggerated.

exposition
An explanation, normally in dialogue, of events preceding the beginning of a dramatic piece which an audience needs to know.

expositor
An actor who pointed a moral for the audience at the end of a morality play—14th to 16th centuries.

expository scene
A SCENE (sense 1) the chief purpose of which is to provide exposition.

expressionism
A non-illusionistic theatrical method by which the playwright, actor, designer, and others stress the inner emotional significance of a play instead of the mere exterior reality; the means are sometimes violent, always unusual; the action may be speeded unrealistically, striking symbols may be brought onstage to express abstractions—Chiefly 1910–1925. Also *expressionist, expressionistic*.

extempore acting
Impromptu acting, without regard for a script. Hence *extemporize*, etc.

exterior (scene)
A scene out-of-doors; a flat representing part of such a scene. Hence *exterior backing, exterior setting,* etc.

extra
An actor who speaks no lines, or speaks lines only as a member of a crowd, but who comes onstage for minor participation in a performance. British: Often SUPER(NUMERARY).

extravaganza
A light entertainment in dramatic form, with music, improbable in plot (which was formerly based on a myth or fairy tale), spectacular in presentation; often resembling BURLESQUE (sense 1). By extension, any extravagant, exaggerated play.

eye shadow
A grease used to accentuate the eyelids in making up.

F

fabulous invalid, (the)
The theatre, always amazingly vital in spite of its chronic financial and artistic setbacks.

face
A rare term for a mask.

face powder
See THEATRICAL FACE POWDER.

facing trim
Part of a door or window casing; a length of wood placed parallel to a flat to conceal the canvas and frame where these meet a thickness piece.

fade in
To increase the illumination of the stage gradually by means of dimmers.

fade out
To decrease the illumination of the stage gradually by means of dimmers, until the stage is totally dark. Also a noun.

fair-ground theatre
A booth or other temporary theatre erected at a fair.

fake
1. To AD LIB (which see). 2. In acting, to omit lines or business, or to execute business in less time than it would require in actual life. 3. To use an imitation of a real object on the stage.

fall
1. To drop; said of a curtain when it is lowered to close an act or scene. 2. See STAGE FALL.

falling action
Dramatic action following a climax.

129

falling flap
A hinged flat, painted on both sides, so that when the upper half is allowed to fall the scene formerly presented is changed to another scene—Chiefly 18th and 19th centuries.

false masque
An ANTI-MASQUE.

false proscenium
A framing construction, placed within the proscenium opening, usually to reduce its dimensions temporarily. It is called *hard* when built of flats, *soft* when made of cloth (as by shifting the position of TEASER and TORMENTORS).

false proscenium border
In British terminology, a movable border directly behind the proscenium opening.

false stage
A stage built above the actual stage.

family box
A box for the use of family parties.

family circle
A seating area in a balcony. The term, now chiefly British, designates an area behind or above the dress circle.

family house
Formerly, a theatre catering inexpensively to families in its neighborhood.

fan
An enthusiastic follower or admirer of the theatre, of an actor, etc. Hence also *fan mail*.

fancy border
A border for an interior setting such as a drawing-room.

fan effect
Formerly, a means of producing a sudden change in scene, as for a transformation, by dividing the back scene into segments which collapsed like a pair of folding fans.

fantastic comedy
A comic extravaganza, far-fetched and farcical.

fantasy
A play or other entertainment which is imaginative, fanciful, rather than realistic; it may, for example, include the supernatural.

fantoccini
Puppets operated by machinery on hidden strings or wires; shows using such puppets—An Italian word ("puppets") used in English. Infrequently anglicized as *fantocine*.

farce
A broadly humorous dramatic composition, or a portion of one, which is based on improbable situations and is unsubtle in idea or characterization; also collectively. Hence *farcical*, etc.

farce-comedy
An entertainment mixing the exaggeration of farce with the realism of comedy. British: Usually *farcical comedy*.

farcetta
A term, especially in British usage, for a short farce—19th century.

farewell
Said of an event supposed to mark an actor's retirement from the stage, as, a *farewell appearance*, a *farewell tour*.

fast
See MAKE FAST.

fat
A role, lines, or business sure to succeed and thus offering an actor an easy opportunity. Hence, a *fat part*, etc.

fauteuil
A seat with arms, usually one well to the front in the stalls— A French word used in British terminology.

feature
To give any actor a billing second only to that of a star, usually by placing his name after the title of the show, preceded by the word "with." Hence *feature man, feature player, feature role*, etc.

feed
1. To help another actor get full effect from some significant speech or action by supplying one's own preparatory speech or action. Hence, a *feed line*. Also, an actor, usually a straight man, who thus feeds lines to another actor, usually a comic actor; the role of such an actor. Called also a *feeder*. 2. Chiefly in British usage, to prompt, as, to *feed him his lines*.

feel
1. *feel the audience:* To feel the emotional stimulus that comes from acting before an audience. 2. *feel the line:* To pull a rope line at the tie-off rail, in trimming, to test its tautness. 3. *feel the part:* In acting, to immerse oneself creatively in the problems of any role.

female impersonator
A man who plays the role of a woman. Hence *female impersonation*.

festival
Short for DRAMA FESTIVAL. Hence *festival theatre*, etc.

festoon
To loop a curtain or similar piece loosely in folds. Thus, a border or curtain or the like hanging in folds, as, a *festoon curtain*.

fettpuder
A make-up powder used to brighten the hair. Often italicized.

Fifteen minutes!
An act warning, fifteen minutes before the beginning of a scene or act. Hence, a *fifteen minutes call*. British: *Quarter of an hour, please!*

figurant; (feminine) **figurante**
A ballet dancer who performs as one of a group; an actor who has a part without lines—A French word used in English.

fillet
In British terminology, a section of the stage floor between STAGE CUTS.

filling
Short for SLIDER (*filling*).

filling-station town
A TANK TOWN.

filter
A COLOR MEDIUM (which see).

filter holder
A COLOR FRAME.

final curtain
The lowering of a curtain at the end of a performance; hence also a closing scene.

finale
The last song, the closing ensemble number of a show—Chiefly Musical shows. See also GRAND FINALE.

finaletto
The ending of the first act—Musical shows. See GRAND FINALE.

finger flash
A flash effect achieved by rubbing collodion paper.

fire a trap
To set a trap apparatus in motion so that someone or something rises through a trap opening in the stage floor.

fire curtain
Short for FIREPROOF CURTAIN.

fire door
Any door to prevent the spread of fire to dressing rooms, etc.

fire effect
The simulation of the noise or appearance of fire.

fire exit
A door in the auditorium through which the audience may escape in the event of fire. British: *emergency door.*

fireman
A person in charge of precautions against fire in a theatre.

fireman drama
A play dealing with the firefighting activities and social life of volunteer firemen—19th century.

fireplace flat
A flat with an opening into which a fireplace unit can be fitted.

fireproof
To apply a chemical solution (*fireproofing*) to a curtain, flat, or other object so that flames cannot spread rapidly in case of fire; to flameproof. Short for FIREPROOF CURTAIN.

fireproof curtain; short forms, (the) **fireproof,
    fire curtain**
The foremost curtain in the proscenium arch, commonly made of asbestos on a steel frame, used to protect the auditorium if fire breaks out on or behind the stage.

firing step
In British terminology, a platform in the flies used for the storage of slack ropes.

first circle
A British term (formerly also U.S.), now rare, for the topmost seating area, above the dress (or royal) circle.

first entrance
1. The stage entrance farthest downstage. 2. An actor's first entry onstage.

first gallery
A balcony seating area above the first tier of boxes—Restoration.

first money guarantee
A guarantee by a producer that a theatre owner's expenses will be met before the money from the sale of tickets is distributed to other claimants.

first night; first-night
An opening night. Hence *first-night audience*, etc.

first-nighter
A member of an opening-night audience, especially a person who habitually attends first nights.

first night list
A list of persons for whom the management reserves free seats for an opening night.

first pipe
The pipe batten (see BATTEN) flied horizontally immediately behind the proscenium, to carry lighting equipment. British: *chamber batten, concert batten, number one batten, proscenium batten.*

fitting
Short for COSTUME FITTING.

fit-up
In British terminology, said of a temporary stage (a *fit-up stage*) and its equipment, formerly often carried by companies

Five minutes to curtain!

touring in small towns; also, a collective noun for such furnishings; a touring company using such a stage.

Five minutes to curtain!
An ACT CALL.

fizzer
In British terminology, a play or production certain to become a hit.

flag
A curtain. See also PRINTED FLAG.

flame effect
A FIRE EFFECT.

flameproof
FIREPROOF (which see). Hence *flame-proofing* (noun).

flap
1. A BACKFLAP HINGE. 2. A hinged curtain or flat used for trick effects and transformation scenes. See also FALLING FLAP.

flare
In British terminology, to place and regulate light and sound equipment.

flash back
A dramatic technique which carries a spectator back to an earlier event, thereby breaking the strict chronological development of the plot. Hence, a *flash-back scene*, etc.

flash box
A box containing powder to be ignited electrically for a flash effect.

flash effect
An optical EFFECT, a device to produce a flash.

flash paper
COLLODION PAPER.

flash powder
LYCOPODIUM.

flat (piece)
A scenic piece, usually a rectangular wooden frame covered with painted canvas, standing as part of a wall or flied as part of a ceiling. Often named for its width in feet, as, a *deuce flat*, a *four flat*. Hence *flat cleat*, *flat scenery*, etc.

flat scene
A painted cloth, or one of a pair of painted flats, used as a back scene—Restoration to mid-19th century.

flesh
LIVE (which see, sense 2), as, *flesh actor*, *flesh show*, etc.

fleshings; fleshing-tights
Tights, especially when flesh-colored.

flexible cable; short forms, **flexible, flex**
British terms for a STAGE CABLE (which see).

flexible control switchboard
A switchboard so wired that each stage electrical circuit is available for connection to any dimming circuit.

flexible dimmer
A dimmer which can handle varying loads.

flexible setting
A UNIT SETTING (which see).

flicker (wheel)
A British term for a LOBSTERSCOPE.

flied
See FLY.

flies
1. In the plural, the space above the stage behind the proscenium, out of view of the audience, used temporarily during

flipper

a performance for the storage of hanging scenery or lighting equipment. British spelling sometimes *flys*. 2. In the plural, in British terminology, a FLY GALLERY; sometimes, the *flys*. 3. See CATCH FLIES.

flipper

1. A flat, usually narrow and short, which is hinged to a larger flat to support the latter at right angles, as, a TORMENTOR FLIPPER. 2. A piece of scenery or part of the floor which can be quickly flipped into another position. 3. Short for FLIPPER SHUTTER.

flipper (shutter)

A CUT-OFF (which see) with a SHUTTER (sense 2) which can be adjusted to produce a square or rectangular beam shape.

flipper switch

A switch which automatically disconnects a resistance dimmer from its power source when the lights are fully dimmed.

float

1. To lower a flat to the stage floor, letting the air cushion its descent, while one holds a foot on the lower rail; usually in the form *floating a flat*. 2. In British terminology, a footlight. The term *float* (commonly used in the plural) is so called because the light was formerly provided by a wick floating in oil. British: Also FOOTLIGHT. 3. In British terminology, a truck for transporting scenery. 4. A pageant wagon or other car used as an outdoor stage.

floating stage

1. A stage in a floating theatre; a FLOATING THEATRE (which see). 2. A stage on supports, which is moved up and off backstage by means of a motor and is then replaced by another stage.

floating theatre

A showboat or other theatre floating on water.

138

float spot
A British term for a FOOTLIGHT SPOT.

flog
To remove the dust from canvas scenery by beating it with a device (*flogger*) consisting of strips of canvas fastened to a wooden handle—British.

flood
1. Short for FLOODLIGHT. 2. To cause a spotlight to give diffused illumination, as, to *flood it.*

(See also the combinations of FLOODLIGHT, with which the combinations of *flood* are almost always interchangeable.)

flood batten
In British terminology, a pipe batten (see BATTEN) carrying floodlights.

flood (light); flood-light; floodlight
1. A lighting unit consisting of one or more lamps in a metal hood, with a reflector or inner reflecting surface and a color frame holder, but commonly without a means of focusing, used to illuminate a large area diffusely; commonly placed in the wings, either hanging from the flies or fastened to a standard. British: FLOAT, *floodlight, flood* (or *flooding*) *lantern, standard flood.* Also, to illuminate the stage with such lights.

floor
See STAGE FLOOR.

floor block
In the counterweight system, a pulley block fastened to the stage floor to receive an endless line.

floor cloth
A GROUND CLOTH.

floor electrician
An electrician in charge of disposing and adjusting the lighting units while the curtain is down.

floor hook
A hook used to attach a guy rope or wire to the stage floor.

floor iron
A SILL IRON.

floor plan
A map of the stage floor, showing the position of everything in a setting.

floor plate
A flat metal device which can be placed on the stage floor to receive the lower end of a stage brace, so that a stage screw will not be needed.

floor plug
A STAGE PLUG (which see).

floor pocket
A STAGE POCKET. British: *dip*.

floor show
An entertainment consisting of various specialty acts, presented informally in a night club, cabaret, or the like.

floor sleeve
A metal tube, fastened to the stage floor, through which a purchase line can be played.

floor stay
A DROP CLAMP.

flop
An utter failure (as stage production or actor). British: Also, *dud*. Also, to fail utterly.

flourish
A trumpet call, usually to herald the entrance of important persons—Elizabethan stage direction.

fluff

In acting, to forget one's lines; or to mumble lines which one cannot clearly remember. Also, a blunder or delay caused by lapse of memory, as, to *commit a fluff*. Hence *fluffy*.

fly

To hang scenery, etc., above the stage by means of lines from the grid, so that it may be raised into the flies out of sight of the audience, or lowered into view. Hence *flying* (noun, adjective), as, a *flying ceiling*, the *flying system*. Past participle and adjective *flied* or *flown*. Past tense *flied*.

fly bridge

See BRIDGE (sense 2).

fly curtain

A curtain which is vertically raised into or lowered from the flies.

fly floor; fly-floor

A fly gallery; sometimes, the lower of two fly galleries.

fly gallery; fly-gallery

A narrow balcony outside the acting area, usually only on one side of the stage, running from front to back at least a few feet above the floor; on it stagehands can stand to fasten lines to the pin rail or to load counterweights; it is sometimes distinguished from a lower balcony of this kind (*fly floor*) when two are used.

flying bridge

A fly bridge (see BRIDGE, sense 2).

flying effect

A mechanical device by means of which actors and objects can be suspended and moved above the stage, on wires or otherwise.

flyings

Formerly, FLYING EFFECTS (which see).

flying space
The space available for the flying (hanging) of scenery above the stage.

Fly it
A command to a stagehand to raise scenery or other equipment into the flies.

fly ladder
A ladder at the side of the stage, used for access to the fly gallery.

fly line
A rope or wire line used to hang scenery or equipment from the flies.

fly loft; short form, **loft**
The upper part of the flies.

fly-man; flyman
A stagehand who handles ropes or equipment by means of which scenery, lighting units, etc., are raised and lowered.

fly plot
A GRID PLOT (which see).

fly rail; fly-rail
1. The upper of the two rows of pins comprising a pin rail, used for tying off lines when scenery has been hauled into the flies. Called also *working rail*. 2. In British usage, a PIN RAIL.

flys
Variant British spelling of *flies*.

fly space
The space above the acting area, below the grid.

focus
1. In acting, to turn to face squarely another actor, an object, etc. 2. In lighting, to adjust a lighting instrument in terms of beam spread or direction. Hence *flood focus, spot focus*, etc.

focus lamp
In British terminology, a lighting unit, such as a spotlight, providing specific illumination controlled by a lens.

F.O.H.
Abbreviation of FRONT OF HOUSE.

foil
An actor or character who sets off or marks the qualities of another.

fold
1. To close, to fail, to end the run of a production. Also as *fold up*. 2. To CLEW.

folding batten
A vertical batten which folds on hinges so that a three-fold may be closed.

foliage border
A border with a foliage design, irregularly edged.

foliage brush
A small paintbrush used to decorate scenery with simulated foliage.

folk drama
A dramatic entertainment involving folklore, traditional (and commonly regional) material, generally presented by natives of rural areas, and often unsophisticated or impromptu; also collectively. Hence *folk theatre, regional folk drama,* etc.

follow
To aim a spotlight so that its beams pursue a moving actor.

follow spotlight
A spotlight so mounted that it can follow. British: Also as *following spotlight*.

follow-through
CONTINUITY (which see).

foot
Short for FOOTLIGHT. Commonly in the plural, *foots.*

foot a flat
To hold a foot, with the sole on the floor, against the bottom edge of a flat, while another person, moving under the flat, pushes it up or lets it down. Hence *footing a flat.*

foot iron
A metal bar, usually with two arms hinged or fixed at a right angle to each other, fastened to the base of a piece of scenery with bolts or screws and to the floor with a stage screw.

footlight; short form, **foot**
A lighting unit with a reflector, installed in a strip on or in the floor across part of the width of the stage, parallel to the curtain line and usually in front of it, and hooded on the auditorium side. Hence *footlight strip.* British: FLOAT or *footlight.*

footlight spot
A small spotlight mounted as one of the footlights; sometimes used elsewhere. British: *float spot.*

footlights trap
Formerly, a long transverse opening at the front of the stage floor, into which the oil lamps of footlights could be lowered for dimming and blackouts, by means of a sliding framework.

footlight trough; short form, **trough**
A narrow section across the front of the stage floor, recessed to contain footlights.

footmen's gallery
The uppermost gallery in a theatre, occupied by servants and other poor classes—Restoration and into 18th century.

foot piece; footpiece
A British term for a GROUND ROW.

fop's alley; fops' alley; fop alley
A space in the pit or on the forestage where fops (dandies) promenaded to display themselves and comment on the play—Restoration.

fop's corner; fops' corner
The section of the FOP'S ALLEY near the forestage.

foreshadow
To hint, in dialogue or by other means, that some later dramatic action will occur. Hence also *(dramatic) foreshadowing.*

fore-stage; forestage
An APRON, though sometimes considered as some extension thereof, or the area downstage of the inner proscenium.

fork
1. A tilting fork (or YOKE, which see). 2. Chiefly in British terminology, a device consisting of wooden blocks or prongs or rollers projecting downward from a board, used to hold the tops of wings—19th century. Called also *fork end.*

form
In the composition of stage settings, the technical consideration given to the distribution of lighting, the arrangement of scenery, etc.

formal
Said of a stage setting which is architecturally simple and generalized in design, a more or less permanent background for a production regardless of changes in locale. Hence *formal stage.*

formal balancing
In stage directing, a symmetrical balancing of the stage picture, such as the placing of the central figure upstage center and two lesser figures down right and down left at points equidistant from the center.

formalism
In scenic design, a method based on the use of a formal stage setting, rather than a realistic one, to indicate the locale. See FORMAL.

Fortuny lighting system
A method of throwing diffused light on the stage, by means of reflection from colored bands (of silk, etc.) and from a sky-dome (of silk, plaster, etc.). Named for its inventor, Mariano Fortuny (1871–1949), Italian scenic designer.

foul
Said of ropes, scenic pieces, etc., hanging in the flies: To become entangled. Hence *fouling* (noun).

fouling pole
A long pole used to release ropes or pieces of equipment which have become fouled.

foundation
A flesh-colored grease paint, used as a make-up base. Also the application of this paint to the face.

four
See IN FOUR.

fourth wall; fourth-wall
The conventional name for the proscenium opening, which replaces one wall in an interior set; sometimes assumed to be the wall behind the audience.

four walls
Said of a theatre rented by the owner to a producer (who assumes all operating expenses) for a fixed figure rather than for a percentage of the profit. Hence a *four-wall basis*.

fox wedge; fox-wedge
A wooden wedge, used on a raked stage under a flat to make it level.

foyer
The theatre area between the outer lobby and the auditorium; or the lobby itself.

frame
1. The wooden framework of a flat. 2. A flat; short for FRAME PIECE. 3. A playwriting device: The plot framework enclosing an inner dramatic action, such as a play within a play. 4. Short for LOBBY FRAME. 5. Short for COLOR FRAME. 6. A false proscenium. 7. For *carriage-and-frame system*, see CHARIOT-AND-POLE SYSTEM.

frame batten
The cross-braced frame for a framed drop.

frame border
A border stretched on a frame of border battens.

frame brace
A FRENCH BRACE (which see).

frame cloth
A FRAMED DROP.

framed drop
A drop curtain, on a steadying wooden frame consisting of stretchers and battens, used as a back wall in the absence of a ceiling and door opening.

frame piece; short form, **frame**
A FLAT.

framing shutter
A cutoff with a shutter which can be adjusted to give a square or rectangular beam shape, as, a *four-way framing shutter*.

free act
A privilege, accorded to gentlemen, of seeing one act free— Restoration.

free list
A door list. Hence, for a person on such a list, a *free-lister*.

freeze
In acting, to HOLD (sense 1), to keep motionless, especially while the audience laughs. Also, a hold of this kind.

French brace
A British term for a BRACE JACK.

French curtain
A festoon curtain (see FESTOON).

French door shutter
A door shutter with small oblong panes.

French flat
In British terminology, a framed canvas piece which can be flied, with practical doors and windows (see under PRACTI-CABLE).

French scene
A scene division marked (as in French drama) by the entrance or exit of any actor.

French shutter
Short for FRENCH DOOR SHUTTER.

French tab
A term, chiefly British, for a DRAW TAB.

Fresnel (lens spotlight)
A powerful step-lens spotlight giving a soft-edged illumination. Hence also *Fresnelite*. Named for the French physicist Augustin Jean Fresnel (1788–1827).

fright wig (or hair)
A wig which, when its wearer pulls a string, gives the effect of hair standing on end as in terror.

front

1. Downstage. 2. All the parts of a theatre which are not backstage, as, *out front*. Sometimes specifically the business offices.

front box

A box facing the stage rather than at the side—Chiefly Restoration and 18th century.

front cloth; front-cloth

1. Chiefly in British usage, a FRONT CURTAIN. 2. *in a front cloth:* See IN ONE.

front curtain

Any curtain hanging across the front of the stage, especially an ACT CURTAIN.

frontispiece

A proscenium—Restoration.

front light

A lighting unit (as, a *balcony front light*, a *front spotlight*) placed somewhere in the auditorium for the illumination of the front of the stage. Hence *front lighting*.

front of house; front-of-house;
front of the house; abbreviation, **F.O.H.**

1. The parts of the theatre in front of the proscenium arch. Hence, said of equipment placed therein, as, a *front of house light*. 2. The audience. 3. The lobby and business offices 4. The personnel and operations of the business staff, including the ushers, as, the *front of house staff*.

front piece; front-piece

A CURTAIN RAISER (which see).

front pipe

A pipe batten downstage, as in *front pipe lighting*.

front row

1. The foremost line of seats in a seating area. 2. The foremost line of a chorus or dancing ensemble.

front scene
1. A scene played downstage, either in front of a painted drop or in a small set in front of a large set, while the set for the next scene is being readied. 2. Scenery near the front of the stage, as, a drop or flat.

front set line
An actual or imaginary line between the inner proscenium and the TORMENTORS, marking the downstage limit of the stage setting and the acting area.

front spotlight
See FRONT LIGHT.

front stage
The forepart of the stage.

frost
1. A diffusing color medium. Hence *frost gelatin, frosted gelatin.* 2. Lacquer. 3. A play that is a failure. 4. To simulate snow by decorating a scene with glittering material. Hence *frosting* (noun).

fruit woman
A woman holding the concession to sell refreshments in a theatre—Restoration. Hence *fruit money* (payable to the theatre for the concession).

full-back (position)
The body position of an actor with his back turned to the audience.

full drop
Any drop curtain other than a CUT DROP.

full-front position; short form, **full-front**
The body position of an actor facing the audience.

150

full-length play
A play of the usual duration, long enough for a full program, in contradistinction to a shorter work such as a one-act play.

full set
A stage setting covering the full width of the acting area.

full stage
A stage used in its general entirety for setting and acting. Hence a *full stage act*, etc.

full up; full-up
Said of lighting at its maximum brightness.

functional property
A property required by the script.

funnel
A metal or cardboard cylinder or box used on a lighting unit to limit the beam spill.

funny man; funnyman
A comedian.

furniture plot
A list of all pieces of furniture to be used in a production, with an indication of their location.

furniture store
A room offstage for the storage of stage furniture (other than scenery or properties).

futurism
An art movement and style breaking with the past and emphasizing new forces; related to expressionism, Dadaism; and sometimes influential upon the theatre—Chiefly early 20th century. Hence *futuristic*, etc.

G

gaff

In British terminology, a portable or improvised theatre or music hall, a fit-up; hence any cheap, low-class theatre or music hall. Also, from the former admission charges, in the forms *penny gaff, twopenny gaff;* and see BLOOD TUB. Hence also, in British terminology, *Gaff Street,* for any street containing several theatres.

gag

An interpolation consisting of lines or business not in the script, introduced by an actor extemporaneously (or seemingly so), and usually comic; also, any stage jest, derived visibly or audibly from lines, situation, business, properties, etc. To introduce such lines, business, etc.; to ad-lib. Hence *gagger* (*gaggist, gagman, gagster*), *gagging* (noun), *gag line.* See also SIGHT GAG.

galanty (galantee, galanti, gallanty) show

A British term for a shadow play (see SHADOW SHOW)—19th century.

gallery

1. In British and rarely in U.S. terminology, a seating area higher than the main floor, usually the topmost balcony with the cheapest seats but sometimes one of two such balconies (*upper gallery, lower gallery*). See PENNY GALLERY. Hence also the spectators in such an area (called also *gallery-ites*), often derogatorily in allusion to an actual or alleged lack of taste or manners; by extension, an entire audience. See PLAY TO THE GALLERY. 2. Any raised working platform at the side of the stage, as, a FLY GALLERY. 3. The UPPER STAGE (which see)— Elizabethan.

gallery door
A term, chiefly British, for a street door through which spectators are admitted to a gallery. Hence *gallery doorman.*

Gallery Gods; short form, (the) **Gods**
The spectators in the topmost gallery or balcony, often with the implication that these are cruder than other spectators but sometimes that they are the most influential critics. By extension, the upper gallery or balcony. Usually capitalized; rarely found in the singular.

galloping hooves
An acoustical effect, simulating the sound of horses' hooves, achieved by such means as the rattling of coconut shells (held in the hands) on a slate. Called also *hoofbeat effect, hooves-heard-off trick.*

gang
To group together (spotlights, dimmers, etc.). A group or grouping of lighting equipment, as *gang control.*

gangway
A British term for an aisle.

garden border
A FOLIAGE BORDER.

garden set
An exterior setting simulating a garden.

garden theatre
A theatre in the open air, making use of hedges or other vegetation for part of the stage enclosure.

garland
A border or other hanging piece simulating foliage.

gas
Illuminating gas, which supplanted the wax candle and oil lamp for theatrical lighting, and which in its turn was supplanted by

gas batten

the incandescent electric bulb—19th century. Hence *gas* (verb), *gaslight* (or *-light,*) *gaselier* (or *gasolier*), etc.

gas batten; gas-batten
A row of gaslights illuminating the stage from above—19th century.

gas dial (or **table**)
A control board with keys or valves, used to regulate the flow of gas for theatrical illumination—19th century.

gas length
A row of gaslights fastened vertically behind the proscenium or wings—19th century.

gas-man; gasman
A person charged with the operation of the gaslights in a theatre —19th century.

gas table; gas-table
See GAS DIAL.

gas-wing
A row of gas LADDER LIGHTS—19th century.

gate
1. A place on a lamp housing at which a shutter is attached. 2. In the plural, temporary properties used to close off the inner stage—Elizabethan. 3. See CRASH THE GATE. 4. The main entrance door of a theatre. See WATCH THE GATE.

gatherer
A collector of admission fees—Elizabethan. Called also *box holder, door keeper.*

gauze
Short for THEATRICAL GAUZE. Also, a curtain made of this material (in British usage, a *gauze cloth*).

gel
Short for GELATIN SLIDE. Also a verb, as in *gel-up* (meaning to replace burnt-out gelatin mediums).

gelatin(e)
Short for GELATIN SLIDE.

gelatin frame
A color frame, for a gelatin slide.

gelatin slide; short forms, **gel, gelatin(e)**
A translucent substance used as a color medium.

general-admission fee
A charge made for admission to a theatrical performance, now commonly for an unreserved seat.

general lighting
Lighting which is thrown over a fairly extensive portion of the stage.

general manager
The business manager of a theatrical production firm.

general utility; short form, **utility**
A UTILITY ACTOR (which see).

genteel comedy
A type of polite comedy lying between the Restoration comedy of manners and 18th century sentimental comedy (comedy of sensibility)—Early 18th century.

gentleman
See WALKING GENTLEMAN.

gentleman's room
A room or box with high-priced seats, in a gallery near the stage, as, the lord's room, the twelve-penny room, etc.—Elizabethan.

George Spelvin
See SPELVIN.

gesture
In acting, a movement of the limbs or body as a means of dramatic expression. Also, to make such a movement.

get across
See GO (*across*).

get a hand
See HAND.

get-away night
The night on which a touring company plays its last performance in a particular theatre.

get in
A British term for TAKE IN (which see). Also, as a noun (hyphenated), taking-in.

get out
A British term for the following: 1. TAKE OUT (which see). Also, as a noun (hyphenated), *taking-out*. 2. Usually when hyphenated, the BREAK-EVEN.

get over
See GO (*over*).

get the bird
To be jeered by the audience for one's acting.

Get the hook!
A command shouted by an audience to get an actor off the stage. See HOOK.

get the raspberry (or razz)
To be jeered by the audience for one's acting.

ghost
1. A company treasurer. Hence, for pay day, *ghost-walking day* or *the ghost walks*; to receive one's salary, *see the ghost walk*;

not to be paid, *the ghost fails to walk;* pay window, *ghost window.* The name is said to come from the ghost in *Hamlet,* an actor in this role having refused to play until he was paid. 2. In lighting, a secondary illumination from a spotlight, showing that the optical system is not in proper adjustment.

ghost glide
A trap mechanism operated through a stage cut, consisting of a small truck on an inclined railway which slowly lifted an actor as it moved across the stage—19th century. Called also CORSICAN TRAP.

ginger
Risqué significance.

give
To move so as to allow another actor to take some important position on the stage. Hence also *give a scene, give stage, giver, given position.*

give a hand
See HAND.

give out the play
Formerly, to announce the play to be given the following night.

give the word (or **line**)
To prompt, as, *Give me the line, He gave him the words.*

G.K.P. projector
An optical apparatus for the projection of scenic effects on a cyclorama. Named for its developers, the former Viennese firm of Gayling, Kann, and Planer.

glass crash
An acoustical crash effect simulating the sound of breaking windowpanes, etc., as by dropping bits of glass offstage.

glaze
To cover the painted surface of scenery with *glazing* (a thin wash of size) to soften its appearance.

glitter
A substance used to add sparkle in a snow effect.

glory
1. A frame covered with taffeta, lighted from behind, used to provide a glowing background for an actor in his role as a divinity—Restoration. 2. A tableau, consisting of an actor in the role of a divinity on an elevator against a colorful background—Renaissance through the 17th century.

go
1. Said of a performance or production: To be successful with an audience or audiences, as, The play didn't *go* at all, The second act *went* well. Also as *go* (or *get*) *across* (the footlights), *go* (or *get*) *over* (the footlights). 2. Change the set—A direction to stagehands.

go back(stage)
To visit an actor in a dressing room or in the green room. Also, *go behind*. British: *go round*.

gobo
A pattern for a lighting effect, either plain, diffusing, or figured, placed in front of a light source so as to cause the projection of the pattern onto the projection surface. Often confused with CUCKALORIS (which see).

go clean
To sell all the tickets for a performance.

god from the machine
See DEUS EX MACHINA.

go down
1. To move downstage—Sometimes, a stage direction. 2. Said of lights: To be dimmed.

Gods
Short for GALLERY GODS.

gold powder
A golden powder for a blond hair effect.

good box office
Said of a production successful in its appeal to the public, having a good run, as, *It's good box office.* See BOX-OFFICE APPEAL.

good house
1. An appreciative audience. 2. A theatre filled with paying patrons.

good theatre
Said (especially in the U.S.) of a theatrically effective play or bit of business.

go off
1. To make an exit—Sometimes, a stage direction. 2. The stage manager's command to an actor to leave the stage.

go on
1. To make an entrance—Sometimes, a stage direction. To substitute for another actor, as, I'm *going on* for him. 2. The stage manager's command to an actor to enter, to go on stage. 3. *go on the stage:* To become a professional actor.

go round
A British equivalent for GO BACKSTAGE.

go the rounds; make the rounds
To go from one agent or producer to another in search of a role. British: *do the agents.*

go to Cain's (Warehouse)
To close a show. Hence also *going to Cain's.* Cain's Warehouse was a storage place in New York City operated by Cain's Transfer Company (1886–1937), which sold and rented scenery to road companies.

gouger
See TICKET GOUGER.

go up
1. To move upstage—Sometimes, a stage direction. 2. To forget one's lines.

grand circle
A British term sometimes used for a DRESS CIRCLE.

grand curtain
A GRAND DRAPERY BORDER.

grand drapery border; short forms, **grand drape, grand drapery**
A border across the width of the stage behind the asbestos curtain, used to provide part of the decorative frame completed by the TEASER and TORMENTORS which are just upstage of it. British: *pelmet* or VALANCE.

grande dame
An actress who plays the role of an imperious elderly woman; particularly, an actress who specializes in such roles.

grand finale
A finale on a grand spectacular scale, in which the principals and ensemble participate—Chiefly Musical shows.

Grand Guignol
A short sensational horror play—A French term (the name of a Paris theatre where such plays are produced) used in English.

grand master control (or **cross-control**)
A locking device on a dimmer board to permit the simultaneous operation of groups of dimmers. Hence *grand master board, grand master handle*, etc.

grand opera
A serious opera, especially a tragic opera, in which all the dialogue is sung; also collectively.

grand tab
An ACT CURTAIN.

grass mat
A map of artificial (or sometimes real) grass fastened to a canvas or other backing.

grave trap
A trap in the shape of a grave, centrally placed in the stage floor, through which actors can be made to appear and disappear, and sometimes containing a mechanism to raise and lower them. Named from its use in the grave scene in *Hamlet*.

gravy
1. HOKUM. 2. In British usage, risqué lines.

grease paint; grease-paint; greasepaint
A waxy cosmetic used in making up for the stage, of oil, spermaceti, and wax, or of similar substances, in various colors. Hence *grease color*, *grease stick*, etc. See also SMELL OF (THE) GREASE PAINT.

great scene
In a WELL-MADE PLAY (which see), the scene embodying the climax.

Great White Way
BROADWAY (which see) in New York City.

green
1. Formerly, a stage. 2. Formerly, a front curtain, especially in the form *green baize;* also called a GREEN CURTAIN. 3. A stage carpet used in tragedy, especially in the form *green baize*—18th and 19th centuries.

greenback
A GREENCOAT (which see).

green baize
See GREEN and GREEN CURTAIN.

green box
A British term for an upper box—18th and 19th centuries.

Green Cloth
Short for BOARD OF GREEN CLOTH.

greencoat; green-coat man
A stagehand dressed in green—Restoration.

green curtain (or **baize**)
A heavy outer curtain, traditional from the time of the Restoration, but now outmoded, serving variously as an act drop, fire curtain, etc.

green room; green-room; greenroom
A lounge offstage where actors may rest or receive visitors; now uncommon. Perhaps so named for its original color. Hence also *green room gossip*, to talk *greenroom* (to indulge in theatre gossip), etc.

green room actor
An actor whose success in the theatre is limited to his self-satisfied green room posturing.

grid
Short for GRIDIRON.

grid connector
In British terminology, a connector box located on the grid.

gridiron; short form, **grid**
An open framework of beams over the entire stage, used principally for the suspension of scenery and lights.

grid plot
A plot or plan made and used by a flyman to indicate his duties in a performance.

grip
1. In British terminology, short for BARREL GRIP. 2. A metal device, consisting of a U-shaped body, with a saddle and nuts,

used to fasten a cable. 3. In U.S. terminology only, a stagehand, usually one who helps the chief carpenter on or below the stage level, especially in scene-shifting. Called also *grip-hand, grips, stage grip.*

groove
1. A wooden channel to receive a sliding flat, especially in a wing setting—17th through 19th centuries. Grooves were numbered from the front of the stage to the back (*first groove*, etc.), and were called *lower* (at the stage level) and *upper* (at the grid level) ; they could be *loose* or *fixed.* An upper groove which could be swung offstage on hinges was called a *groove-arm.* 2. A channel or bracket affixed to a lighting unit to receive a color frame.

gross (receipts)
The total income from ticket sales, computed weekly, used as a basis for determining such financial arrangements as the author's royalties.

grotesque
Said of a drama which is fantastically unrealistic, as, a *grotesque comedy.*

grouch bag
An actor's purse.

ground cloth
A canvas or other covering stretched on the floor of the stage. British: *stage cloth.*

groundling
A member of the audience standing in the yard (that is, pit)— Elizabethan.

ground plan
A FLOOR PLAN of the stage.

ground row; ground-row; groundrow
1. A long, low set piece, commonly built and painted like a flat, with the upper edge cut irregularly, used to simulate a more or less distant view, as of a landscape, buildings, or a wall, and often also used to conceal lights or the edge of the backdrop. Called specifically a *horizon row,* a *sea row,* etc. 2. Originally (19th century) a gas strip light; now a strip light behind a ground row (sense 1).

ground row strip
A strip light used to illuminate a ground row from the front.

group
Short for STAGE GROUPING.

group drama
MASS DRAMA.

grouping
Short for STAGE GROUPING.

group scene
A scene in which several actors participate.

guest actor (or **artist** or **star**)
A distinguished actor playing temporarily with a repertory or stock company.

guest-direct
To direct a production at the invitation of an amateur company, in place of the usual director. Also, *guest-directing* (noun), *guest director.*

guest performance
A performance by a guest actor.

guide (counterweight) arbor
A counterweight arbor (see COUNTERWEIGHT SYSTEM) with a bar, through which run guide wires, fastened to an eye.

guide line (or **wire**)
1. One of two steel lines placed vertically behind the proscenium to guide the movement of a curtain. 2. Any line, permanent or temporary, which guides the movement of stage scenery or rigging. British: BRAIL (LINE).

Guignol
See GRAND GUIGNOL.

Guild, (the)
1. Frequently, in the U.S. only, short for the *Dramatists' Guild*, an association of playwrights which has established a basic contract with theatre managers to protect the interests of dramatic authors. 2. Short for the (New York) *Theatre Guild*.

guild play; guild-play
A play produced by a guild of craftsmen or tradesmen—Medieval.

guiser; guisard
A British term for a mummer, masquer, disguiser.

gyp
An agent who charges more than the legal ticket premium.

H

habit
See COSTUME.

hair powder
A powder used to gray or otherwise color the hair, beard, mustache, or eyebrows.

Half (an) hour!
An act warning, about half an hour before the first rise of the curtain. Hence, *half-hour call*.

half keystone
A KEYSTONE trimmed at an angle, used to fasten a diagonal to a stile.

half leg drop
A LEG DROP which is attached to a solid, or at least rounded, tree trunk, column, or similar piece, and which does not itself extend to the stage floor.

half-price
A reduction to half the usual admission charge, effective at a stipulated time during a performance—18th and 19th centuries. Hence *at half-price (time)*, the *half-price system*.

hall
Short for MUSIC HALL.

hall backing
See BACKING.

hall-keeper
A British term for a STAGE DOORMAN.

ham
To act badly, or to overact, especially from vanity. Hence *hamming* (noun), *ham acting*, *hammy*. Also, an actor who so

performs, especially when he is unaware of his poor showing; formerly sometimes used in the form *hamfatter*.

hamartia
A doctrine in Aristotle's *Poetics*. See TRAGIC FLAW.

hand
Applause, usually in the forms *get a hand* or *give a hand*. See also SIT ON ONE'S HANDS.

handbill
A printed theatrical notice of a forthcoming production or performance, identifying the theatre, title of the piece, players, date, and hour.

handcuffed
Said of an audience which does not applaud, as, They're *handcuffed*.

hand line
A line on which a stagehand pulls.

hand property
A property which is handled by an actor onstage, especially one which he carries on or off with him, such as a tray.

hand-worked house
A theatre using ropes which are hauled, rather than a counterweight system.

hang
1. To suspend or trim any piece of scenery or equipment. Hence (of a hung piece) *hanging flood*, etc. 2. To put up a set and all that goes with it, as, *hang the show*.

hanger
Any of several devices used to suspend scenery, equipment, etc. Hence CURTAIN POLE (or *drapery*) HANGER, PICTURE FRAME HANGER, etc.

hanger iron; hanging iron
A short strip of steel or iron used in hanging framed scenery. It is pierced with holes, and can be screwed or bolted to the frame of a flat; one end is fitted with a ring or eye through which a line can be passed, and the other end is sometimes hooked to pass under the bottom rail of the framed piece.

hanging clip
A British term for a PIPE CLAMP (which see).

hanging iron
See HANGER IRON.

hanging length; short form, length
In British terminology, a line of lights, fastened to a portable wooden casing which is hooked to the rail of a flat or is otherwise suspended from scenery, used to illuminate doors and windows. U.S.: STRIP (LIGHT).

hanging plot
A plan used to indicate the position of hanging pieces.

hanging space
The space available for hanging scenery.

hanging unit
A group of scenic pieces, such as the components of a cyclorama, suspended as a unit rather than as separate parts.

happy ending
In the plot of a dramatic composition, a termination which is felicitous, fortunate, and favorable for the characters in whose fate the spectator (or reader) is expected to be especially interested.

hard
See FALSE PROSCENIUM for the meaning of *hard false* (or *inner*) *proscenium*.

hardware
Short for THEATRICAL HARDWARE.

hard wood; hardwood
Collectively, special tickets sold at bargain rates, when a show is not drawing well; also, tickets on sale to standees.

Harlequin
Originally, a minor character (Arlecchino, a servant of Pantaleone) in the *commedia dell' arte*. Later, Columbine's lover and the principal figure in a HARLEQUINADE (which see), especially in PANTOMIME (which see, sense 2). Former spelling also *Arlequin*. Also (uncapitalized) a trickster, buffoon, or performer in a Harlequin role.

Harlequina
Feminine form of HARLEQUIN (which see).

harlequinade
A type of entertainment featuring a HARLEQUIN (which see); especially, in British usage, though now reduced in importance, the traditional second part of a PANTOMIME (which see, sense 2), featuring the characters of Harlequin, Columbine, Pantaloon, and Clown. Also, a harlequin role. The first letter is sometimes capitalized.

harmony
In production, a regard for the appropriate total effect of the various elements of design.

Hasait
A kind of roll cyclorama (trade-marked). Named for Max Hasait, a German supplier of theatrical curtains, its inventor. See also SCHWABE-HASAIT LIGHTING.

hat
In lighting, a *tin hat*, a type of FUNNEL (which see).

head
Short for CREW HEAD, *department head.* Also, said of a crew head, as, the *head electrician.*

head block
A frame at the side of the grid, containing pulleys over which pass lines between the loft blocks and either the pin rail or the counterweight cradle.

header
A small flat placed between two flats to fill in the space above a door, window, or arch.

headline
To obtain star billing, as, We *headlined* on the Orpheum circuit—Chiefly Vaudeville. Hence *headlining* (noun) for billing as the leading actor (British: *topping the bill*), *headliner* for an outstanding actor (British: *top liner*), *headline system.*

head rail
The top RAIL of a flat.

head room
The height of the over-stage space available for the flying of scenery.

Heads up!
A warning call by a flyman who is moving scenery overhead.

heart
A padding used in tights worn by actors, acrobats, etc.

heaven
1. A KUPPELHORIZONT (which see). 2. As *a heavens* or *the heavens,* a wooden roof over part of the outer stage, on columns —Elizabethan. 3. See NIGGER HEAVEN and PEANUT GALLERY.

heavy
1. Said of intensely serious drama, as, a *heavy play.* 2. Said of a comic role which requires an actor to pretend to be serious, as, a *heavy comedy part.* 3. Short for HEAVY LEAD (or MAN).

heavy lead (or **man**); short form, **heavy;**
  (feminine) **heavy woman**
The role of any solemn leading character, especially (though now becoming rare) a villain; an actor who plays such a role.

hell
The CELLAR (which see) under the stage—Medieval and Elizabethan.

hero; (feminine) **heroine**
The central figure in a dramatic work, the protagonist; the romantic lead.

heroic acting
An acting style marked by physical force, by emphasis on major traits of character rather than on detail, by the strong delineation of passion rather than subtlety, spirituality, or intellectuality.

heroic drama
Dramatic works, collectively or individually, in which a central figure struggles to decide between the conflicting claims of love and honor—Restoration. Hence *heroic comedy, heroic tragedy,* etc.

heroine
Feminine form of HERO.

high comedy
A comedy which is subtle and articulate, giving rise to thoughtful laughter; also collectively. Sometimes limited to the COMEDY OF MANNERS (which see). Hence *high comedian.*

high light; highlight
To accentuate part of the face by means of a spot or line of light-colored make-up. Hence *highlighting* (noun). Also, a spot or line so used.

high tragedy
Tragedy at its noblest, loftiest.

hinge

An ordinary household hinge, used on the stage under various specific names to join flats and other pieces; commonly the original pin is replaced with a looser one which can more easily be removed.

hireling

A person employed by the sharing members of a theatrical company to serve as actor or as musician, book holder (prompter), etc.—Elizabethan and Restoration. Called also *hired man,* etc.

hiss

A noise made by a spectator, expelling air through the teeth, to express disapproval. Also, to make such a noise.

historical drama

A dramatic composition based on historical events; also collectively. Hence *historical tragedy*, etc.

history (play)

Short for CHRONICLE HISTORY PLAY.

histrio; histrion

A rare term for an actor.

histrionic

1. Of or pertaining to acting or actors; theatrical. Hence *histrionical*, etc. 2. As a plural noun, stage shows; dramatic representation; over-emotional acting; acting.

hit

A successful stage production, acting performance, etc. Hence *hit show, make a hit*, etc.

Hock-Tuesday play

A folk drama performed at Coventry on the third Tuesday after Easter, which in its late literary form depicted a victory of English knights over Danes who were led off as prisoners by Englishwomen. It probably developed from an earlier rural festival in which women caught ("hocked") men and extracted forfeits from them—Medieval. Called also *Hock play, Hocktide play*, etc.

172

hokum; hoke
A situation, a piece of business, or lines, which can be relied on to produce a predictable (usually a sentimental) response from an audience; time-worn claptrap.

hold
1. In acting, to pause, as for the audience's laughter or applause. Also, a delay, intentional or unintentional, by an actor (British: Usually *wait*). 2. A command from the director at a rehearsal to stop acting so that comment can be made. 3. Of an actor or scene, to capture and retain the attention of the audience.

hold a scene
In acting, to remain in one's position at the close of a scene.

holdover
A show continuing after the announced closing date.

hold the boards
To HOLD THE STAGE (which see).

hold the book
To serve as prompter.

hold the stage
Said of dramatic compositions: To continue to be produced. By extension, applied also to dramatic authors.

hold up the backdrop (or **scenery**)
To have no (or few) lines to speak, as (of a show girl) to appear onstage only to display one's clothes or body.

homiletic tragedy
Domestic tragedy (see DOMESTIC DRAMA).

hood
1. A funnel for a lighting unit. 2. The box-like metal body of a spotlight or floodlight.

hoof; hooves
See GALLOPING HOOVES.

hoofer
A dancer, especially a tap dancer—Musical comedy, Vaudeville.
Hence *hoofing act.*

hook
A hook on a pole used to pull an unwanted actor off the stage on
amateur night—Vaudeville, late 19th century. Also, *be hooked.*
The expression *Get the hook!* survives with the meaning "Take
him off the stage!" when an actor does badly.

hook up; hook-up
To compare production and operating costs in budgeting. Also,
such a comparison.

horizon
See DOME HORIZON.

horizon cloth
A cyclorama, as of canvas.

horizon floodlight
A type of HORIZON LIGHT.

horizon light
A light used to illuminate a cyclorama from below.

horizon pit
A CYCLORAMA TROUGH.

horizon row
A GROUND ROW simulating a view of the horizon.

horizon strip
A cyclorama strip light.

horizont
Short for DOME HORIZON, KUPPELHORIZONT.

horror play
A play emphasizing the horror of torture, bloodshed, etc. Hence
horror tragedy, etc.

horseshoe

1. An auditorium, or a portion of an auditorium (as, a tier of boxes), in the shape of a horseshoe. Hence, *horseshoe theatre*, etc. 2. Hyphenated: In British terminology, a clamping device used to fasten a wooden batten to an iron batten.

hot

1. Said of any electrical device through which current is passing, particularly to convey the idea of its possible exposure to human touch. 2. Said of a performer who seems likely to become a star. Also, to *be hot*.

hot spot

1. An area which is brightly illuminated. 2. The brightest rays of a light beam.

house

1. An auditorium or other area open to the audience in a theatre; hence an audience, as, an *empty house*, a *full house*, a *good house*. Also a theatre, as, a *vaudeville house*. 2. The permanent management operating a theatre which a company is occupying only temporarily. Hence *house crew*, *house staff*, etc. 3. A MANSION (which see)—Medieval and Renaissance. Called also *players' house*.

house board; house-board; houseboard

1. In the plural, a fairly permanent posting-place for play advertisements, outside but next to a theatre. 2. A fixed switch-board, usually controlling the house lights only.

house curtain

The FRONT CURTAIN (behind the asbestos curtain), which may or may not also be used as an act curtain.

house full

A British equivalent for SOLD OUT (which see); used as the wording on signs displayed at a theatre entrance.

house full of paper
See PAPER.

house-keeper; housekeeper
1. A person employed to clean or supervise the cleaning of a theatre building. 2. An owner, proprietor, or controller, in whole or in part, of a theatre, who was paid a portion of the admission receipts and was responsible for the building itself—Elizabethan. He might, or might not, also be a sharing member of a theatrical company and an actor. Hence *housekeeping*.

house light; houselight
Any light in a theatre except an exit light or a light on or back of the stage.

house list
A DOOR LIST (which see).

house main
A box where electrical connections must be made to bring the current to the switchboard for stage use.

houseman
A flyman who is temporarily stationed in the auditorium during the preparation for a production to see that the trimming of scenery is accurate.

house manager
The business manager in charge of the theatre building with its staff.

house seat; house-seat
Short for PERSONAL HOUSE SEAT.

house spotlight
A front spotlight (see FRONT LIGHT).

house tab
An ACT CURTAIN.

housing
Short for LAMP HOUSING.

humanist drama
Drama based on classical models—Especially, Renaissance.

humors; humours
See COMEDY OF HUMORS.

hurry music
Music played very fast to accompany the swift action of melodrama.

hut; huts
The superstructure of a theatre, a building or buildings over the acting area from which descents could be made or properties lowered through a trap door in the heavens, and where certain sound effects could be produced—Elizabethan.

hutch
See RABBIT HUTCH.

I

I.A.T.S.E.; I.A.
An abbreviation of *International Alliance of Theatrical Stage Employees and Motion Picture Operators,* a union of stage-hands.

ice
A tip, premium, or commission given by a ticket agent to a box-office treasurer or attendant or to a producer for theatre tickets; a premium charged on a ticket purchased from a ticket agent.

ice-breaker
A fast song for chorus girls—Musical comedy.

idea
See DRAMA OF IDEAS.

idler
A FLOOR BLOCK (which see).

I hope it keeps fine for you
In British usage, a call boy's greeting to wish an actor success.

I hope you break a leg
A superstitious good-luck wish exchanged by actors.

illegitimate drama
Formerly, in British terminology, dramas, collectively or individually, in which songs and instrumental music were interpolated in order to circumvent the theatre laws that gave a monopoly to certain London playhouses (the *patent theatres;* see PATENT) for the production of plays containing only spoken dialogue (the LEGITIMATE DRAMA)—Especially 19th century. Hence *illegitimate theatre,* etc.

illumination
1. Light thrown on the stage. 2. The science or technique of lighting the stage.—In both senses, also in the form *stage illumination.*

178

illusion
In stage production, a method or style which attempts to create the illusion of reality, to simulate real life, to ignore theatrical conventions. Hence *illusionary, illusory,* etc.

imitation
An Aristotelian principle in playwriting: The transformation of materials from real life into a synthesized dramatic substance, as opposed to the indiscriminate copying of such materials.

imitative setting
A representational, realistic, non-abstract setting.

impersonate
To act a role, assuming the character of one of the dramatis personae. Hence *impersonation* (rarely, *impersonification*), *impersonative, impersonator* (feminine, rarely *impersonatress* or *impersonatrix*). See FEMALE IMPERSONATOR, MALE IMPER-SONATOR.

impracticable; impractical
Said of a scenic piece which appears to be an ordinary usable object but which cannot actually be used.

impresario
A producer, especially of musical entertainments. Plural, *impresarios* or *impresari*. Hence also *theatrical impresario,* etc.

impressionism
A theory and technique in dramatic writing and production, aiming at the suggestive rather than the realistic representation of actuality.

improvisation
1. See IMPROVISE. 2. In the Stanislavski method, the acting out of scenes not in a script but invented by an actor for practicing his role offstage.

improvise
To invent lines or business not in a script, to ad-lib. Hence
IMPROVISATION (which see), etc.

improvised comedy
The COMMEDIA DELL' ARTE (which see).

in
1. Said of a setting, curtain, etc., which is ready in position.
2. Said of an actor who has a part in a particular production,
as, John Gielgud *in* "Hamlet."

in a front cloth
A British equivalent for IN ONE (which see).

in association with
A publicity formula by means of which a producer or director
acknowledges a sharing of the responsibility for a production.

incident
Any small event forming part of the dramatic action.

incidental music
Instrumental music played during a dramatic performance,
especially that which is written for, but is not essential to the
completeness of, the dramatic piece itself.

inciting moment
In a dramatic plot, the moment at which an EXCITING FORCE
(which see) begins to operate.

independent
Said of a lighting circuit which is not subject to group control,
though it is operated from a DIMMER BOARD.

index strip light
A strip light used to illuminate small numbers marking the sets
of rope lines on a LOCK RAIL.

indirect footlight
A footlight placed so that the illumination strikes the stage from a reflecting surface rather than directly from the lamp.

indirect lighting
The illumination of a scene by means of a reflecting surface, so that the light rays do not directly reach the stage.

individual set
An ordinary stage setting, consisting of separate pieces; the opposite of a UNIT SETTING.

induction
An expository first portion of a dramatic work, such as a PROLOGUE.

inevitability
A feeling developed in the spectator that the rest of the plot ought to and will follow the logical consequences of the preceding dramatic action.

inflection
The variation in the pitch of an actor's voice as he reveals emotion.

informal balancing
In directing, an asymmetrical balancing of the stage picture, as the placing of the central figure to one side, upstage center, and two lesser figures downstage together on the other side.

in four
Said of a scene played in an acting area bounded on the upstage side by an imaginary line across the stage from the left wing farthest upstage to the right wing farthest upstage, and on the downstage side by the IN THREE area.

in front
A British equivalent for OUT FRONT.

ingénue
The role of a sweet, naïve girl; an actress who plays such a role or roles.

initial incident
In a dramatic plot, the incident which first alters the initial situation.

initial situation
The DRAMATIC SITUATION (sense 1) at the beginning of a dramatic work.

inner proscenium
A FALSE PROSCENIUM.

inner proscenium batten
A TORMENTOR BATTEN.

inner stage
A curtained back portion of a stage—Chiefly Elizabethan. The term itself is not Elizabethan; the period terms are *alcove* and *study*.

Inns of Court plays
Plays based on classical models, acted by fashionable amateurs at the Inns of Court—16th century.

inn-theatre; inn-yard playhouse
An early type of English theatre, consisting of a trestle stage in the yard of an inn; later, a theatre converted from an inn.

in one
Said of a scene played in an acting area bounded on the upstage side by an imaginary line across the stage from the left wing farthest downstage to the right wing farthest downstage. Also said of a curtain position at the same line. British: *in a front cloth*.

**in order of their appearance; in the order in
  which they appear**
Said of actors, in listing their names on a program: In the order
of their entrance or in the order in which they speak onstage,
rather than in the order of their importance in the cast.

in person
Said of a motion picture or other non-theatrical actor who is
making an appearance in a stage show.

inset (piece, scene)
A scene, or a small scenic piece, placed inside another for rapid
scene-shifting.

inside joke
In a play dealing with the theatre, a humorous allusion to the
theatrical world.

inside stile
A STILE (which see) used on an opening in a flat.

intensifier
A lens on a projector lamp used to concentrate the direct rays
which would otherwise diverge.

inter-act
An ENTR'ACTE (which see, both senses).

interchangeable unit scenery
Scenery for a UNIT SETTING, constructed for combination and
interchange.

interior
Short for INTERIOR SETTING.

interior border
A border which simulates a ceiling in an interior setting that
has no ceiling.

183

interior monologue (or **dialogue**)
In dramatic writing, a device consisting of lines introduced to reveal what passes at random in a character's mind, in contradistinction to the more organized thinking put into the conventional aside and soliloquy.

interior setting; short form, **interior**
The setting for an indoor scene. British: *chamber setting*.

interlocking
Said of dimmers which can be controlled in groups by means of a mechanical locking device. Said also of equipment used in connection with such dimmers. Hence *interlock*.

interlocutor
A performer in the seated semicircle who has the role of STRAIGHT MAN and announcer. Called also *middleman*—Minstrel shows.

interlude
A short dramatic piece, usually comic but sometimes didactic, played independently, or as part of a longer entertainment, or in an intermission—Chiefly 16th century. Hence also *interluder, interludial,* to *interlude.* The name *interlude* has survived for any short dramatic piece or other entertainment, commonly one performed during an intermission, as, a *ballet interlude,* a *dance interlude,* etc.

intermedio
An ENTR'ACTE (sense 2)—Chiefly Renaissance and Restoration. Plural, *intermedii*. Often italicized.

intermezzo
An ENTR'ACTE (sense 2)—Chiefly Renaissance and Restoration. Plural, *intermezzi*.

184

intermission
A period between acts or scenes. Sometimes more specifically labeled, as, an *act intermission,* a *scene intermission.* British: *interval* (rarely *intermission*).

intermission drop
An ACT DROP.

interpolation
A portion of dialogue or a bit of business inserted in a script or ad-libbed (as, a gag), or a dance, song, or bit of music added in a stage production. Hence *interpolate, interpolator.*

interval
A British term for an intermission. Hence *interval music,* etc.

in the order in which they appear
See IN ORDER OF THEIR APPEARANCE.

in the round
1. Said of a scenic piece, simulating an object (for example, a tree trunk) which is three-dimensional rather than flat. 2. Said of an actor who is seen from three or four sides, as on an arena stage, rather than from one or two sides only, as on a proscenium stage. Hence (to) *play in the round,* (of a play) *be played in the round.* See THEATRE IN THE ROUND.

in three
Said of a scene played in an acting area bounded on the upstage side by an imaginary line drawn across the stage from the left wing to the right wing three quarters of the way upstage.

intimate theatre
A small theatre, in which the presence of a small audience to witness a production by a small cast favors a sophisticated intimacy. Hence *intimate play, intimate revue,* etc.

intrigue
1. The plot complications of a play. 2. See COMEDY OF INTRIGUE.

in trim
See TRIM.

in two
Said of a scene played in an acting area bounded on the up-stage side by an imaginary line drawn across the stage from the second left wing position to the second right wing position.

iris
An adjustable cut-off device on a lighting unit, with overlapping leaves that form a variable circle through which the light beam passes. Called also *iris diaphragm* and *iris shutter;* in British usage, commonly *diaphragm.* Also, to control the size of a spot of light with such a device. Hence *iris down, irising* (noun); see IRIS IN and IRIS OUT.

iris in
To adjust an iris shutter so that the leaves open and enlarge the circle through which the light beam passes, bringing up the light from blackout to full intensity.

iris out
To adjust an iris shutter so that the leaves close, and diminish the circle through which the light beam passes, until the light vanishes.

iris shutter
An iris diaphragm (see IRIS).

iron curtain; short form, (the) iron
A British term for a FIREPROOF CURTAIN.

irony
Short for DRAMATIC IRONY.

It will be all right on the night
A reassuring comment among theatrical people: In spite of the usual preliminary difficulties, by opening night everything will work out perfectly—19th century.

J

jack
Short for BRACE JACK.

jack-knife stage; jackknife stage
A stage used for rapid scene-shifting, consisting of a platform or two on casters pivoted at one corner to swing offstage and onstage. Hence *jackknife set*. See WAGON STAGE.

jack-roller
A device used in scene-shifting, consisting of a lever, hinged to the lower edge of a piece of scenery, and a roller or caster, onto which the lever lifts the scenery for movement on or off the stage.

Jacobean drama
The English drama of the reign of James I (1603–1625), or by extension of a longer period, and then usually to 1642.

jazbo; jazzbo; jasbo
1. Rough, vulgar comic action. 2. A Negro performer—Chiefly in Minstrel shows.

jell
Variant spelling of GEL.

Jessner treppen; Jessner-treppen; Jessnertreppen; Jessner('s) steps
A system of stage levels or platforms, sometimes used in expressionistic staging. Named for the German director Leopold Jessner (1878–1945).

jeune premier (feminine, **première**)
A French term used in English for the juvenile lead (see JUVENILE). Often italicized.

jig
A lively dance, or a humorous song accompanying such a dance, sometimes performed as part of a theatrical entertainment; more particularly, a type of comic afterpiece (in the Elizabethan theatre and surviving among strolling players into the Restoration), consisting of songs with dances, often ribald or libelous.

jobber
An actor who is employed for a particular part (*job*) in a given production; now especially referring to a minor part in summer or touring stock; formerly (*job actor*) often any actor unable to find regular employment. Hence, to *job* in (or to be *jobbed* in) a show; *jobbing* (unengaged).

Joe Miller
An old joke. Named for Joseph Miller, an English comedian of the 18th century. Hence *Joe-Millerize*.

Joey
A clown—Especially in Pantomime, Puppetry, and Circus. The name comes from Joseph Grimaldi (1778–1837), an English actor who played clown roles in the first quarter of the 19th century. Thus Joey the Clown, Punch's friend in the Punch and Judy play.

jog
A narrow flat placed at right angles to another flat, especially in an interior setting, and used to form a corner or to vary a wall surface. British: RETURN PIECE (which is also U.S.). Also, to put up such a flat. Hence *jogging* (noun), as in *jogging the set*.

join
To fasten scenic pieces together, as with a rope line. Also, any such fastening. See also BAD JOIN.

joy-plank
A British term for a RUNWAY.

Judy
Punch's wife (see PUNCH AND JUDY SHOW). The name, until the 19th century, was given as Joan.

juice
An electric current. By extension, an electrician (called also *juiceman*, etc.).

juicy part
A role which is flavorful, rich in opportunity for an actor.

jump
1. In acting, the omission of some of one's lines while speaking, from forgetfulness. Also, to omit lines in this way. 2. A one-night stand, or the distance to be traversed between one-night stands.

jump (a rail)
To add an extra RAIL (which see) to a flat, as for the mounting of electrical fittings. Hence *jumping* (noun).

jumper
A short length of stage cable fitted with connectors at both ends and used to extend a longer length of cable.

jury
An opening-night audience.

juvenile
The role of a boy or young man; an actor who plays such a role. Sometimes also the role of a girl or young woman; an actress who plays such a role. Hence also *juvenile lead* (male; female, INGÉNUE).

Juvenile Drama
Sets of printed sheets issued in England as toy-theatre plays which could be mounted on cardboard and cut out—19th century. See PENNY PLAIN, TWOPENCE COLOURED.

juvenile powder
A make-up powder used to give the effect of youth.

K

katharsis
Variant spelling of CATHARSIS.

keep alive
To keep scenery easily accessible. See also LIVE.

keeper
See BOX-KEEPER, DOOR KEEPER, HALL-KEEPER, HOUSE-KEEPER, STAGE-KEEPER (also as THEATRE-KEEPER).

keeper hook
An S-shaped hook used to fasten a door or window or, attached to a batten, to stiffen a back wall of flats.

keep the stage
To HOLD THE STAGE (which see).

key set
A UNIT SETTING.

keystone
A small piece of profile board in the shape of a wedge or trapezoid, used to strengthen a flat when a toggle is fastened to a rail by means of a butt joint. British: *plate*.

kill
To eliminate, suppress, or subdue; as, to remove excess light, to remove a needless piece of scenery or a property, to spoil the effect of a line, a laugh, or the like by bad timing.

King of Misrule
See MISRULE.

King's Box
Formerly, in British terminology, a box for the king. Now ROYAL BOX.

kitchen border
A beam border (see BEAM).

klieglight; klieg-light
In popular use, any powerful spotlight unit. Originally, a carbon arc spotlight developed by the brothers John (1869–1959) and Anton (1873–1928) Kliegl, American citizens of German birth.

knockabout
Said of stage action which is rough, boisterous. Thus *knockabout business, knockabout comedian,* etc.

knock-out
A show which is or seems likely to become tremendously successful.

knuckle
A joint formed by two flats cleated together.

kuppelhorizont; short form, **horizont**
A cyclorama, especially a true half-dome, as of plaster—A German word ("dome horizon") used in English. Sometimes italicized.

L

L.; L

Abbreviation of *left*, meaning *stage left, left stage*, LEFT OF STAGE. "Left" means to the actor's left, the spectator's right.

This abbreviation is used as a stage direction, either alone or in combination with other abbreviations. Thus, followed by a number, it is used as a symbol chalked on the back of a flat to indicate its place at the left side of the stage in front-to-rear sequence, as, L1.

Also, but now rarely, L.1 or L.1.E. (sometimes without periods) is used to designate LEFT FIRST ENTRANCE; and similarly for LEFT SECOND ENTRANCE, LEFT THIRD ENTRANCE. Thus also L.C. for LEFT CENTER, L.C.E. for LEFT CENTER ENTRANCE, L.S.E. for LEFT SECOND ENTRANCE, L.U.E. for LEFT UPPER ENTRANCE.

laboratory theatre

A theatre for the training of actors and technicians and for experimentation and research. See also DRAMA WORKSHOP.

labor theatre

Theatrical activity concerned with the problems of the laboring class in a capitalistic society, intended for an audience of workmen, laborers, and labor union members, and commonly produced and performed by union members non-commercially as amateurs. Hence *labor drama, labor stage*, etc.

lacopodium

Variant spelling of LYCOPODIUM.

lacquer

THEATRICAL LAMP DIP.

ladder

1. Any common ladder used on the stage, such as an A-ladder. See also FLY LADDER. 2. A ladder-like pipe device used for hanging lighting instruments, sometimes the lights themselves.

ladder (light)
A British term for a PROSCENIUM LIGHT.

lady
See WALKING GENTLEMAN.

lamp
A light source, now an incandescent lamp or an arc lamp, lit by electricity, but formerly an oil or gas lamp; usually synonymous with LANTERN and LIGHT.

(See also the combinations of LIGHT, with which the combinations of *lamp* are commonly interchangeable.)

lamp dip
Short for THEATRICAL LAMP DIP.

lamp housing; short form, **housing**
A HOOD (sense 2).

lampoon
A kind of satirical play, usually offering extreme ridicule of an individual.

lantern
1. A term, chiefly British, for a lamp, light, or lighting unit. 2. In British terminology, short for LANTERN LIGHT. 3. Short for MAGIC LANTERN.

(See also the combinations of LIGHT and LAMP with which the combinations of *lantern* are commonly interchangeable, especially in British usage.)

lantern light; lantern-light; short form, **lantern**
In British terminology, a skylight in the stage roof, which is constructed in such a way that its windows may be opened outwards, automatically or by hand control, in the event of fire. See SMOKE DOOR (U.S.).

lantern slide
A plate, as of painted glass, used in a magic lantern or other projection machine to produce a visual effect (see EFFECT).

lash
To pull two flats together, edge to edge, by winding a lash line over lash line cleats.

lash cleat
Short for LASH LINE CLEAT.

lash knot
A special knot, easy to undo, used in tying a lash line to a flat.

lash line
A rope line used to fasten flats or other scenic units to one another. British: *cleat line, throw line.*

lash line cleat; short forms, **lash cleat, line cleat**
A small metal piece which can be screwed into the back of a flat frame, with a projecting tip over which a lash line can be slipped.

lash line eye
A metal eye which can be screwed into the back of a flat frame, and to which a lash line can be tied.

lash line hook
A metal hook for holding or tying off a lash line when the use of a lash line cleat is impracticable.

latent business
Minor physical action not specified or implied in a text but invented by the actor or the director.

lattice box; lettice box
In British terminology, a private box separated from other seating areas by a lattice or screen—18th century.

laugh
1. *to be laughed off the boards:* Said of a play which is received badly. 2. See BAD LAUGH, PLAY FOR A LAUGH.

laugh line
A line of dialogue which is calculated to produce a laugh from the audience.

lay an egg (or **omelet**)
Said of a production or an actor: To fail miserably; especially, said of an actor who makes an unsuccessful joke.

lay 'em in the aisles
To make an audience laugh hilariously, and thus achieve a successful comic performance.

layout; lay-out
A diagram, as, a *light layout*, a *lay-out sheet*.

L.C.; LC
Abbreviation of LEFT CENTER. See also L.

L.C.E.
Abbreviation of LEFT CENTER ENTRANCE. See also L.

lead
1. A principal role (called also *lead role*); also, an actor playing a principal role. Hence *heavy lead, juvenile lead*, a *leading actor*, etc. 2. A stage electrical cable. 3. A cue.

lead block
A HEAD BLOCK.

leader
Short for ORCHESTRA LEADER.

leaf
A frame section of a ceiling, as, a *one-leaf ceiling*.

leak
To *leak light:* Said when the crack between two flats lashed together lets light show through.

Leblanged

Said of a show supported by ticket sales through cut-rate agencies in New York City such as Joe Leblang's—20th century but now obsolete. Hence, to *Leblang*.

left; abbreviation, **L.**

Short for LEFT (OF) STAGE, *stage left*. Towards the left side of the stage (the audience's right)—Sometimes, a stage direction. See also DOWN LEFT, UP LEFT.

left center; abbreviation, **L.C., LC**

A stage position or area, the center of the stage to the left (the audience's right)—Sometimes, a stage direction.

left center entrance; abbreviation, **L.C.E.**

A stage entrance at the back of the stage and to the left (the audience's right)—Sometimes, a stage direction.

left center stage

LEFT CENTER (which see).

left first entrance; abbreviation, **L.1.(E.)**

A stage entrance at the left (the audience's right), the one farthest downstage—Sometimes, a stage direction.

left (of) stage; short form, **left**; abbreviation, **L.**

The entire left half of the stage (the audience's right) or some portion thereof—Sometimes, a stage direction.

Left second entrance; abbreviations, **L.2(E.), L.S.E.**

A stage entrance at the left (the audience's right) between the left first entrance and the left upper entrance—Sometimes, a stage direction.

left stage

LEFT (OF) STAGE (which see).

left third entrance; abbreviation, **L.3.(E.).**

A left upper entrance. (*Left third entrance* is not used in the professional theatre.)

196

left upper entrance; abbreviations, **L.U.E., L.3(E.).**
A stage entrance at the left (the audience's right), the farthest
one upstage—Sometimes, a stage direction.

leg
1. A LEG DROP (which see). British: *tail* or *leg*. 2. An upright
support for a platform. 3. See I HOPE YOU BREAK A LEG.

leg cloth
A British term for a LEG DROP (which see).

leg (drop)
A narrow flat, or strip of canvas or other cloth, hung vertically
from a border to the stage floor, usually simulating a tree trunk
or column; often used in a pair to mask the side of the stage,
like a wing, and commonly forming part of an inverted U-
shaped cut-out. British: *leg, leg cloth,* and sometimes *tail.*

legitimate drama; short forms, (the) **legit,**
    (the) **legitimate**
Now usually plays, collectively—presented by actors who speak
their lines on a stage before their audience—in contradistinction to other dramatic forms such as vaudeville, puppetry, pantomime, motion picture, television, radio, opera, operetta, musical comedy, etc. Hence *legitimate actor, legitimate theatre,* etc.
Sometimes musical comedy and other musical forms are called
legitimate. Formerly and sometimes now, plays of literary merit.
See ILLEGITIMATE DRAMA, STRAIGHT (*play*).

legmania; leg mania; legomania
1. A craze for dancing. 2. Said of a dancer possessing remark-
able acrobatic skill, a *legmania dancer.*

leg piece
A LEG DROP (which see).

leg show; leg-show
An entertainment relying on the physical charms of scantily
dressed chorus girls—Chiefly Burlesque or Revue.

197

leisure
See AT LIBERTY.

length
1. A unit of forty-two lines of dialogue, used in measuring the number of lines in an acting part, as, a part of four *lengths*.
2. A row of lights fixed together as a unit, now a row of strip lights in a casing. See HANGING LENGTH, PROSCENIUM LENGTH, etc.

lens
A transparent material, commonly glass, with one surface curved and the other either flat or curved, used in a lighting unit or projector to focus light rays, as, a CONDENSER LENS.

lens unit
A lighting instrument with a lens, used to illuminate the stage.

lessee
A producer or another person who operates a theatre on a rental basis.

let in; let-in
To lower scenery into place.

letter-perfect
In acting, knowing one's lines perfectly.

level
A collapsible platform on the stage upon which an actor can stand. See also ACTING LEVEL, STAGE LEVEL.

level guide
One of several short strips of wood screwed into a ceiling batten to keep it level along a visible joint when two one-leaf ceilings are flied.

liberty
See AT LIBERTY.

library
A British term for a TICKET AGENCY.

libretto
The text of a musical comedy or other dramatic piece chiefly composed of sung dialogue. Plural, *librettos* or *libretti*. Hence also *librettist*.

license; (British, noun) **licence**
1. An official authorization sometimes required for the operation of a theatre, the production of a particular dramatic piece or kind of piece, acting, etc. Also, to grant such an authorization. Hence *licenser, licensing* (noun). For British usage, see also LICENSING ACT, THEATRES ACT, LORD CHAMBERLAIN, PATENT. 2. The permission granted to an acting company by a nobleman to use his name as its patron—Elizabethan. Also, to grant such permission.

Licensing Act
An Act of Parliament (Statute 10 of George II, c. 28), 1737, which forbade the production of plays or acting on the stage unless a license could be obtained from the Lord Chamberlain, and which (with little success) further forbade professional performances by provincial companies. This Act followed less specific regulation through earlier acts (sometimes given the same name) and was itself superseded by the THEATRES ACT (which see).

lift
1. To raise a curtain or other stage equipment. 2. An elevator used on the stage or in the auditorium, as, an *orchestra lift*. 3. In British terminology, a bridge, or an elevator by means of which a bridge can be moved vertically.

lifting jack
A JACK-ROLLER.

lifting stage
An ELEVATOR STAGE.

lift jack
A JACK-ROLLER.

lift stage
A British term for an ELEVATOR STAGE.

light
1. To illuminate. Also, illumination. 2. Short for LIGHTING UNIT.
3. In the plural, a nickname for an electrician.

(See also the combinations of LIGHTING, with which the combinations of *light* are commonly interchangeable.)

light area
A portion of the stage which is, or is to be, illuminated.

light batten; light-batten
In British terminology, a pipe batten (see BATTEN) from which lights are hung.

light border
A BORDER (sense 1) used to mask lighting units.

light box; light-box
The body or case of a lighting unit.

light bridge
A BRIDGE (sense 2) for the operation of lighting equipment.

light comedian
A comedian whose wit is more important than his appearance and movement.

light comedy
A comedy which offers gay, witty, and pleasant entertainment without pretending to touch depths of feeling, characterization, etc.; also collectively.

light console; short form, **console**
A mobile switchboard resembling in appearance an organ console, used in any convenient location to control stage lighting.

light cue; light-cue
The cue for the commencement of some planned change in illumination. Hence, a *light cue sheet*.

light dip
THEATRICAL LAMP DIP.

light distribution; short form, **distribution**
The placement of rays from a lighting unit.

light ground row
A row of lights placed on the stage floor.

lighting
Short for *stage* (or *theatre*) *lighting:* The illumination of a theatre, and especially of the stage, by means of artificial light.

(See also the combinations of LIGHT, with which the combinations of *lighting* are commonly interchangeable.)

lighting booth
A BOOTH (which see) from which theatre lights are operated.

lighting flies
A FLY GALLERY used for the operation of lighting units.

lighting plot; light plot
A list, with diagrams, showing the lighting to be used in each scene of a production.

lighting unit; short form, **light**
Any source of light, with its stage accessories (such as a reflector) if any.

light layout
A diagram to show the disposition of lighting units.

light man
A person who operates lighting units.

lightning effect
The simulation of lightning; the means by which this is achieved, as by the projection of slides or the ignition of lycopodium powder.

lightning lantern
An electrical device containing a lightning-striker.

lightning stick
One of two sticks of carbon brought together to produce an electric flash effect—19th century.

lightning-striker
An electro-magnetic device operated by remote control to produce a flash effect from a carbon arc.

light opera
A comic opera, usually one which deals with a romantic love story; also collectively.

light operator
A person in charge of the operation of the lights in a theatre.

light pipe
A pipe batten (see BATTEN) used to carry lighting equipment. See also FIRST PIPE.

light pit
A trap or hollow in the stage floor, in which lighting units can be placed.

light rehearsal
A rehearsal of all the lighting operations for a production.

Lights
A nickname for an electrician.

light stand; short form, **stand**
An upright wood or metal standard to which a lighting unit can be fastened.

light tormentor
A TORMENTOR LIGHT; a TORMENTOR BATTEN.

light tower; short form, **tower**
A tall movable structure of wood or metal, often with ladder and platform, mounted on casters, used at the side of the stage to carry side lighting units; sometimes simply a length of pipe fastened vertically for the same purpose.

lime-light; limelight; short form, **lime**
1. Formerly, a lighting unit containing a piece of lime upon which a jet of mixed gases was directed to produce a bright beam of light generally used for spotlighting at the front of the stage; also called a *calcium light*—19th century. Also, the light from such a unit. Now, in British terminology, any electrical lighting unit, but especially a spotlight (called also *following spot*) shining on the front of the stage. 2. By extension of the preceding meanings, the most desirable acting position on the stage, well lighted, at the front, and in the center. Hence *share the limelight, be in* (or *fond of*) *the limelight*, and, in British terminology, a *limelight man* (in charge of the operation of the limes).

limited engagement
As applied to an actor or a production, an engagement advertised as of limited duration.

line
1. A rope or wire used to hang scenery, etc. 2. A portion of dialogue occupying a single row in the script. Hence *be up in one's lines* (to know one's part). 3. A make-up mark drawn with *lining color* (grease paint, etc.) on the face or body. Also, to make such a mark, as with a *lining pencil, lining stump* (see STUMP), etc. 4. Short for LINE OF BUSINESS.

line cleat
Short for LASH LINE CLEAT.

line cue
A cue which is spoken rather than otherwise indicated.

line grip
A BULL-DOG (which see).

line (of business)
An actor's specialty in the way of roles.

line of sight
A SIGHT LINE.

line of vision
A SIGHT LINE.

line plot
A diagram to show the flyman the location of all lines hanging from the flies.

liner
1. A thin stick of lining color (see LINE). 2. A small brush used in scene-painting to make a fine line. Called also *lining brush*.

line rehearsal
A rehearsal for spoken lines rather than for body movements.

lining
For *lining brush*, see LINER. For other combinations, see LINE.

link man; link-man; linkman
In British terminology, from "link" (torch), a DOORMAN (sense 1).

Linnebach projector (or lantern)
A projecting device using a powerful light source to throw scenic images through a glass or gelatin slide onto a drop or other surface, usually from behind. Named for the German inventor of the process, Adolf Linnebach (1876–).

liquid board
A DIMMER BOARD which controls liquid dimmers.

liquid dimmer
A resistance dimmer in the form of a jar, containing a solution of salts and two plates or cones which can be brought together or drawn apart to increase or decrease the amount of electric current delivered to the lighting units.

liquid make-up
A cosmetic used in making up for the stage, of a coloring pigment in a gelatine-like solution, as, specifically, *liquid white* (or *whitening;* or *liquid powder*).

literary drama
Dramatic works, collectively or individually, which are considered to possess value as literature (in contradistinction to the POPULAR DRAMA), or which are intended primarily for reading rather than for stage production (the CLOSET DRAMA), or which exhibit ignorance of practical stagecraft; or written drama (in contradistinction to improvisation or drama without dialogue).

little theatre
Any small theatre, but especially one for amateur productions, often with an interest in experimentation. In British usage, any small theatre, but especially one housing a professional repertory company.

liturgical drama
Sacred dramas, collectively or individually, based on the Bible and performed during some special festival in connection with the ritual of the Roman Catholic Church—Medieval.

live
1. Said of a property, a scenic piece, etc., which will be needed again during a performance, as (of a scene pack) a *live pack* or a *live stack*. See also KEEP ALIVE. 2. Said of drama which is performed before its audience on a stage, rather than in the motion pictures or on radio or television. Hence *live actor, live* (or *living*) *theatre*, etc.

live-front board
A stage switchboard on the front panel of which are exposed controls carrying the full electric current.

living newspaper
A play in which social and political events are dramatized, and which is realistic, stylized, based on the disjointed news of the day rather than on a smoothly woven plot, concerned not with individual experience or a personal story but rather with a general social situation.

loading door
A door through which scenery can be passed, between the stage and an alley.

loading platform
A high, narrow platform near the counterweight lines, on which flymen can store or load counterweights; sometimes synonymous with FLY GALLERY. British: *loading flies*.

load range
The possible variation in load upon a dimmer, as compared to its maximum rated load, without materially affecting the characteristic of the dimming curve.

lobby
A place in a theatre building where spectators may wait, walk, smoke, etc. Hence *box lobby, lobby bell*, etc. Especially, the area (or the outermost part of the area—the *outer lobby*) between the main entrance doors and the auditorium (British: *entrance-hall, foyer*). See FOYER.

lobby frame; short form, **frame**
A framed display space in a lobby for theatre advertisements.

lobsterscope
An optical effects machine used to simulate a slow-motion running effect or some other flickering light; it consists of a slotted disc rotated in front of a lighting unit. British: *flicker (wheel)*.

locale
The place where the action of a dramatic work is supposed to occur.

locality board
A placard displayed on the stage, to designate the place where the action is supposed to occur— Elizabethan.

lock off
To clamp a hauling rope so as to fasten counterweight equipment in a desired position.

lock rail; locking rail
A rail at one side of the stage floor, bearing clamps which lock the rope lines of a counterweight system in place.

loft
A part of the stage region above the grid. See BARREL LOFT, FLY LOFT.

loft block
A block on the gridiron, with one pulley sheave over which a rope line passes between a piece of scenery and a head block.

loge
A box or a stall.

long
Short for LONG LINE.

long arm
A CLEARING POLE (which see).

long center (line)
In a set of four lines used to fly scenery, the line between the short center line and the long line.

long (line)
In a set of lines used to fly scenery, the line farthest from the pin rail.

long load
A pack of flats exceeding 16 feet in length, which needs a special truck for transportation.

loop curtain
A drape curtain (see DRAPERY).

loose grid
A grid counterweight system which makes use of rope ties at the pin rail, instead of a union counterweight.

loose line
In the counterweight system, any rope line from which lights or scenic pieces are hung, when it is fastened to the pin rail rather than to the cradle.

loose-pin hinge
See PIN HINGE.

Lord Chamberlain
In British terminology, a government official, whose permission, by the Theatres Act of 1843, must be obtained before any new theatrical entertainment may be publicly performed by professionals, and who licenses the theatres in London and in certain other places. His control over the theatre goes back to Tudor and Stuart times, when his responsibilities included also the general supervision of court entertainments. See also MASTER OF THE REVELS.

Lord of Misrule
See MISRULE.

lord's room
A seating area, originally reserved for the patron or for other noblemen—Elizabethan. See GENTLEMAN'S ROOM.

lounge
A resting-place for theatre patrons between the acts. Hence *lounge bell,* etc.

louver; louvre
A metal shield used on a lighting unit to control the rays so as to sharpen the beam.

love-and-honor; (British spelling) **love-and-honour**
See HEROIC ACTING. Also used adjectivally of heroic plays.

love interest
1. That part of a plot which deals with romantic love. 2. The principal role or roles concerned with romantic love.

low comedy
A comedy which is obvious, elementary, or crude, such as that involving slapstick and knockabout business; also collectively. Hence *low comedian, low-comedy part,* etc.

lower gallery
A term, chiefly British, for a balcony seating area below other galleries.

lower (out)
To let scenery descend into place.

low light; lowlight
To simulate a hollow on the face by means of a spot of dark-colored make-up. Hence *lowlighting* (noun).

L.S.E.
Abbreviation of LEFT SECOND ENTRANCE. See also L.

L.U.E.
Abbreviation of LEFT UPPER ENTRANCE. See also L.

lycopodium
A powder, of resin or a mossy plant (*lycopodium*), which can be ignited for flash and flame effects in a *lycopodium flask* (blow-pipe), box, or pot, etc.

lyric
1. Pertaining to drama which is sung rather than spoken, as, a *lyric role*, the *lyric stage*, etc. The *lyric drama:* Musical drama (in the collective sense). A *lyric* (or *lyrical*) *drama:* A dramatic composition in poetic form, for, or as for, singing. 2. The text of a song—Musical comedy, Musical plays. Hence *lyricist* (writer).

M

Macbeth trap
A trap with an elevator, used for such purposes as the appearance of a ghost.

machine
A piece of stage equipment, as a crane, a trap door, a means of producing optical or acoustical effects, etc. The term is obsolete, except in combinations (RAIN MACHINE, etc.), or collective terms (*theatre, theatrical,* or STAGE MACHINERY).

machine for theatre
A production theory which regards the stage setting as a machine used by the actors to bring a play into being.

machinery
Short for *theatre, theatrical,* or STAGE MACHINERY.

machine-theatre
A theatre using elaborate stage machinery.

machinist
An obsolete term for the following: A stage carpenter; a designer of theatrical machinery.

Macready
In acting, a marked pause, a catching of the breath (a glottal stop) before certain words. Named for William Charles Macready (1793–1873), a British actor whose acting style was marked by pauses of this kind.

magazine
See COMPARTMENT.

magic lantern
A projection machine used for optical effects such as lightning, clouds, etc.

magnetic amplifier dimmer
A self-controlling type of REACTANCE DIMMER (which see), using the feed-back principle.

magnifying lens
A lens which enlarges the image thrown by a magic lantern or projector.

main play
The principal part of the bill or program offered at a performance, when an afterpiece or the like is also presented.

main plot
In a dramatic work, the principal plot, when there is a subplot.

Main Stem; short form, **Stem**
Broadway, as the principal avenue in the New York theatre district.

maître de ballet
See BALLET.

major (theatre)
In British terminology, one of the two or three London theatres licensed to produce legitimate drama—18th and 19th centuries. Hence *major stage*, etc.

make a break
See BREAK.

make an ascension
In acting, to forget one's lines or business—chiefly British.

make an entrance
See ENTRANCE.

make fast
To tie a rope line, to tie off. But sometimes *make fast* implies a more permanent fastening than TIE OFF.

make off
A British expression for the following: 1. To tie a line. 2. One of the two flats farthest downstage in a stage setting.

make one's bow
To appear as an actor, especially in some kind of debut, as, He *made his local bow* in *Macbeth.*

make one's debut
See DEBUT.

make the rounds
See GO THE ROUNDS.

make-up; makeup
To change the appearance of one's face and other exposed surfaces of the body for acting, by means of cosmetics, false hair, etc., in order to emphasize characteristics appropriate to one's role or to compensate for the exaggerating effects of stage lighting and distance. Also, the cosmetics (in full, *stage make-up* or *theatrical make-up*) so used; the art, action, or process of applying these (also as *making-up,* noun); the result of applying them. Hence *make-up box, make-up pencil, make-up table,* etc.

male impersonator
A woman who specializes in male roles. Hence also *male impersonation.* Not to be confused with BREECHES PART (which see).

manager; (feminine) manageress
1. A British term for PRODUCER. 2. Short for BUSINESS MANAGER, COMPANY MANAGER, HOUSE MANAGER, PERSONAL MANAGER, STAGE MANAGER, THEATRE (or *theatrical*) MANAGER—Hence also *manage, management.*

manet
"He remains" (onstage)—A Latin word used in English as a stage direction. Often italicized.

manners
See COMEDY OF MANNERS.

mansion
One of several structures of wood and canvas in a stage setting, simulating a building or other place before which a scene could be played—Medieval and Renaissance. Also, a *mansion stage*, a stage showing several *mansions* simultaneously.

manuscript; short form, script
The unprinted text of a dramatic composition.

marionette
A doll (commonly made of wood), simulating a person, animal, etc., used on a miniature stage as a performer and controlled from above (now by strings only, formerly by rods or wires) by manipulators (*marionettists*), who speak the dialogue, if any. Sometimes interchangeable with PUPPET (which see). Also, to make such a figure move. Hence *marionette play* (or *show*), *marionette theatre*, etc.

marquee
A canopy or roof which projects over a theatre entrance towards the street, usually bearing lettering to advertise the names of the theatre, the current production, the star, etc.

mask
1. A covering worn by an actor to conceal his face or head. Also, to put on, to wear such a covering. 2. To conceal part of the stage from the audience, by means of a masking piece. Often in the forms *mask in* or *mask off*. 3. To adopt a position, while acting, which deprives the audience of a clear view of another actor. 4. Short for MASKING CONTROL. 5. Variant spelling of MASQUE.

masked comedy
The COMMEDIA DELL' ARTE (which see).

214

masking
Short for MASKING PIECE.

masking control; short form, **mask**
A diaphragm or other means of shaping the beams emanating from a lighting unit.

masking (piece)
A scenic piece, such as a teaser, a flat, or a backing, used to conceal part of the stage. Hence, more specifically, *masking border*, etc.

masque; (formerly) **maske** or **mask**
A procession of masked figures in various mumming performances, in medieval times; later (especially first half of 17th century) an entertainment, commonly presented as part of a special celebration, with or without dialogue, typically allegorical or mythological, elaborate and spectacular, with pageantry, music, songs, dances, and impersonations by actors wearing masks. Hence *masquer* (or *masker*), *masque* (or *masking*) *house*, etc. See also ANTI-MASQUE.

mass
In directing, the grouping of actors considered as an element in composition.

mass drama
A dramatic work in which groups of actors rather than individuals become the principal characters.

mast
A standard used to support a flat, fastened to a weight which was under the stage, and slipped along a groove in the stage floor—19th century.

master
1. Short for MASTER CONTROL, MASTER SWITCH. 2. The head of a children's acting company—Early 17th century. 3. The head of a theatrical company—Restoration.

master carpenter
A STAGE CARPENTER (sense 1).

master control
A handle, lever, or wheel, used to operate interlocking dimmers or switches. Hence *master-control lever, master handle,* etc.

master dimmer
A dimmer which can control groups of lighting units simultaneously.

master electrician
A CHIEF ELECTRICIAN.

master of ceremonies; abbreviations, **Emcee, M.C.**
An announcer, commentator, and director—Chiefly Vaudeville; but sometimes in mixed forms of drama with musical comedy elements. British: *chairman.*

master of costumes
A wardrobe master (see WARDROBE).

master of properties
A PROPERTY MASTER.

master of (the) revels
A British term for the following: 1. The government official (under the Lord Chamberlain) charged with the supervision of dramatic entertainments at the royal court; later, the dramatic censor—Late 15th to 18th centuries. Also in the forms *Master of Revels* and *Revels* (or *Revel*) *Master*. The initial letters are capitalized. 2. Formerly, a master of ceremonies.

master (switch)
A theatre switch used to control all electrical circuits or selected groups of circuits.

mat
1. Short for MATINEE. 2. A CUT-OFF (which see) made of metal or cardboard, commonly used in a frame. 3. See GRASS MAT.

matinee; short form, mat
An afternoon, or sometimes a morning, performance. Hence *matinee day*, etc. Sometimes an acute accent is placed over the first *e*.

matinee call; matinee-call; short form, call
A posted notice to cast and crew of a matinee performance.

matinee idol
A male actor whom female theatregoers admire extravagantly.

mazarine floor
Variant obsolete spelling of MEZZANINE (*floor*).

M.C.
Abbreviation of MASTER OF CEREMONIES.

mechanical dimmer
Any device, such as a serrated iris or a shutter of the Venetian-blind type, which decreases the intensity of a light without materially affecting the beam form.

Medieval drama
The drama of the Middle Ages, in England a period generally understood to cover the 10th through the 16th centuries, overlapping at the end with the RENAISSANCE (which see).

medium
Short for COLOR MEDIUM.

meller drama; mellerdrama
A misspelling and mispronunciation of MELODRAMA, used humorously.

melodrama
1. A play which is sensational, implausible in characterization, dialogue, and situation, abounds in thrilling struggles between exaggerated heroic and villainous figures, and ends happily in the romantic triumph of virtue; also collectively. Formerly, such a play, interspersed with song and orchestral music to

217

circumvent the licensing laws in London—First half of 19th century. Also, any play or portion of a play, which, though not conforming (strictly speaking) to the type, embodies some of its characteristics. Hence *melodramatic*, etc. 2. A bustle of stage business, during which the actors had no lines in the script—A stage direction, 19th century.

Melpomene
The Muse of tragedy—Greek mythology.

member
An actor belonging to a theatrical company, especially a stock company. See also RESIDENT. A regular member of a company as distinct from a hired man (see HIRELING) or APPRENTICE—Elizabethan.

memory play
A play in which past events, as the protagonist recalls them, become the principal portions of the dramatic action.

Menace, (the)
The VILLAIN (which see).

mending batten
1. A batten used temporarily to hold flats together. 2. A MENDING PLATE.

mending plate
A small flat metal plate used to strengthen scenery at a crack or joint.

merciful darkness
Humorously, a lighting designer's term for a dimly lighted scene, especially one which is boring or badly acted and fortunately calls for low-level lighting intensity.

merry andrew; merry-andrew
A clown. Sometimes the initial letters are capitalized.

merry-merry
A chorus—Musical comedy.

metallic dimmer
In British terminology, a dimmer made with coils of resistance wire.

metaphor
See DRAMATIC METAPHOR.

Method, (the)
See STANISLAVSKI METHOD.

metteur en scène
A French expression used in English for a STAGE DIRECTOR. Usually italicized.

mezzanine
1. A seating area just above the orchestra, or the forward part of such an area; the first balcony. British: DRESS CIRCLE, or less frequently *grand circle, royal circle,* etc. 2. A space under the stage used for the manipulation of traps, etc. Hence also the *mezzanine* (*mazarine,* or *mezzonine*) *floor,* the *mezzanine level.*

middle-class tragedy
A bourgeois tragedy, a domestic tragedy; also collectively.

middle gallery; mid-gallery
Formerly, in British terminology, a balcony seating area between two other balcony levels.

middle line
A CENTER LINE (sense 2).

middleman
An INTERLOCUTOR (which see)—Minstrel shows.

mid-gallery
See MIDDLE GALLERY.

miles gloriosus
The role of a boastful, cowardly soldier—A Latin term ("braggart soldier"), from a comedy by Plautus, used in English. Often italicized. Plural, *milites gloriosi*. See BRAGGART SOLDIER.

milestone
The achievement of the hundredth performance of a production.

milk
To work hard to get as much response as possible from the audience to one's acting; thus, of a scene, to *milk it dry* for laughs, tears, or applause.

milk jump
A one-night stand accessible to an acting company only by milk train, inconveniently early.

Miller
See JOE MILLER.

mime
To act; especially, to act in PANTOMIME (sense 1). An actor, especially a comic actor; also as *mimer* (rarely, *mimester*). PANTOMIME (sense 1); a pantomimed dramatic piece. Hence *miming* (noun), *mimology*, etc.

mimesis
Imitation; representation by gesture and movement without words. Hence also *mimetic*, etc. See PANTOMIME.

mimic
To imitate, copy, simulate, impersonate. One who represents on the stage; (in an obsolete sense) a mime. Mimetic; (in an obsolete sense) like or otherwise relating to a mine. Hence *mimicry*.

mimo-drama
A pantomimed entertainment, conceived as serious drama at a high artistic level.

minimum basic agreement
A standard agreement which an American producer (producing manager) must sign in order to obtain the right to produce a dramatic work by a member of the Dramatists' Guild.

minor business
Stage business which is of secondary importance.

minor part
A small acting role.

minor (theatre)
In British terminology, a London theatre not licensed to produce legitimate drama, and therefore producing burlettas, melodramas, and other illegitimate entertainments—18th and 19th centuries. Hence also *minor drama, minor stage.*

minstrel
1. A performer in a minstrel show. 2. A musical entertainer, sometimes acting in dramatic performances—Especially, Medieval and Elizabethan.

minstrel black
A cosmetic used in making up for Negro roles on the stage, of burnt cork and glycerine, but generally superseded by brown grease paint.

minstrel show
A kind of comic stage entertainment, typically consisting of dialogue, song, and dance in a set pattern, ostensibly but unrealistically imitating Negro manners and speech, performed by white actors (an interlocutor, as master of ceremonies and straight man; two end men in blackface, as comic speakers; and a chorus in blackface seated in a semicircle)—mid-19th through early 20th centuries, now surviving only in the amateur theatre. Thus MINSTREL, MINSTRELSY, *Negro minstrel, Negro minstrelsy* —the *N* either capitalized or uncapitalized. After the Civil War, all-Negro minstrel shows also flourished.

minstrelsy
Collectively, minstrel shows.

miracle (play)
A type of play based on a Biblical or other sacred story; more particularly, a play dealing with the miracles associated with a saint—Especially, Medieval. See also MYSTERY PLAY.

mirror arc
In British terminology, a carbon arc light used with a reflector of mirrored glass and special lenses.

mirror spot
In British terminology, a spotlight behind which is an ellipsoidal reflector that directs the beam through a focusing lens and cut-off.

miscast
To cast an actor in a role for which he is not fitted. Said of an actor so cast. Also *miscasting* (noun).

mise en scène; mise-en-scène
The stage director's arrangement of all the elements that comprise the stage picture, such as the scenery, actors, lighting, etc. —A French expression used in English. Often italicized.

Misrule, Abbot (or **King** or **Lord**) of
A MASTER OF REVELS. Scottish: *Abbot of Unreason*—Medieval.

mixed bill
A program calling for two or more separate items.

mixed notices
Reviews in the press which differ markedly in their reception of a new production.

mob scene
A scene in which a crowd of actors participates.

modern drama
The contemporary or recent drama; the drama of Europe and America, beginning with the plays of Ibsen; the drama of the modern world, in contradistinction to the classical drama of ancient Greece and Rome.

modern dress; modern-dress
Said of a dramatic production which is costumed in the dress of today rather than in the dress ordinarily worn in the period in which the action is supposed to be taking place. Hence, *in modern dress*.

modern play
A play belonging to the modern drama.

moko
In British terminology, a paint distempered with oil, chiefly used to give a glossy surface to scenic pieces.

Momus
The god of ridicule, of clowns—Greek mythology. Hence, a clown, and a name for a clown.

money taker; money-taker
In British terminology, a ticket seller at one of the theatre entrance doors (but not at the box office). See also PAY BOX and WICKET (both British).

monkey pole
In British terminology, a stick with a hole through which a lash line can be drawn, used to guide the line in lashing flats together.

monodrama
1. A dramatic entertainment calling for a single speaking actor.
2. A dramatic entertainment in which the action is supposed to occur in the mind of a single person.

223

monologue; monolog
1. A dramatic entertainment consisting of a recital or performance by one person (a *monologuist* or *monologist*). Also, the
lines in such an entertainment, collectively. 2. A soliloquy.

monumental
Architectural, formal, as especially of large massive structures
used in stage settings.

mood
ATMOSPHERE (which see).

mood play
A play in which a mood, rather than plot or characterization,
is emphasized.

moon box
An optical effect machine used to simulate the moon. A container holding a lamp is moved on lines behind a transparent
drop.

moral
Short form of MORALITY PLAY.

moral drama
Collectively, plays considered by moralists to be suitable for
public representation—19th century.

moral lecture
A term sometimes used in the U.S. to cover a dramatic reading
or performance in order to avoid possible censorship—18th and
19th centuries.

morality play; short forms, **moral play, morality, moral**
An allegorical play, with characters personifying abstractions,
originally (in medieval times) serious and theologically didactic; later often dealing with pedagogical, political, and other
non-theological topics, and sometimes containing comic elements; also collectively. The type survives in various forms.

moral play
A MORALITY PLAY.

morgue
1. A theatre which is currently showing an unsuccessful production. 2. A company's collection of press cuttings and production records.

morning performance
A matinee in the morning.

motion
A puppet play—Chiefly in the plural; 16th and 17th centuries.

motion picture
A series of photographs thrown on a screen by a projector to give spectators the impression that they are watching moving persons and objects; a form of entertainment, complete in itself, consisting of such pictures. Sometimes used in connection with stage productions. Called also *movie, moving picture,* etc. British, and sometimes U.S.: *cinema.* For (*motion*) *picture rights,* see RIGHTS.

motivating light
An optical effect, the introduction of sunlight, firelight, etc., onto the stage, in addition to the general lighting. Hence *motivating sources, motivated lighting.*

motivation
1. Part of the DRAMATIC PREPARATION (which see); the forces which lie behind the words and actions of a character. 2. In lighting, the use of MOTIVATING LIGHT (which see).

motor-driven auto-transformer
An AUTO-TRANSFORMER DIMMER which is operated by a motor, the motor in turn being controlled from a remote point by a switch or other control device.

motor-positioned auto-transformer
A form of MOTOR-DRIVEN AUTO-TRANSFORMER (which see), in which the motor is controlled by a miniature potentiometer marked with conventional dimmer-scale readings.

mount a production
To stage a dramatic entertainment; to provide a substantial part of the initial cost of production; to provide the scenery, costumes, and other furnishings for a production.

mounting
1. The staging of a production, including the settings, costumes, music, etc. 2. The equipment to which a lighting unit may be fastened, as, a *vertical pipe mounting*, or a device for fastening a lighting unit to such equipment, as, a YOKE.

mouth the lines
To speak one's lines in an exaggerated, declamatory manner.

movement
Short for STAGE MOVEMENT.

move off
To walk off the stage or away from the center of the stage towards the side.

move on
To walk onto the stage or towards the center of the stage from the side.

moving effect
An optical effect machine, consisting usually of a cylinder on which are mounted transparent painted discs, rotated electrically or by clockworks in front of a light source. See EFFECT.

moving picture
A MOTION PICTURE (which see).

mug

In acting, to assume an exaggerated facial expression. Hence *mugging* (noun). Also, *mug* or *mugger*, a comic actor who puts on such an expression.

multi-capacity dimmer

A FLEXIBLE DIMMER (which see).

multiple set; multiple setting

A stage setting displaying three or more localities as acting areas. Hence *multiple scenery, multiple stage* (or *staging*). Called also *simultaneous setting, simultaneous scene, décor simultané.*

mum; mumm

To act; more particularly, to act in a MUMMERS' PLAY (which see), masque, or disguising. Hence *mummer, mummery, etc.*

mummers' play; mummer's play; mumming play; mumming

In British terminology, a folk drama of death and resurrection with certain stock characters (including St. George and the Turkish Knight), played and danced by village amateurs— Medieval, with rare survivals.

municipal theatre

A theatre owned by a municipality.

murder

A great demand from the public for theatre tickets. Hence, a hit (also as *murder at the box office*); terrific box-office sales (*It's murder*); etc. But see also DEATH AT THE BOX OFFICE.

murder drama

A drama about a murder (real or fictitious). Hence *murder mystery*, etc.

Muse

See THALIA (Muse of Comedy) and MELPOMENE (Muse of Tragedy).

music

1. An art form of structured and expressive sound, frequently a part of the drama or of stage representation. Hence a *musical* (for MUSICAL COMEDY, etc.), the *musical stage* (or *theatre*), a *music drama, musician,* etc. 2. An ORCHESTRA (sense 2)— Elizabethan and Restoration, spelled *musick* or *musique*. 3. Short for ACT-MUSIC, CURTAIN MUSIC, etc.

musical adaptation

An adaptation of a straight play into a musical play or comedy.

musical (comedy)

A dramatic entertainment, with a light comedy plot, dances, songs, spoken dialogue, and spectacle; also collectively; not always distinguishable from such types of entertainment as ballad opera, light opera, opera comique, operetta, etc.

musical director

In a dramatic entertainment accompanied by music, the person responsible for everything related to that music.

musicalize

To adapt a play for production in a musical version. Hence *musicalization.*

musical (play)

A play to which music has been added, a type of drama usually more substantial and realistic than musical comedy but interspersed with songs.

musical (show)

A MUSICAL COMEDY.

musical tent theatre

See TENT THEATRE.

musical version

An adaptation of a non-musical dramatic (or other) composition for production as a musical comedy, musical play, etc.

music cue

A cue for the commencement of music. Hence *music cue sheet.*

music hall; music-hall

1. In British terminology, a vaudeville theatre; vaudeville in general; originally (mid-19th century) the place for an entertainment consisting of a series of turns by individual performers before an audience seated at supper-tables, and the entertainment itself. Short form, *hall.* 2. A motion picture theatre in which vaudeville or similar entertainment is provided between film showings.

music house

An obsolete term for a MUSIC HALL or MUSIC ROOM (both of which see).

musicomedy

A MUSICAL COMEDY.

music plot

A list of the musical items to be played during a performance, with cues.

music room

A room for musicians, usually near the stage, either a lounge or (especially in the Elizabethan theatre, where a gallery behind and above the stage commonly served for the purpose) a place for the performance of instrumental and sometimes vocal music.

music show

A musical show.

mystery (play)

1. A play based on a Biblical story; more particularly, a play dealing with the life of Christ—Especially, Medieval. See BIBLE-HISTORIES. 2. A play based on the detection of crime. Hence *mystery-comedy*, etc.

N

naked stage
A bare stage, a stage without any scenic decoration.

name actor (or **performer** or **star**)
A principal actor, one whose reputation is expected to attract the public. Hence also *name act, name billing.*

name part
The role of the character from whose name a dramatic composition takes its title.

name performer (or **star**)
See NAME ACTOR.

narrator
An actor whose role is that of a commentator on a dramatic production, whether or not he is also a participant.

national company
An American acting company organized for a nationwide tour.

national drama
Collectively, the native dramatic works of a country; works produced at the British NATIONAL THEATRES (sense 2) ; the drama of a country, considered as representing broadly the drama cutting across social lines.

national theatre
1. A theatre subsidized by a national government, or, if privately supported, officially recognized by a national government as of nationwide importance. Typically, it is professional but non-commercial, and produces native rather than foreign dramatic pieces. 2. A nickname for Drury Lane and Covent Garden Theatres, London, in recognition of their pre-eminence as British theatrical institutions, and of their former government-sanctioned monopoly as patent theatres. 3. National drama, drama which is native, not foreign.

Nativity play
A religious drama based on the birth of Christ—Especially, Medieval.

naturalism
1. Realism; especially, extreme anti-conventional realism in dramatic writing and production, aiming at photographic objectivity rather than imaginative selectivity in duplicating the details of real life on the stage, and emphasizing the scientific treatment of man in his environment, particularly a lower-class environment—Especially, a late 19th century movement. 2. Stage representation, especially a style of acting, which is or seeks to be unaffected, without exaggeration.—Hence, in both senses, *naturalistic*.

nautical drama
An AQUATIC DRAMA (which see). Also called *nautical melodrama, nautical piece*, etc.

neo-classic(al) drama
Drama which attempts to imitate Greek or Roman models in the unities, decorum, the balance of characters, etc.—Especially, 17th and 18th centuries. Thus also *neo-classicism, neo-classicist*. See CLASSIC(AL) DRAMA and PSEUDO-CLASSIC(AL) DRAMA.

net
Short for THEATRICAL NET.

netting compound
A glue used to fasten cut-out foliage to a net, etc.

neutral stage
A stage which does not visually designate a locality, as (frequently) the Elizabethan platform stage.

New Drama
The British drama of the 1890s, influenced by Ibsen.

new play
A play which has never before been produced.

newspaper
See LIVING NEWSPAPER.

New Stagecraft; New Theatre movement
A movement in stage production, aiming at the harmonious synthesis of setting, lighting, acting, etc., and embracing a wide range of techniques such as theatricalism and expressionism—Late 19th century and first third of 20th century.

nifty
A joke, a wisecrack; the punch line or tag of a joke.

nigger heaven
The topmost seats in a theatre.

nigger show
A minstrel show—19th century. Hence also *nigger minstrel*.

night, (the)
The opening night. See IT WILL BE ALL RIGHT ON THE NIGHT.

night club
A place where FLOOR SHOWS (which see) are exhibited and where patrons dine, dance, and listen to music.

night man; nightman
A stagehand employed for night work.

night stand; night-stand
Short for ONE NIGHT STAND.

nitrogen spot
Formerly, a spotlight using an incandescent bulb containing nitrogen.

nod
To take a bow.

noise(s) off
Off-stage sound effects—Sometimes, a stage direction.

non-commercial
Said of a (or the) theatre, in contradistinction to COMMERCIAL (which see). A non-commercial theatre may be professional, wholly or partly, or amateur.

non-professional
Said of a (or the) theatre, etc., in contradistinction to *professional* (see PROFESSION), to avoid the derogatory connotation sometimes understood in AMATEUR.

non-stop
Said, in British terminology, of a show which runs continuously through many hours, repeating itself—Revue and Vaudeville. U.S.: *continuous* (which is also British).

nose putty; nose-putty; nose paste
A plastic substance used to alter the appearance of an actor's nose, chin, etc.

notice
1. A review of a production in the press. 2. An actor's or producer's notification of an intent to terminate an engagement. 3. An announcement posted on a call board.

notice board; notice-board
1. A CALL BOARD (which see). 2. In British terminology, a display (on a board or cloth) used on the stage to give the audience dialogue or other information which could not be spoken in theatres unlicensed for legitimate drama—First half of 19th century.

novelty act
A skit, acrobatic feat, etc., which is unusual and perhaps new—Vaudeville.

number
A distinct portion of a production, such as a song or a dance—Musical comedy, Vaudeville.

number one batten
A British term for the FIRST PIPE (which see).

number two company
A company which tours while the original company continues to play.

nursery
Short for STAGE NURSERY.

nut (of the show)
The actual or estimated cost of producing a show, commonly figured on a weekly basis. A show that has begun to make a profit is said to be *off the nut;* if money reserved for overhead is being drawn upon, the show is said to be operating *on the nut.*

O

Oakley
See ANNIE OAKLEY.

objective lens
In optical effects machines, any lens or composition of lenses placed between the slide and the projection surface so as to cause an image of the slide to appear on the surface.

obligatory scene
A scene which becomes necessary in a dramatic work because the dramatist has led the audience to expect it.

oblique
Said of scenery that is not placed at a right angle to the center line of the stage.

odeum
Originally, a roofed theatre used for Greek and Roman musical and poetic contests; now (sometimes) a building or portion of a building used for dramatic performances. Plural, *odea*.

off
1. Short for OFF STAGE. 2. Off the stage, from the center, as, to *move off*. 3. See also CARRY-OFF, GO OFF, LOCK OFF, MAKE OFF, *open off* (see OPEN), TIE OFF.

off Broadway; off-Broadway
Said of a professional theatre in New York City which is not located in the usual Broadway theatre area; also collectively. Hence *off-Broadway show*, etc.

off-cast
To play a role with considerable freedom from the specifications in the script.

offer
To present a production to the public. Hence also an *offering*.

office actor
An actor who tries to get a part by behaving pretentiously during an interview with a producer.

Office of the Revels; Revels Office
The office of the MASTER OF THE REVELS (which see). Hence *Officers of the Revels*.

off set; off-set
Said of scenery which is placed at a right angle to the center line of the stage.

off stage; off-stage; offstage
1. That part of the stage which is not visible to the audience and which lies outside the acting area; also, off, or away from the center of, the stage. Short form, *off*. Hence *offstage action, off stage speech*, etc. 2. Supposedly or actually outside the theatre.

off-stage character
A character who is mentioned in a dramatic work but who never becomes one of the dramatis personae.

off-stage cue
A cue given for, or by, someone offstage.

off-stage effect
A noise or other special effect produced offstage.

off stage noise
A NOISE OFF (which see).

off the nut
See NUT (OF THE SHOW).

Old Comedy, (the)
English comedy of former times, as from Shakespeare to Sheridan; or more specifically the artificial comedy of manners of the Restoration period, satirizing aberrations in social behavior and dwelling on amorous intrigue.

236

old man; (feminine) **old woman**
An actor who plays the role of an elderly man; particularly, an actor who specializes in such roles; the role itself.

old play
A play which has been produced, which is not new, which is being revived.

old pro
An old professional, a veteran actor.

old stager
A veteran actor.

Old Tragedy, (the)
Elizabethan tragedy.

old woman
Feminine form of OLD MAN (which see).

olio; oleo
1. A scene consisting of a specialty act (see SPECIALTY) played IN ONE (which see) while another scene is being set farther back—Especially, Vaudeville. Also as *olio act* (or *scene*). 2. A backing, drop, or tableau curtain for a FRONT SCENE (which see)—Especially, Vaudeville. Also as *olio drop*, etc. 3. A medley of songs, dances, comic sketches, and the like—Especially, Vaudeville, and as the typical second part of a Minstrel or Burlesque show.

olivette
A floodlight of the simplest kind, with a single lamp bulb.

omnibus box
A term, chiefly British, for a BOX (sense 1) capable of containing a large number of persons—19th century.

on
1. Short for ON STAGE, as, to be *on.* 2. On the stage, towards the center, as, to *move on.* 3. See also GO ON, *open on* (see OPEN), WALK ON.

one
See IN ONE, TWO FOR ONE.

one-acter
A ONE-ACT PLAY.

one-act play
A play in one act, usually longer than a sketch, concentrated, economical of detail, unified in effect; analogous to the short story in contrast to the novel.

one night stand; one-night stand; short form, night stand
A single evening performance given by a visiting company, or the town or theatre in which such a performance is given.

one-sheet
To give an ACT (sense 4) minor billing. From the name of the smallest size of theatrical advertising poster used on billboards (see SHEET).

one-week house
A term, now rare, for a theatre usually booked for one week by a company on the road.

on its dead
See DEAD.

on one's card
A British expression meaning: Upon the presentation of one's theatrical calling card (to obtain free admission to a theatre). U.S.: *courtesy of the profession.*

on spike
Said of scenery, furniture, or a property that has been moved into its proper final position. British: *on its* (or *the*) *dead.*

on stage; on-stage; onstage
1. That part of the stage which is visible to the audience and which is used for, or is available for, acting; also, on, or to-

wards the center of, the stage. Short form, *on*. Hence GO ON (the stage manager's command to an actor), *Goes on* (a stage direction), *on-stage space*, etc. 2. An act call, to summon actors.

on the book
be on the book: To serve as prompter.

on the dead
See DEAD.

on the dog
See TRY IT ON THE DOG.

on the nut
See NUT.

on the road
See ROAD.

on tour
See TOUR.

on trim
See TRIM.

O.P.
1. Abbreviation of OPPOSITE PROMPT SIDE. Also in the forms O.P. SIDE, O.P.S. 2. Old prices. The O.P. Riots in London were disturbances lasting 61 nights in 1809, occasioned by an increase in admission charges to cover the cost of rebuilding the Covent Garden Theatre after a fire.

open
1. To bring a dramatic work to the stage, to produce, to begin a run. 2. Short for OPEN UP. 3. Said of a door or window: To open towards or away from the playing area, as, *open on, open off*. 4. In various compounds, applied to lighting units which have no lens or similar cover, as, *open-box, openfaced*. 5. To reveal part of the stage area by pulling the wings apart—Restoration.

open-air theatre
An OUTDOOR THEATRE (which see). Hence *open-air production, open-air stage,* etc.

open box
A BOX (sense 1) for spectators, which is not enclosed by curtains, lattices, etc.

open cold
To OPEN (sense 1) in New York City without a try-out elsewhere.

opener
A short play given before a longer play, or as the first in a series; an opening number (see NUMBER).

open-faced; openfaced
Said of lighting units which are uncovered, as, *openfaced strip lights.*

open flat scene
A CUT FLAT SCENE (which see).

opening
1. Short for OPENING NIGHT. 2. In British terminology, in a PANTOMIME (which see, sense 2), a dramatic entertainment in one or more acts preceding the harlequinade, originally (18th century) in dumbshow, later (from 1814) with spoken dialogue (the *speaking opening*), and now the principal and sometimes the only portion of the (Christmas) pantomime.

opening (night)
The first performance of a production. Hence *opening-night ticket,* etc. British: *first night,* which is also U.S.

opening situation
The INITIAL SITUATION (which see).

open out a speech
In acting, to lengthen a speech, to vary the delivery, by changing the tempo, the pauses, etc.

240

open time
Dates free for an actor's or a company's engagements.

open (up)
1. In acting, to turn the body towards the full front position for emphasis. 2. To emphasize in one way or another, as in *opening up a prop* (picking it up).

open white; abbreviation, **O.W.**
Said of a lighting unit which is operated without a color medium.

opera
A dramatic composition for the stage, in which all or most of the lines are sung, a musical drama more elaborate than a musical comedy or the like. Hence *operatic*, etc. See COMIC OPERA, GRAND OPERA, LIGHT OPERA.

opéra bouffe
A French expression ("comic opera," "burlesque opera") used in English for a COMIC OPERA. Plural, *opéras bouffes*. Often italicized.

opera buffa
An Italian expression ("comic opera") used in English for a COMIC OPERA. Plural, *opere buffe*. Often italicized.

opera glasses
Binoculars used for viewing the stage. Sometimes in the singular; but seldom monocular.

opera house
A theatre building for opera, and sometimes for plays and other entertainments.

operating crew
The stage crew, from the stage manager to the GRIP (sense 3).

operating line
1. A CURTAIN LINE (sense 3). 2. A line used for moving counterweight equipment.

241

operator
1. A person who operates theatre lights; an assistant electrician.
2. See also CURTAIN OPERATOR.

operetta
A light dramatic entertainment with much singing and little speaking; formerly, and sometimes now, equivalent to musical comedy.

opposite
See PLAY OPPOSITE.

**opposite prompt (side); abbreviations, O.P.,
  O.P.S., O.P. side**
A term, now chiefly British, for a section of the stage outside the acting area and opposite the prompt corner; usually downstage right.

opry-house
An opera house, so spelt and pronounced facetiously, and commonly derogatively, to indicate a run-down theatre used by a touring company.

optical effect
See EFFECT.

option
The privilege, paid for by a producer, of producing a dramatic work within a given time, if he so desires. Also, to buy this privilege.

orange girl (or wench)
A girl who sold fruit and candy to theatre audiences under the direction of a concessionaire (*orange woman*)—Restoration.

oratorio
A sacred musical drama without stage action.

orchestra
1. The seating area on the main level of an auditorium. Hence, the *orchestra floor*, an *orchestra seat*. British: (the) *stalls*, a

STALL; but orchestra seats extend to the rear of the auditorium, into the area which the British call the PIT. 2. Collectively, the persons who play music in a theatre, the instrumentalists. Hence (of music for an orchestra) *orchestral, orchestrate,* etc. 3. Short for ORCHESTRA PIT. 4. A seating area for the nobility, near the stage—Elizabethan.

orchestra circle
A term, now rare, for a PARQUET CIRCLE.

orchestra divan
A particularly comfortable wide seat with folding arms, now sometimes used in the front rows of the orchestra.

orchestra leader; short form, leader
The person in charge of the theatre musicians, their director during a performance. British: *conductor,* which is also U.S.

orchestra pit; short form, pit
A place assigned to musicians, immediately in front of or wholly or partly under the stage, and sometimes sunk below the level of the floor of the auditorium.

orchestra stall
In British terminology, a seat in the front rows of the stalls on the main floor of an auditorium. Infrequently, in U.S. terminology, an orchestra seat.

orchestra well
An alternative British term for ORCHESTRA PIT.

order
1. A term, chiefly British, for admission PASS. 2. See IN ORDER OF THEIR APPEARANCE.

organ-loft
A SCENE DOCK.

original cast (or company)
An acting company which has played in the first run of a show, or is still playing in it, or is playing in a revival of it, rather

243

than a road company or a company composed wholly or partly of new players.

original production
The first production of a dramatic piece, in contradistinction to a revival. Hence *original play*.

ornamental property
A DECORATIVE PROPERTY (which see).

outdoor flood light
A strong floodlight used in outdoor productions.

outdoor theatre
A theatre in the open air, with no roof or at least not completely roofed. See also PUBLIC THEATRE.

out front
In the auditorium; or wherever the audience may circulate in a theatre. British: *in front*.

outlet box
A STAGE POCKET.

outer stage
A PLATFORM STAGE or large APRON (sense 1)—Elizabethan.

overact
1. To overemphasize, to exaggerate, in acting. Hence *overacting* (noun). An obsolete term for the following: 2. To surpass, in acting. 3. To act over again.

overhaul line
A rope line used over a pulley to haul scenery into place.

overhead lighting
The illumination of a scene from above, and usually from behind the proscenium.

overlap
In acting, to move or speak before another actor has finished moving or speaking.

overplay
To overact.

overture
1. Introductory music played before the beginning of a performance (or act). 2. Short for OVERTURE AND BEGINNERS!

Overture (and beginners)!
An ACT CALL (sense 1) for the beginning of a performance.

O.W.
Abbreviation of OPEN WHITE.

owner
Short for THEATRE OWNER.

P

P.A.
Abbreviation of PRESS AGENT.

pace
The speed at which a dramatic performance or any part of it is played. Also, to play at a certain speed.

pack
1. Short for SCENE PACK. Also, to group flats or cloths in a scene pack. 2. To fill an auditorium with spectators, as *pack 'em in, pack the house.* Hence also a *packed house,* etc. 3. To introduce friends or hired persons to applaud or to hiss, as, *pack the audience,* etc.

package
An arrangement by means of which a summer theatre pays for the temporary importation of a touring guest company, usually one rehearsed in New York. Hence, *package company, package show,* etc. Sometimes only a star, or a star with a few other actors, is so "bought." Hence *star package, packaged stars.*

pad
To add lines or business to a script to make an actor's role more important, as, *pad a part.*

pageant
1. A type of entertainment (play, sketch, tableau, or procession), usually produced outdoors, usually performed by a large number of people of the locality where it is played, usually spectacular, and usually historical or patriotic (formerly often religious) in nature, now and sometimes formerly usually given a musical background; also, a scene in such an entertainment. In medieval times, often performed on a wheeled stage as one of a series of religious scenes. Hence *pageant-drama, pageanteer, pageantry,* etc. 2. A fixed or movable stage (as, a *pageant,* a

246

pageant wagon) for such an entertainment—Medieval and Renaissance. 3. A structure of wood and canvas used as a stage machine in the setting of a masque—15th and 16th centuries. 4. Short for PAGEANT LAMP (or LANTERN).

pageant lantern (or lamp)
A British term for a narrow-beam PROJECTOR UNIT (which see).

paint bridge
See BRIDGE (sense 2).

paint frame
A wooden support used to hold scenery which is to be painted.

paint room
A working place backstage for a scenic artist.

palmy days
The best days, the times of greatest success, of plays and players of legendary fame.

pam
Short for PANORAMA.

pan
1. Short for PANORAMA. 2. To ridicule or criticize severely. 3. See DEAD PAN.

panorama; short forms, pam, pan
A scenic device, a kind of cyclorama, used to present a distant (and often moving) view, usually on a painted canvas which rolls from one cylinder to another at the back of the stage. Called also a *panoramic cloth*. Hence *panoramic,* etc. See also DIORAMA.

panorama floodlight
A CYCLORAMA LIGHT.

panorama-groove
A groove in the stage floor in which the edge of a panorama can be inserted.

Pantaloon

Originally, a major character (Pantalone or Pantaleone, an avaricious old merchant, Harlequin's master) in the *commedia dell' arte*. Later, Columbine's jealous father (husband, guardian), the Clown's dupe, and a principal figure in a HARLEQUINADE (which see), especially in PANTOMIME (sense 2). Hence *pantaloonery*.

pantomime; short form, panto

1. In acting, expressive movement of the body (arms, legs, face, head); called also *stage action* (see ACTION), STAGE BUSINESS. Silent drama, mime, dumbshow, as part of a stage performance or as a performance complete in itself, often spectacular and with dance and musical accompaniment. To mime, to act silently. Hence *pantomime theatre, pantomimist*, etc. 2. In British (and formerly occasionally U.S.) terminology, a spectacular entertainment, first (early 18th century) a silent harlequinade, then a speaking harlequinade, later a burlesque and extravaganza; later still and now an olio of acrobatics, clowning, tableaux, songs, music, dances, and dialogue (usually comic), with gorgeous settings, and a plot drawn from a nursery or other fantastic popular tale. Since the 1820s it has usually opened during the Christmas season; hence such designations as CHRISTMAS PANTOMIME. 3. A dance drama, a spectacular ballet afterpiece—18th century.

Pantomime the business

A director's instruction to the actors, in rehearsals, before properties become available, to perform in pantomime any stage business calling for the use of a property.

paper

1. A free admission PASS. Hence, *paper the house*, to issue free admission passes so that the auditorium will be filled and the entertainment will appear to be successful. Hence a *house full of paper*, a *paper house*. 2. Theatrical advertising sheets posted outdoors.

248

paper set
An interior stage setting, the walls of which are decorated with wallpaper rather than with paint.

parabolic reflector
A paraboloid reflecting surface, used in certain lighting units to obtain powerful parallel rays.

paradise
The topmost seating area in a theatre.

parallel
A hinged trestle which, unfolded, supports a stage platform (PLATFORM, or *parallel top*).

parallel action
1. The balanced stage movement of two actors, or of two groups of actors. 2. The balancing of two equally important dramatic actions, as in *King Lear*.

parallel top; short form, **top**
A platform which fits on a PARALLEL (which see).

parley
A trumpet call announcing an embassy or a pause in fighting— Elizabethan stage direction.

parody
A dramatic composition, or any stage activity, which imitates in order to burlesque or ridicule. Also, to burlesque. Hence *parodist*, etc.

parquet; parquette
A term, now rare, for the main floor of an auditorium or part of it (sometimes the portion not covered by balconies, or certain portions at the side or back) ; also, the seats in such an area.

parquet circle
A term, now rare, for that portion of the main floor of an auditorium which is covered by balconies; also, the seats in such an area. Also called *orchestra circle, parterre.*

part
1. An actor's role. 2. An actor's lines, typed or written down for his use in conning them, with indications of business and cues.

parterre
A PARQUET CIRCLE. Thus also a *parterre box.* Sometimes, the pit—Restoration.

party
See THEATRE PARTY.

party claps; party-claps
Collectively, a claque—18th century.

pass
A permit to admit a person into a theatre without a ticket. British: *complimentary ticket.*

pass check
A re-admission pass for a spectator who leaves the theatre temporarily. British: *pass-out check.*

pass door; pass-door
A door for the use of theatre people, between the side of the stage and the auditorium.

Passion play
A religious drama based on the trial and crucifixion of Christ.

passout
A term, chiefly British, for a spectator who leaves the theatre temporarily. Hence *pass-out check* (a re-admission pass). U.S.: Usually *pass check.*

250

paste
In stage use, a mixture of glue, whiting, and cold water, used to fasten canvas to the frame of a flat.

pasteboard
A theatre ticket.

pastoral (drama)
A romantic, artificial drama, in a stylized rustic setting, commonly dealing with shepherds and shepherdesses; also collectively—Chiefly Renaissance.

patch panel
Any of a variety of electrical systems allowing the complete interconnection of any stage electrical circuit to any dimming circuit; the principal types are the cord and plug, the bus bar and slider, and the rotary selector switch.

patent
In British terminology, a royal license conferring certain privileges, especially the authorization to produce legitimate drama —1660–1843. The term usually refers to two London theatres, the Drury Lane and Covent Garden. Hence *patent company, patentee, patent theatre*, etc.

Paternoster play
A dramatization of the Lord's Prayer—Medieval.

pathetic drama (or **tragedy**)
A kind of tragic play seeking to elicit the spectator's pity; also collectively—Restoration and 18th century.

patron
1. A supporter of the theatre, especially a paying spectator. 2. A royal or noble person who supported and protected an acting company, usually granting a patent or license—Elizabethan, and later. Hence *patronage*.

patsy
1. A "fall guy," an assistant who does all the work, as in the theatre or in an agency. 2. An actor on whom a director vents his spleen.

patter
A set of amusing lines rapidly and fluently spoken or sung by an actor, or the words for such lines—Musical comedy, Comic opera, Vaudeville, Revue, etc. Also, to deliver such lines. Hence *patterer* (or, if very successful, *patterist*), *patter song*, etc.

pattern projector
An ellipsoidal reflector spotlight, designed to be used with a drop-in shutter holding any of a variety of patterns cut out of metal.

pause
In acting, a short delay in dialogue, gesture, or movement, in order to achieve emphasis, suspense, etc. Also, to delay for this purpose.

pay box, pay-box, paybox
In British (formerly also U.S.) terminology, an office where patrons pay cash at the time of admission.

pay off
To pay the production costs of a show from the producer's pocket rather than from the box-office receipts.

peanut gallery (or heaven)
A term, used in the U.S. only, for the topmost seating area in a theatre.

peep hole; peep-hole
1. An opening in a curtain through which persons on the stage may peek into the auditorium. 2. Said of a play which is realistic. 3. Said of a PICTURE FRAME STAGE (which see). Called also *peep-show theatre*.

peg
Short for STAGE PEG.

pelmet
A British term for a VALANCE, or a GRAND DRAPERY.

penny gaff
See GAFF.

penny gallery
The upper of two galleries—Elizabethan. Called also *two-penny gallery*, since the admission charge was one penny at the theatre door and another penny at the gallery.

penny plain, twopence coloured
A nickname (from the original prices) for printed sheets of drawings, scenes, etc., copied from the contemporary stage and issued by various British publishers 19th century. These sheets were intended to serve as cut-out materials for the JUVENILE DRAMA (which see) or as souvenirs or decorations. Sometimes the word "and" (or "or") is placed before the word "twopence."

people's theatre
A theatre which professes to serve all the people in a community, usually aiming neither at profit nor at intellectual achievement; also collectively.

Pepper's ghost
A transparent ghost, a trick effect achieved by presenting on an inclined sheet of plate glass the image of an actor moving in the orchestra pit. Named for its British inventor, Professor John Henry Pepper (1821–1900).

percentage basis
In a contract between a producer and a theatre owner, an agreement providing that the producer shall pay the owner a percentage of the gross receipts rather than a fixed sum for the rental of the theatre.

perch

A term, chiefly British, for a small platform just behind and above the proscenium opening, to the right or the left, used for the operation of strong lighting units which illuminate the front of the stage; the lighting units so placed. If two platforms are used, they are called *upper perch* and *lower perch*. Hence also *perch lime, perch spot.*

perform

To ACT (which see), to take part in a theatrical performance. Hence (*stage* or *theatrical*) *performer* (actor, dancer, singer, etc.).

performance

1. A showing of a dramatic entertainment. Also in the forms *dramatic* (or *stage* or *theatrical*) *performance*. 2. An actor's execution of his role.

period

Said of any theatrical representation of a past age, as, *period acting,* a *period costume,* a *period play* (equivalent to a *costume play*).

peripeteia; peripety

A DRAMATIC REVERSAL (which see). The first spelling comes from the Greek.

permanent company

An acting company, resident or touring, which remains intact indefinitely rather than for the production of only one dramatic work. Hence *permanent stock company,* etc.

permanent control switchboard

A stage switchboard wired so that the circuits remain permanently hooked up.

permanent cyclorama

A fixed cyclorama made of a rigid material, such as plaster, rather than of fabric.

permanent footlight
A footlight which is fixed rather than portable.

permanent frame
A PERMANENT SETTING.

permanent setting
A stage setting in which the chief components remain fixed in place for an entire performance and lesser components are moved about or replaced. See also PERMANENT UNIT SETTING.

permanent unit setting
A stage setting in which a framework of flats remains fixed in place for an entire performance and units of scenery called inset pieces are used to effect minor changes in appearance for different scenes.

person
See IN PERSON.

personae
See DRAMATIS PERSONAE.

personal house seat; short form, house seat
One of several choice seats in the auditorium reserved at each performance for the use of the theatre owner, the manager, an actor, etc.

personal manager
A person who represents a theatre manager, actor, author, or the like.

personal property
A HAND PROPERTY (which see) worn or carried on the person of an actor, such as a handkerchief.

personate
To impersonate. Hence *personation, personator,* etc.

personify
To characterize; also, to embody an abstract characterization.
Hence *personification,* etc.

perspective
A depiction of the proportions and relationships of objects in
a view in such a way that the audience will receive an impression of distance; the view so depicted; the art of so depicting
a scene. Hence *in perspective, perspective scenery, perspective
setting, perspective sketch, perspective stage.*

photograph call; short forms, photo call, call
A notice to actors and certain technicians to come to the theatre
for the taking of photographs.

piano-case dimmer; piano-board dimmer
A portable switchboard and bank of dimmers in the shape of
an upright piano.

pick up
In acting, to speed up, and especially to speed up one's responses
to cues (*pick up cues*).

pick up an audience
To act so successfully that members of the audience are carried
away emotionally to the point of wishing to intervene in the
drama being represented before them, as in the form *picking
up an audience into their arms*—19th century.

pictorial scenery
PICTURE SCENERY (which see).

picture
1. Any picture used in a projection machine for effects. 2. See
STAGE PICTURE. 3. A tableau—A stage direction.

picture-ending curtain
A TABLEAU CURTAIN (sense 2).

picture frame hanger
A hanger, consisting of a hook and socket, used on the stage to attach a picture, lamp, or other object of light weight to a flat.

picture-frame stage; short form, **picture stage**
A stage which is framed like a picture by a proscenium arch. Hence *picture-frame theatre.*

picture scenery
Scenery used in a PICTURE SETTING (sense 1).

picture screen
A PICTURE SHEET (which see).

picture setting
1. A stage setting which emphasizes the pictorial possibilities of stage depth and proscenium frame; a pictorial presentation of locality. Called also *pictorial setting, picture scene.* 2. A stage setting in which distant perspective scenes appeared through doorways—Renaissance.

picture sheet (or **screen**)
A drop curtain on which pictures can be projected.

picture stage; picture-stage
Short for PICTURE-FRAME STAGE.

picturization
In directing, the positioning of actors so as to add visual meaning to the dramatic situation.

piece
1. A drama, especially a play. 2. A scenic piece, a unit or element of scenery, especially one which is built up. 3. A share in the financial risk of a show, as, to own a *piece* of the show.

pièce à thèse
A French expression used in English for a thesis play, a DRAMA OF IDEAS (which see). Usually italicized.

pièce bien faite
A French expression used in English for a WELL-MADE PLAY
(which see). Usually italicized.

pierrot show
In British terminology, a type of light entertainment featuring
singing, dancing, comic acts, etc., performed usually by touring companies of actors (*pierrots*) and actresses (*pierrettes*)
freely imitating in costume and make-up the white clothing and
whitened face of the Pierrot of the French stage—Late 19th
and early 20th centuries. Hence *pierrot troupe*.

pigeon hole; pigeon-hole
1. A box for spectators, with a small arched opening. 2. A top
gallery seat.

pigtail (outlet)
A short length of stage cable, as from a lighting unit, for making a quick connection. British: *tail*.

pilot lamp (or light)
1. A work light. 2. A lamp on a switchboard which shows
whether or not a circuit is functioning. 3. A lamp on a dimmer
which shows the amount of the current and the color of the
light being supplied to a lighting unit. 4. A burner at the end
of a row of gaslights—19th century.

pin connector
A STAGE CABLE CONNECTOR (which see).

ping
In acting, to speak lines softly, without heavy emphasis.

pin hinge; pin-hinge
An ordinary household hinge (fitted, however, with a pin or
wire which can easily be pulled out) used to fasten scenic
pieces together. Called also a *butt* (or *loose-pin*) *hinge*. To
fasten scenic pieces together with such a hinge.

pin rail; pin-rail; pinrail
A rail on a gallery, or at the stage level, or on a wall, holding two rows of belaying pins or cleats (upper, *fly rail* or *working rail;* lower, *tie-off rail* or *trim rail*) to which flying lines can be fastened. British: Usually *fly rail.*

pin spot
A spotlight which has been focused to a very small beam, used to illuminate a small portion of the stage. Hence *pin-spotting.*

pin wire
A piece of wire used as a pin in a pin hinge.

pipe (batten)
See BATTEN.

pipe clamp
A clamp used to fasten a lighting unit or a scenic piece to a pipe or batten. British: *barrel clamp* (or *clip* or *grip*).

pirate
To produce or publish a dramatic piece without authorization. A person who does so. Hence *piracy,* etc.

pit
1. Short for ORCHESTRA PIT. 2. In British (and formerly U.S.) terminology, an unreserved seating area behind the stalls, that is, at the back of the ORCHESTRA (sense 1); formerly, the entire lower floor of the auditorium. Hence that part of the audience which occupies such an area. 3. A space without seats, for standing spectators, in the center of a public playhouse; or with seats, in a private playhouse—Elizabethan.

pitch
In acting, the height to which a voice is raised. Also, to raise or lower the voice, not in volume but according to the musical scale.

pit circle
In British terminology, a seating area above the pit in one or another of the galleries.

pit stall
In British terminology, a stall in the front rows of the pit.

pittite
In British terminology, a spectator in the pit.

pivot (leg) arm
An adjustable device used to link curtains or other scenic pieces to a batten or other carrier.

Places!
A call to summon the actors to take their positions on the stage when the curtain is about to rise. British: *Beginners, please!*

plan
A seating chart used in the box office.
(See specific entries, such as FLOOR PLAN, for other kinds of *plan*.)

plano-convex lens spotlight
A spotlight with a CONDENSER LENS (which see), the lens having one curved surface and one flat surface, the latter nearer the light source.

plant
1. In dramatic construction, and hence in acting, to introduce an idea or object which will later become significant in the dramatic action; a line, bit of business, property, character, etc., so introduced. Hence *planting* (noun). 2. To place an actor among the spectators; an actor so placed. 3. See THEATRE PLANT.

plaster dome; short form, **dome**
A dome horizon (see CYCLORAMA).

plastic
Said of scenery which is three-dimensional. Also said of a setting or a stage which is three-dimensional, especially when the setting is emphasized by light falling on non-realistic sculptured shapes. Hence *plasticity*, etc.

plate
1. In British usage, a keystone. 2. A board bearing controls for the illumination of the stage by gas—19th century.

(See specific entries such as CEILING PLATE, for other kinds of *plate*.)

platea
A level, unlocalized, neutral playing space between MANSIONS (which see)—Medieval.

plate dimmer
A stud contact dimmer, with an arm pivoted to make contact between studs arranged in a circle and one of a set of resistance coils fastened to a circular plate.

platform
An acting surface resting on a parallel.

(See specific entries, such as LOADING PLATFORM, for other kinds of *platform*.)

platform stage
A stage using an acting area which extends into the auditorium without a proscenium picture frame.

platform theatre
A WAGON STAGE (sense 2).

platt
A plot, a play synopsis, used by the stage staff—Elizabethan.

plaudit
Applause. Also (but rare), to applaud. Hence *plaudite* (applause), *plauditor*, etc.

play
1. A piece of writing composed for, or as if for, stage production, telling a story by means of dialogue (or pantomime); a DRAMA (sense 1). 2. To act, act the role of, represent by acting, perform in (a place), etc. 3. Said of a script: To be actable, as, It *played* well. 4. To produce a dramatic composition on the stage.

play agent
A person who serves as a broker to help a dramatic author find a producer. Hence (*play*) *agency*.

play-bill; playbill
A theatrical program or bill; a poster.

play book; play-book; playbook
1. A play manuscript, as an acting text—Elizabethan. Short form, *book*. 2. A book of plays.

play broker; playbroker; short form, broker
A PLAY AGENT (which see). Hence *play-broking*.

play carpenter
A dramatist who constructs plays without originality from non-dramatic works or changes plays to suit different audiences.

play coach
See COACH.

play doctor
A person employed to revise a script in order to remedy its obvious shortcomings. Hence *play-doctoring*, and to *play-doctor*.

play down
1. In acting, to underemphasize important dialogue or action. 2. In acting, to strive to make obvious to spectators who are considered to be unintelligent.

262

player
An actor.

players' house
A MANSION (which see).

play for a laugh (or **for laughs**)
In acting, to stress lines or business in order to make the audience laugh.

play-goer; playgoer
A spectator, especially one who makes a habit of attending the theatre. Hence *playgoing*.

play house; play-house; playhouse
A theatre.

playing
1. Acting. 2. Said of a dramatic piece which is currently being performed, as, (*now*) *playing*.

playing area
The acting area, or a portion thereof.

playing space
The ACTING AREA.

playing time
The length of time required for a dramatic performance.

play it straight
See STRAIGHT (sense 1).

playlet
A short play.

play-maker
A dramatist.

play of atmosphere
A play in which an emotion, rather than character study, plot, etc., is dominant, as, *Riders to the Sea, The Cherry Orchard.*

play of character
A play in which character study, rather than atmosphere, plot, etc., is dominant, as, *Macbeth*.

play of ideas
A DRAMA OF IDEAS (which see).

play of situation
A play in which events rather than character or atmosphere dominate.

play opposite
To have a leading male or female role, corresponding to the leading role of the other sex which is being played by a more noted actor or actress. Also as *appear opposite*.

play out
In acting, to project one's efforts towards the auditorium rather than towards the rest of the stage.

play package
A group of plays available for purchase for amateur production.

play-production
See PRODUCTION.

play reader; play-reader; playreader;
     short form, **reader**
A person who evaluates scripts for a producer, a publisher, or a company. Hence *playreading* (noun and adjective). Also as *script-reader*.

play-reading
1. The reading aloud of plays for amateur entertainment. 2. See PLAY READER.

play reviewer
A DRAMA CRITIC.

play right; play-right
In British terminology, a copyright in a dramatic composition.

play scout
A representative of a producer or of some other person who watches productions in order to report on new plays which might be bought for use elsewhere.

playscript
See SCRIPT.

play society
A British term for a STAGE SOCIETY (which see).

play's the thing, (The)
A proverbial expression, quoted from *Hamlet,* meaning that the play itself should be the center of interest in a stage production, not the scenery, costumes, acting, etc.

play the first spot
To be the first actor, or actors, to appear at the rise of the curtain. British: *play them in.*

play them in
A British equivalent for PLAY THE FIRST SPOT.

play tinker
A PLAY DOCTOR.

play to (or for) the gallery
To act with special regard for the plaudits of the spectators in the gallery (balcony), alluding to the actual or supposed lack of taste of such spectators; to overact.

play to the gas
To play before an almost empty auditorium.

play up
To emphasize important dialogue or action.

play up the curtain
To perform instrumental music just before the rise of the curtain.

play up to
To act in such a way as to support another actor.

play within a (or **the**) **play**
A simulation of a dramatic performance as part of a play.

play with music
A legitimate play, with a substantial amount of music.

playwright
A dramatist.

playwrite
An incorrect spelling of PLAYWRIGHT, originating in a confusion of "wright" with "write."

playwriting
The writing of plays.

Plinge, Walter
The British equivalent of *George Spelvin* (see SPELVIN), dating from about 1900.

plot
1. The amplified story of a dramatic piece, as a succession of unfolding situations. Hence *plotting* (noun), *plot structure*, etc. Also, to develop the story of a dramatic piece in this way. See also PLATT. 2. A plan, scheme, or list having to do with production arrangements, as, a GRID PLOT, a *light plot*, etc. Also, to prepare such a plan.

plot action
PLOT BUSINESS (which see).

plot business
STAGE BUSINESS (which see) essential to the unfolding of the plot of a dramatic composition.

plot line
Usually in the plural: Dialogue essential to the unfolding of the plot of a dramatic piece.

plot movement; plot-movement
Dramatic action (see ACTION, sense 2).

plot play
A PLAY OF SITUATION (which see), especially when characterization is sacrificed to melodramatic action.

plot structure
DRAMATIC STRUCTURE (which see).

plug
1. A small flat used to fill in an opening between other scenic pieces, to conceal the underpinning of a staircase, etc. Hence such combinations as *door plug, plain plug*. Also, to use a small flat for such purposes. 2. To emphasize or overplay, as, *plug a line, plug for laughs*. 3. See STAGE PLUG.

plugging box; plug-in box
A portable box, which can be plugged into a stage pocket or switchboard, and which contains a set of electrical outlets into which plugs may be inserted to provide circuits to lighting units. British: *connector box, plug box*.

plugging strip
A duct containing a series of plug outlets.

plus and minus dimmer; plus or minus dimmer
British terms for an AUTO-TRANSFORMER DIMMER.

pocket
Short for STAGE POCKET.

podium
Short for LYCOPODIUM.

poet
An author of plays in verse; formerly, a prose dramatist as well.

poetic(al) drama
A dramatic work composed in verse; also collectively. Infrequently, applied also to works of a poetic quality in prose. Hence *poetic dramatist*, etc.

poetic(al) justice
Applied chiefly to tragedy: The reward of virtue or innocence and the punishment of vice; but in modern usage also a logical and motivated catastrophe satisfying the tragic necessity of catharsis despite the death of the sympathetic central figure or figures.

poet's night
Formerly, a benefit performance for a dramatist.

point
In dramatic construction and acting, to stress (*point* or *point up*) certain lines, movements, or gestures, called *pointers*, by directing the attention of the audience to something of dramatic importance, as in order to create suspense. Hence *pointing* (noun).

point business
PLOT BUSINESS (which see).

point line
A PLOT LINE (which see).

poison at the box office
An actor, author, play, etc., unable to attract audiences.

pole
See CHARIOT-AND-POLE SYSTEM.

police light
In British terminology, a light such as an exit light, which laws or ordinances specify shall remain on throughout a performance.

pong
1. In acting, to ad-lib when one forgets one's lines. Also, *pong-ing it*. 2. In acting, to speak lines firmly, with heavy emphasis.

pop
1. A nickname for a STAGE DOORMAN. The initial letter is capitalized. 2. Short for POPULAR PRICES; thus *pop theatre*.

popular drama
Drama which has its origin in folk ritual; drama which has little value as literature; drama which succeeds with the public, whatever its merit or lack of merit. Hence *popular theatre*.

popular prices
Comparatively low admission prices. Hence *popular-priced theatre*, etc.

portable
Said of a stage or of stage equipment which is movable for use wherever it is temporarily needed. Hence *portable footlight, portable stage, portable switchboard, portable theatre*.

portal (opening)
1. In U.S. terminology, a FALSE PROSCENIUM. 2. A door or other opening in a proscenium thickness or in a false proscenium. Formerly, one of two permanent doors or arches downstage, one on each side of the stage. Also as *portal door*.

portal set
A stage setting in which flats downstage remain unchanged throughout a performance, while other flats are rearranged.

position
The place where an actor stands at any given moment; especially, a STAGE POSITION (which see).

(See specific entries, such as BRIDGE POSITION, POSITIONS FOR CURTAIN, for other uses of this term.)

positions for curtain
The places which the members of the cast are to occupy for a curtain call.

poster
A theatrical notice, such as an announcement of forthcoming performances, which is affixed to a theatre wall or elsewhere. Also as *theatrical poster*.

post the bond
To give the financial guarantee required of producers by the Actors' Equity Association.

pot dimmer
A British term for a LIQUID DIMMER.

practicable; practical; short form, **prac**
Said of scenery or a property which is not merely simulative or decorative but functional, workable, as, a *practical door*, a *practical stair*, a *practical tree*. In the plural, often *practicables*.

pratfall; prattfall
In acting, a stage fall on the buttocks, with humorous exaggeration.

prelude
In British terminology, a short entertainment played before the principal entertainment. More specifically, a satirical sketch dealing with contemporary theatrical affairs, presented usually at the opening of a new theatre or season—Especially, late 18th century.

premier
See JEUNE PREMIER.

premier danseur; (feminine) **première danseuse**
A ballet dancer in a leading role—A French expression ("first dancer") used in English. Plural, *premiers danseurs* (feminine, *premières danseuses*). Often italicized.

270

première
1. The first public performance of a dramatic composition. Also, to give such a performance, as *premièring X's play*. 2. The leading lady in a stage production (see also JEUNE PREMIER).— Often italicized in both senses.

preparation
Short for DRAMATIC PREPARATION.

presence
Short for STAGE PRESENCE.

present
To offer a theatrical production or star to the public; to introduce a performer to an audience.

presentation
1. An introduction. See PRESENT. 2. Theatrical production, as, a method of theatrical *presentation*. 3. A theatrical production, ready for performance. 4. A particular style of staging. See PRESENTATIONAL.

presentational
Said of a dramatic work, or of a style of acting and staging: Anti-naturalistic; direct; using the artifices of the theatre instead of attempting to represent actual life realistically in every outward detail. Hence *presentationalism*.

pre-set switchboard
1. A stage switchboard so wired that groups of circuits can be controlled by master switches. Hence *pre-set lighting control*, a *pre-set*, to *pre-set*. 2. A stage switchboard equipped with duplicate controllers which are set in advance for the various dimmers and are activated when required. Hence, a *two-scene pre-set*, an *infinite pre-set*, etc.

press agent; abbreviation, **P.A.**
A publicity representative, as for a producer. Hence *press agentry*. Also as *press representative, theatrical press agent*.

press book
A collection of clippings about an actor or a dramatic work.

press list
A list of drama critics who are to receive free admission passes.

press matter
See SET OF PRESS MATTER.

press representative
A PRESS AGENT.

preview
A try-out performance before an invited audience.

prima donna
A leading female singer in opera, operetta, etc., especially one who is temperamental—Originally an Italian term ("first lady"). Plural, *prime donne* or *prima donnas*.

principal (actor)
1. An actor who has an important (especially, a leading) role; or an actor who speaks, rather than a walk-on. 2. A member of an acting company, in contradistinction to a hireling; also, an apprentice in a leading woman's role—Elizabethan.

principal boy; short form, (the) **boy**
In British terminology, the role of the dashing hero, conventionally (but not invariably) played by a woman—Pantomime (sense 2).

principal girl
In British terminology, the role of the sweet lovable heroine—Pantomime (sense 2). Not to be confused with PRINCIPAL BOY (which see), also conventionally played by a woman.

printed flag
In British terminology, a kind of NOTICE BOARD (sense 2)—19th century.

prism
A glass or crystal body with two or more plane faces which are not parallel, used in a magic lantern to turn a projected image upright.

private box
An enclosed box for a private group of spectators, now commonly called merely *box*—18th and 19th centuries.

private life, (in)
In one's life (as an actor) outside the theatre.

private performance
A theatrical performance not open to the general public. Especially in current British usage, a theatre club's production "for members only" of a dramatic work which is not licensed by the Lord Chamberlain.

private theatre (or **playhouse**)
1. A theatre not open to the public, as, a private house used for amateur theatricals (PRIVATE THEATRICALS). Hence also *private stage*. 2. An indoor theatre, smaller and more expensive than a PUBLIC THEATRE (which see), but open to the public—Elizabethan.

private theatricals
Stage performances by amateur actors, held elsewhere than in a theatre open to the public. See PRIVATE THEATRE.

problem play (or **piece** or **drama**)
See DRAMA OF IDEAS, for comment on *problem play* and related types.

produce
To bring a theatrical piece to the stage.

producer
1. The person who arranges for the stage production of a dramatic work, including the financing and management. Also as

production

theatrical producer. British: MANAGER (formerly STAGE MANA-GER). 2. In British usage, a STAGE DIRECTOR.

production
1. Collectively, the staging (or the arrangements for the staging) of a dramatic work, or of dramatic works in general, including some or all of the following (and other) theatrical matters: financing, management, direction, acting, costuming, lighting, making-up, scenic design and construction. 2. A dramatic composition on the stage.—Also as *theatrical* (or *dramatic* or *stage*) *production,* for both senses.

production notes
Notes made by members of the stage staff at a play reading, to remind themselves of their responsibilities.

production number (or **routine**)
A spectacular ensemble NUMBER (which see)—Revue, Musical comedy, Vaudeville.

production stage manager
A term, used in the U.S. only, for a stage manager for a dramatic production. See STAGE DIRECTOR and STAGE MANAGER.

profane drama
Dramas, singly or collectively, which are not religious or liturgical, in contradistinction to SACRED DRAMA.

profession, (the)
The theatrical occupation or calling, and the body of people who practice it for money; more particularly, acting, and actors; sometimes restricted in meaning, as by the exclusion of vaudeville. Also in the forms (the) *theatrical profession,* (the) *dramatic profession.* Hence *professional* (or *pro,* or *professional actor,* an actor who is paid for performing), *professional performance,* *professional production rights* (see RIGHTS), *professional theatre,* etc.

274

professional matinee
A theatrical performance, in the afternoon or evening, offered on a day not usually chosen for an afternoon or evening performance, so that actors from other shows, or out-of-town visitors, may attend.

profile
1. Short for PROFILE BOARD. Hence, constructed of profile board, as, a *profile drop* (which is a CUT DROP), a *profile strip* (which is a CUT OUT). Also, to saw a profile board. 2. Short for PROFILE POSITION.

profile block
See PROFILE BOARD.

profile board; short form, **profile**
A piece of thin wood, such as plywood, to which canvas or other cloth is glued, and which is then sawed to show an irregular edge in silhouette for the simulation of scenic objects such as rocks, columns, and foliage. Also as *profile block*.

profile position
The body position of an actor whose right or left side is turned towards the audience.

profiling
A PROFILE BOARD.

program; (chiefly British) **programme**
1. A printed announcement given or sold to a theatre audience to provide information concerning a production which is about to be performed; a playbill. Hence, pertaining to programs, as, a *programme girl,* a *program-seller.* 2. Collectively, a series of plays or vaudeville acts.

projected scenery
Scenic effects obtained by means of projection.

projection
1. The throwing of an image onto the stage by means of light, for an optical effect. Hence, pertaining to such a throwing, as, a PROJECTION BOOTH. 2. The means by which an actor, through voice, movement, or gesture, reaches an audience effectively.

projection booth
A compartment at the rear of an auditorium for the operator of lights.

projection lantern; projector lantern
British terms for a PROJECTOR UNIT.

projection machine
A scenic effect machine used to project pictorial or moving effects, such as clouds, onto the stage.

projection screen
A cloth or other smooth surface onto which images can be transmitted from a projection machine.

projector
1. A projection machine; short for SCENERY PROJECTOR. 2. Short for PROJECTOR UNIT.

projector lamp
1. A lamp used in a projector unit, or (chiefly in British usage) a projector unit. 2. A type of incandescent lamp consisting of a blown glass bulb with an inside reflecting surface surrounding the lamp filament.

projector unit; short form, **projector**
A narrow-beam lighting instrument, consisting of a high-powered lamp, (currently) a metal parabolic reflector, and a device such as a shield or louver, used as a spotlight or as a directed floodlight; according to its position and type, it may be known by some more limited name, as, a FRONT LIGHT. British: *pageant lantern, projection* (or *projector*) *lantern.*

prologue; prolog

1. A speech or scene preceding the first act of a dramatic work, to which it may or may not be related. 2. An actor who delivers lines in a prologue.

prompt

To tell an actor what speech or action is required of him, especially when he forgets during a performance. Also, such a reminder, as in *take a prompt*. Hence *prompt corner, prompting* (noun), etc.

prompt-bell

A bell by means of which an actor can be summoned to take his place onstage.

prompt board

A panel on which the house telephone, and certain signals such as the act call bell, are placed.

prompt book; promptbook

A play text containing production notes, including cues, for the use of the stage manager, prompter, etc.

prompt box; prompt-box

A hooded recess at the front of the stage where a prompter may be concealed.

prompt copy; prompt-copy

A PROMPT BOOK.

prompt corner; prompt-corner

A term, chiefly British, for a position for the prompter, offstage, usually downstage left.

prompt-desk

A desk for the prompter in the prompt corner.

prompter

A person who is charged with prompting.

prompter's box
A PROMPT BOX.

prompter's table
A PROMPT TABLE.

prompt-script
A PROMPT BOOK.

prompt side; prompt-side; abbreviation, **P.S.**
A term, now chiefly British, for the left side of the stage as one faces the audience; not necessarily the PROMPT CORNER side.

prompt table; prompt-table
A PROMPT-DESK.

prompt wing
The space where the prompt corner is located, whether or not it is set off with wing flats.

prop
1. Short for PROPERTY. 2. A nickname for a property man, with the initial letter capitalized.
   (See also the combinations of PROPERTY, with which the combinations of *prop* are commonly interchangeable.)

propaganda play
A play which is intended to influence an audience in favor of some idea, particularly some political idea.

property; short form, **prop**
Any object used on the stage, except scenery, lights, and costumes. Also as *theatrical property*. Hence *property sword*, etc.
   (See also the combinations of PROP, with which the combinations of *property* are commonly interchangeable.)

property box
A box in which properties are kept when not in use. Also, in British terminology, as *property basket*.

property crew; property master's crew
The property men, the stagehands who work under the property master.

property department
A stage department consisting of a property master and his property crew.

property list
A term, used in the U.S. only, for a PROPERTY PLOT.

property man; property-man
A member of the property crew under the property master; sometimes the property master himself. Called also PROP, *prop boy* (or *hand* or *man*), *Props.*

property master; property-master
A stage department head, responsible for the handling, storage, and sometimes operation of properties. Called also *master of properties* and sometimes *property man.*

property master's crew
See PROPERTY CREW.

property mistress
Feminine form of PROPERTY MASTER.

property plot; property-plot
A list, often with a diagram, showing the properties to be used in each scene of a production.

property room; property-room
A storage place, and sometimes a workshop for properties.

property shop
A rare term for a working place where properties and scenery are prepared.

property table; property-table
A table offstage on which hand properties can be laid ready for use.

property truck
A wagon offstage on which properties can be placed until needed.

prop gag
A comic effect depending upon a property.

prop loft
A PROPERTY ROOM.

proportion
BALANCE (which see).

proportional dimming; proportionate mastering
The dimming of lights by means of a master control, so that their relative intensities are not altered.

prop rehearsal
A rehearsal during which actors can familiarize themselves with the properties they will encounter during their performance.

proprietor
Short for THEATRE PROPRIETOR.

props
1. Plural of PROP: Properties. 2. A nickname for a PROPERTY MAN, with the initial letter capitalized.

pros
1. When followed by a period: Short for PROSCENIUM. 2. In the plural: Short for *professionals* (see [the] PROFESSION), as *old pros.*

proscenium; short form, pros.
1. Commonly, in the modern theatre, the proscenium opening (through which the spectator sees the acting area), the proscenium arch (which frames this opening), and the wall of which the arch is a part, considered together; or the proscenium arch alone. 2. Formerly, the forestage.

280

proscenium arch; proscenium-arch
The framing arch through which, in most modern theatres, the stage setting is revealed to the audience.

proscenium balcony
A BALCONY (sense 2) overlooking the forestage—Restoration and 18th century, with traces surviving into the 19th century.

proscenium batten
A British term for the FIRST PIPE (which see).

proscenium border
A British term for a TEASER (which see).

proscenium box
A BOX (sense 1) near or over (and originally in) the proscenium.

proscenium door
Formerly, one of a pair (or two or three pairs) of doors, usually permanent openings in the proscenium wall, through which actors could move onto or off the forestage.

proscenium ladder
In British terminology, a strip of proscenium lights.

proscenium length; short form, length
A row of strip lights in a casing, fastened overhead, behind and to the side of the proscenium arch.

proscenium light
A proscenium strip; a lamp in a proscenium strip.

proscenium opening; proscenium-opening
The space bounded by the proscenium arch.

proscenium splay
A section of the theatre auditorium in which the proscenium wall slopes to meet the auditorium side wall.

281

proscenium stage
A stage which is framed by a proscenium arch.

proscenium strip
A strip of low-power lamps fastened to a vertical pipe batten behind the proscenium arch. Called also *proscenium light.* British: *proscenium ladder* (or *light*).

proscenium theatre
A theatre the stage of which is framed by a proscenium arch.

proscenium thickness
The depth of a proscenium arch from front to back.

proscenium wing
One of the wings closest to the proscenium arch.

prose drama
A dramatic work composed in prose; also collectively.

protagonist
The central figure in a dramatic work; often, the hero.

protasis
The opening lines of a dramatic work. Hence *protatic*, pertaining to such an introduction, and *protatic character*, for one of the dramatis personae who appears only at the beginning.

protean
An actor who plays several roles in a dramatic performance, usually by making quick changes in his appearance while performing alone—Especially, 19th century Vaudeville. Called also *protean actor*, *protean artist*. Hence *protean act*, *protean drama*, etc.

provinces
In British terminology, the theatre towns outside of the London region. (The term is also sometimes used in the U.S. for towns and theatres outside of New York or, infrequently, other American cities.) Hence *provincial drama*, *provincial stage*, etc.

P.S.
Abbreviation of PROMPT SIDE.

pseudo-classic(al) drama
NEO-CLASSIC DRAMAS (which see), collectively or individually, especially when modified, in whole or in part, to conform to the taste of the modern world—Especially, 18th century. Hence *pseudo-classicism*. See also CLASSIC(AL) DRAMA.

P. side
Abbreviation of PROMPT SIDE.

psychodrama
A dramatization by a patient in a mental hospital of a social situation in which he feels himself to be involved. He outlines the scenario and appears in the role he plays in real life; fellow patients, staff members, and sometimes other persons participate as actors. This therapeutic psychiatric technique is also now used in programs for group discussion of problems in social adjustment, but is then more accurately termed "role-playing" or "sociodrama." See also CATHARSIS.

psychologic(al) drama
A play which emphasizes mental problems or other psychological subject-matter; also collectively. Hence *psychological theatre*, etc.

psychological lighting
Lighting which seeks to match the mood of a dramatic piece.

public
Spectators, actual or potential members of the audience, collectively, as, to give the *public* what it wants.

publicity agent
A person, such as an advance man, in charge of advertising and news items for a stage production. Also as *publicity man*.

public performance
Considered as the basis for the determination of royalty payments due to a copyright-holder, a dramatic performance given before an audience.

public theatre (or playhouse)
1. A theatre open to the public. 2. An outdoor theatre, the central portion (yard) of which was unroofed—Elizabethan. See also PRIVATE THEATRE.

puff
A notice such as a review or publicity announcement, praising extravagantly or by way of advertisement a dramatic piece, performance, actor, etc. Also, to write, or praise by means of, such a notice. Hence *puffer*.

punch
To emphasize part of one's dialogue, in acting.

Punch and Judy show
A type of comic puppet show with a fairly fixed plot, featuring Punch, a hook-nosed hunchback in Italian costume, who, amidst much rough-and-tumble and slapstick, slays his wife Judy and other persons—19th century and since. Originally Punch (or Punchinello) was brought into puppet plays of all kinds as a kind of clown, his character deriving from the native medieval Vice as well as from the French Polichinelle and the Italian Pulcinella (of the *commedia dell' arte*); gradually his traits and the present plot were developed—Restoration and 18th century. See also JOEY and JUDY.

punched paper
A free admission PASS.

Punchinello
An early form of the name Punch (see PUNCH AND JUDY SHOW); hence, a buffoon, an actor playing a buffoon, or a show featuring Punch.

punch line
A line of dialogue which carries particular emphasis for dramatic or comic effect.

puppet
A doll, simulating a person, animal, etc., appearing on a miniature stage, and operated by the hand of a manipulator (*puppeteer*) inside it, or on a handle or otherwise. Sometimes interchangeable with MARIONETTE (which see). Hence *hand puppet, puppet play* (or *show*), *puppetry*, etc.

purchase line
An endless rope to move a counterweight cradle up or down, running over pulley wheels above and below the counterweight track.

pure
Applied to comedy or tragedy: Without the admixture of other elements such as sentimentalism.

purgation
See CATHARSIS.

pusher
A British term for a SCENE SHIFTER.

putty nose
A nickname for a low comedian (see LOW COMEDY).

Put up your lights!
A stage manager's command to the electrician: Increase the illumination.

pylon
A movable device used in a stage setting to carry a light pipe, constructed of a FLAT and REVEALS.

Q

Quarter of an hour, please!; Quarter-of-an-hour, please!
In British terminology, a fifteen minutes call

quarter position
The body position of an actor one side of whose body is turned halfway between the profile position and the full front position.

queue
A term, chiefly British, for a line of persons waiting to buy tickets at a box office. Also, to take one's place in such a line (usually as *queue up*).

quick change; quick-change
1. The rapid substitution of one costume for another during a performance. Hence, a *quick-change artist*. Also, to make such a change. 2. A rapid scene-shift.

quick change room; quick-change room
A dressing room, either an actual room conveniently near the stage or an enclosure constructed of flats in the wings, where actors may make quick changes.

quick-cue
A cue picked up immediately, without a pause. Also, to pick up cues quickly.

quick curtain
A sudden dropping of a curtain to close a scene.

quick study
A hasty memorizing of an acting part; an actor who can memorize quickly.

R

R.; R
Abbreviation of RIGHT, meaning STAGE RIGHT, RIGHT STAGE, RIGHT OF STAGE. "Right" means to the actor's right, the spectator's left.

This abbreviation is used as a stage direction, either alone or in combination with other abbreviations. Thus, followed by a number, it is used as a symbol chalked on the back of a flat to indicate its place at the right side of the stage in front-to-rear sequence, as, R1.

Also, but now rarely, R.1 or R.1.E (sometimes without periods) is used to designate RIGHT FIRST ENTRANCE; and similarly for RIGHT SECOND ENTRANCE, RIGHT THIRD ENTRANCE. Thus also R.C. for RIGHT CENTER, R.C.E. for RIGHT CENTER ENTRANCE, R.S.E. for RIGHT SECOND ENTRANCE, R.U.E. for RIGHT UPPER ENTRANCE.

rabbit hutch
A THUNDER BOX.

rack
1. Short for TICKET RACK. Hence, to place tickets which are for sale in the box-office ticket rack, as *rack the tickets*. See also COUNT THE RACK. 2. A support for spotlights, which can be hooked to the balcony rail. 3. A board near the stage door, with hooks or nails on which dressing-room and other keys can be hung.

radial arm dimmer
A STUD CONTACT DIMMER, with an arm pivoted to make contact between studs arranged in a semicircle and a single resistance coil.

rag
A term, chiefly British, for an ACT CURTAIN or a TABLEAU CURTAIN.

rail
1. One of the two outer horizontal wooden crosspieces on the frame of a flat, specifically the *top rail* and the *bottom rail*. 2. A safety handrail used on the off-stage portion of a platform or a flight of steps. 3. A counterweight track. 4. Short for RAILING. 5. In lighting, specifically, balcony front lighting (see BALCONY FRONT).

(See specific entries such as BRACE RAIL, for other kinds of *rail*.)

railing; short form, **rail**
A handrail separating a seating area or some other part of an auditorium from an aisle or from some other section.

rain barrel
A British term for a RAIN PIPE (which see).

rainbow wheel
An optical effects machine for producing changing colored light by the rotation of a slotted disc, with color mediums, in front of a lighting unit.

rain box; rain-box
A RAIN MACHINE (which see).

rain drum
A RAIN MACHINE (which see).

rain effect
An acoustical or optical simulation of rain, as by a rain machine or rain pipe.

rain machine
A container (*rain box* or *rain drum*) of wood or metal which can be tilted or turned so that dried peas or beans, or small metal shot, are rolled about inside to simulate the sound of rain.

rain pipe; rain-pipe; rainpipe
A steel or iron pipe, closed at one end and perforated with small holes on the under side, through which water can escape to give the appearance of rain. British: Also as *rain barrel.*

raise
1. To lift; to fly scenery, etc. 2. *raise the dead:* In British terminology, to tell an audience from the stage what the next week's program will be—19th century.

rake
1. The slope of an auditorium or (now rarely) a stage, upward towards the rear. Also to build an auditorium or stage with such a slope—Usually in the passive voice. Hence *raked stage, stage rake.* 2. To place the side walls of a stage, or any scenic piece, at an angle or slope. Hence, a RAKING PIECE (which see, sense 2).

raking piece
1. A slanting or sloping piece of scenery, especially a triangular masking piece covering the downstage side of a ramp. 2. A wedge used to level scenic pieces on a raked stage.

rally
A British term for the following: 1. In acting, to speed up dialogue and movement in order to produce a more dramatic effect. 2. In the harlequinade, the pursuit of Harlequin and Columbine—Pantomime (sense 2).

ramp
A sloping platform on which an actor may walk. Hence *ramped platform,* etc.

rant
In acting, to deliver one's lines noisily, extravagantly. Hence also *ranter, ranting* (noun).

raree show; rarity show
A peep show; any show, but especially a cheap street show.

raspberry; razz
See GET THE RASPBERRY.

rat
A DIGGER (which see).

rave
An enthusiastic review of a dramatic production by a drama critic. Also as *rave notice*. To review a piece enthusiastically.

R.C.; RC
Abbreviation of RIGHT CENTER. See also R.

R.C.E.
Abbreviation of RIGHT CENTER ENTRANCE. See also R.

reactance (or reactor) dimmer
A remote-control dimmer (often called a *saturable-core dimmer*) operated by the electrical principle of reactance.

read a play
1. To go over a play aloud; to partake in a rehearsal reading.
2. To evaluate a play script as a PLAY READER (which see).

reader
Short for PLAY READER, READER OF PLAYS.

reader of plays; short form, reader
A British term for a dramatic censor—19th and 20th centuries.

read for a part
In trying out for an acting part, to read one's lines aloud to a casting agent or to a stage director.

reading
1. A rehearsal at which a company hears a dramatic composition read aloud, as by its author; or a rehearsal at which the actors read their parts aloud without stage movement or stage business. 2. An actor's interpretation of his lines. 3. A play-reading (see PLAY READER). 4. A dramatic reading (see DRAMATIC READER).

reading edition
The published text of a play, intended for reading and therefore differing in certain respects from the acting edition of the same play.

reading fee
1. A fee charged by an author or play agent for a playreading.
2. A fee charged by an author or his representative for a public reading.

realism
In composition and production, an aesthetic attempt to make a dramatic piece reproduce real life. Hence *realistic*. See NATURALISM.

real life
Life as it actually is, has been, or may be, in contradistinction to life as it is simulated in a theatrical representation.

rear stage
The inner or alcove stage—Elizabethan.

receiver
A theatre treasurer—17th century.

recitalist
A DISEUR (which see) or diseuse.

recognition
In a dramatic plot, a discovery of identity. Hence *recognition scene*. See also ANAGNORISIS.

recognize
See DO YOU RECOGNIZE THE PROFESSION?

recreational
Non-commercial, intended chiefly to benefit the participants through social activity, as *recreational dramatics, recreational theatre*.

red-nosed comedian (or **comic**)
The role of a low comedian, whose red nose indicates inebriation; an actor playing such a role.

reflector
A reflecting surface of metal or glass, behind a light source, which controls the direction or intensity of light beams. Also, short for REFLECTOR UNIT.

reflector lamp
Any lamp with a reflector, now commonly an incandescent lamp consisting of a sealed two-piece molded glass bulb with an inside reflecting surface surrounding a carefully positioned filament.

reflector (unit)
A lighting instrument, consisting of a high-powered lamp, a metal parabolic reflector, and a fastening device such as a universal joint, used as a spotlight (*reflector spotlight*) or as a floodlight (*reflector floodlight*).

reformed comedy
Sentimental comedy (see SENTIMENTAL DRAMA).

reform stage
A SLIDING STAGE.

regie-book, regie-buch; short form, **regie**
A notebook in which a director enters his production notes prior to or during the rehearsal period—A German word used in English.

regional
1. Said of dramatic compositions which deal with life in a given geographical region, as *regional drama, regional theatre.* See also FOLK DRAMA. 2. Said of the theatres of a particular region, or of theatres in general outside of major theatrical centers, individually or collectively.

régisseur
A director, especially in the modern theatre (since the 1870s), who unifies the entire production artistically—A French word used in English. Often italicized.

rehearsal
A practice session to prepare a production for public perform-ance. Hence *in rehearsal* (said of a production), *rehearsal room,* etc.

rehearsal call; short form, call
A written notice to actors and other theatre personnel to report for a rehearsal.

rehearsal light
A light, usually a floodlight, used to illuminate the stage during rehearsal.

rehearsal scene
In a dramatic work, a distinct portion of the action, beginning with the entrance and closing with the exit of one or more principal actors.

rehearse
To hold, or to participate in, a rehearsal. Hence *over-rehearse, under-rehearse, rehearsing* (noun).

release
A let-up in dramatic tension, achieved by interposing an inter-mission or a calmer scene.

relief
1. A scene or incident introduced into a play to give the audi-ence a momentary respite from emotional tension before further tension is required, or to intensify serious action. Often, a comic scene for this purpose; COMIC RELIEF. 2. See RELIEVE SCENE (*scene of relief*).

relief stage
A technique in staging which emphasizes the actor by placing him well forward and close to a flat background.

relieve
A flat partly cut out, used to obtain perspective by revealing a shutter or backcloth behind it—Restoration.

relieve scene
A vista, seemingly in relief, composed of a series of cut-out pieces seen in perspective against a backcloth, and revealed when back shutters (*relieves*) were drawn apart—Restoration. Called also *scene of relief*.

religious drama
Dramas, collectively or individually, which deal with religious subjects.

remote color control
The changing of color slides in a lighting unit from a distance, as by a color boomerang.

remote control (or **remotely controlled**) **switchboard**
Any switchboard which controls the various lighting circuits by sending electrical impulses through pilot switches and controls to operate a main switchboard. Also, hyphenated.

remotely-operated colour change
A British term for a COLOR BOOMERANG.

Renaissance drama; Renascence drama
The drama of the Renaissance, in England a period including the reign of Queen Elizabeth (see ELIZABETHAN DRAMA) and commonly a number of decades before and after it.

renewal clause
The right reserved by a producer, in his contract with an author, to renew his option during a specified period.

rep
Short for REPERTORY.

repeater
A popular play in the repertory of a touring company.

repertoire
A REPERTORY (which see).

repertory; short form, **rep**
1. A group of plays which a company has been trained to perform and which are usually played alternately or in turn and are repeatedly revived; a system based on such productions. Hence also *repertory company, repertory show, repertory theatre*. 2. A stock company, or stock theatre in general. 3. Collectively, the parts which an actor has learned.

repetition
An obsolete term for a REHEARSAL.

répétition générale
A performance or dress rehearsal not open to the public, before opening night—A French expression (meaning "general"— that is, "dress"—"rehearsal") used in English. Usually italicized.

representation
1. A performance. Also in the form *theatrical representation*. 2. Realism; ILLUSION (which see). Hence also *representational, representationalism*, etc.

reprise
A repetition, with variations, of a song or dance—Especially, Musical comedy. Also, to perform such a repetition.

reserved seat
A seat specifically held for a theatregoer by ticket or by some other arrangement.

resident
Not touring, more or less permanent, as, a *resident company*, a *resident manager*, etc.

resin box
A shallow box in which an actor may rub resin on his shoes for better footing.

resistance dimmer
A dimmer in which a variable resistance in series with a lighting circuit is used to regulate the intensity of the light.

resolution
The final unfolding of the solution to the complications in the plot of a play.

responsibles
A British term for small but important roles in British touring and repertory companies; an actor who plays such roles (a *responsibles*, a *responsible man*, a *responsible player*).

resting
AT LIBERTY (which see).

Restoration drama
The English drama of the period from 1660, date of the restoration of the Stuarts to the British throne, to 1700 or to some convenient terminal date early in the 18th century. Hence *Restoration comedy* (the OLD COMEDY, the *Restoration comedy of manners*) and *Restoration tragedy* (*heroic tragedy, neo-classic tragedy, pseudo-classic tragedy*), etc.

retire
To conclude one's acting career. Hence *in retirement*.

retiring room
1. A public room in a theatre, such as a rest room. 2. A GREEN ROOM (which see)—18th century.

return

1. Short for RETURN PIECE. 2. A report on ticket sales for each performance, or (in the plural) the ticket stubs used in preparing such a report. 3. Unsold tickets returned to the box office for re-sale. 4. In the plural, play reviews.

return date (or **engagement**)

An engagement for a company or an actor to come back to a theatre.

return (piece)

A flat or drapery downstage, used to mask the off-stage view between the tormentor, which it parallels, and the rest of the set.

revamp

To make over a dramatic work or some part of it.

reveal

A THICKNESS PIECE, or an imitation of one.

revels

Masques, pageants, and the like provided at a celebration. More particularly, such entertainments, given at the royal court—16th to 18th centuries. Hence *the Revels;* also *Revels books, Revels* (or *Rouel*) *Master, Revels Office,* etc. See MASTER OF THE REVELS and OFFICE OF THE REVELS.

revenge play (or **tragedy**)

A tragedy emphasizing a struggle for vengeance. Especially, 16th and 17th centuries.

reverberator

A lamp with one or more reflectors, used to light the apron—Restoration.

reversal

Short for DRAMATIC REVERSAL.

reverse roller curtain

A curtain which rolls down on a cylinder, instead of up—17th century. See also SINKING CURTAIN.

review
1. A published critical comment on a stage production, especially in a newspaper or magazine. Also, to write such a comment. Hence *dramatic review*, (*play*) *reviewer* (a DRAMA CRITIC, which see), *reviewing* (noun). 2. Occasionally, a revue.

revive
To bring a dramatic work to the stage again after a lapse of time. Hence (*stage*) *revival*.

revolve
A British term for the following: 1. A TURNTABLE, or an entire REVOLVING STAGE. 2. A stage set which can be turned on casters to bring into view the other side of painted flats. U.S.: *revolving set*.

revolver
A TURNTABLE; a REVOLVING STAGE.

revolving platform
A TURNTABLE.

revolving stage
A stage with a turntable on which two or more sets can be constructed, so that one set may be quickly substituted for another. Hence *revolving set*.

revue; (infrequently) **review**
A type of gay, spectacular entertainment, consisting of burlesque topical sketches, with little continuity, accompanied by music, song, and dance. Hence *revuette* (diminutive), *revuist* (writer). The wittier, more sophisticated forms are sometimes distinguished from those which emphasize sentiment, music, lovely girls, gorgeous costumes, etc., by the designations *intimate revue, smart revue, topical revue*. See also NON-STOP *revue*.

rework
To revise a piece of dramatic writing so as to remove supposed defects.

rheostat
An electrical device, adjustable so that the amount of current passing through resistance wires to a dimmer can be increased and reduced. Used in RESISTANCE DIMMERS (which see). British: *wire resistance.*

rhythm
A principal or technique in acting, directing, and other aspects of production, concerned with the harmony of movement in all its implications.

Rialto, (the)
A theatrical area, especially BROADWAY in New York City, named for the business center in Venice.

rig
To fasten all the necessary rigging lines, with other equipment; as *rig a set.*

rigging
Collectively, the ropes, wires, blocks, pulleys, pins, counterweights, and other pieces of equipment needed in the manipulation of scenery. Also as *stage rigging.*

rigging line
A rope or wire used for hanging scenery.

rigging loft
A FLY LOFT.

right; abbreviation, **R.**
1. Short for RIGHT (OF) STAGE, *stage right.* Towards the right side of the stage (the audience's left)—Sometimes, a stage direction. See also DOWN RIGHT, UP RIGHT. 2. See RIGHTS.

right center; abbreviation, **R.C., RC**
A stage position or area, at the center of the stage and to the right (the audience's left)—Sometimes, a stage direction.

right center entrance; abbreviation, **R.C.E.**
A stage entrance at the back of the stage and to the right (the audience's left)—Sometimes, a stage direction.

right center stage
RIGHT CENTER (which see).

right first entrance; abbreviation, **R.1.(E).**
A stage entrance at the right (the audience's left), the farthest one downstage—Sometimes, a stage direction.

right (of) stage; short form, **right;** abbreviation, **R.**
The entire right half of the stage (the audience's left), or some portion thereof—Sometimes, a stage direction.

rights
1. The powers of a copyright-owner to grant or withhold permission to publish, produce, or otherwise make public use of a dramatic piece—*acting rights, amateur production rights,* DRAMATIC RIGHTS, *foreign rights, motion picture rights, performing rights, production rights, professional production rights, public reading rights, publication rights, radio broadcasting rights, recitation rights, stock rights, translation rights,* contractions of these, etc. 2. Income from the exercise of such rights.

right second entrance; abbreviations, **R.2.(E.).**
or **R.S.E.**
A stage entrance at the right (the audience's left), between the right first entrance and the right upper entrance—Sometimes, a stage direction.

right stage
RIGHT OF STAGE (which see).

right third entrance; abbreviation, **R.3.(E.)**
A right upper entrance. (*Right third entrance* is not used in the professional theatre.)

right upper entrance; abbreviations, **R.U.E., R.3.(E.)**
A stage entrance at the right (the audience's left), the farthest one upstage—Sometimes, a stage direction.

ring down (the curtain)
To drop or close the act curtain, and hence to end the performance, to close the show. Also, a command to the flymen to drop
or close the curtain.

ring in the band
In British terminology, to signal the musicians that they should
go into the orchestra pit.

ring up (the curtain)
To raise or open the act curtain. Also, a command to the flymen
to raise or open the curtain.

rise
Said of a curtain: To go up. The going up of a curtain (also as
the *curtain rise* or the *rising*). See AT RISE.

rise and sink
Formerly, a method of changing a back scene (to disclose a
scene behind it) by raising the upper half into the flies and
dropping the lower half into the cellar—Especially in the transformation scene of a Pantomime (sense 2).

riser
1. A stage platform of much greater width than a rostrum or a
parallel. 2. The vertical backing of a step, in a flight of stairs.
3. The step portion of a spotlight lens.

rising action
The dramatic action preceding the climax or turning point.

road, (the)
A circuit of towns, usually any localities outside the New York
metropolitan area, in which a touring company plays. Hence
on the road (touring), *road company, road show*. See TOUR.

road apple
An actor on tour.

road-card
A certification by the Actor's Equity Association that an actor may join a touring company.

road shoe
A device consisting of two metal arms at right angles to each other, which is fastened to the corner of a flat to protect it.

Robin Hood play
A rural play celebrating the exploits of Robin Hood and his Merry Men, written by a minstrel and performed outdoors with dialogue and dance at a May Day festival—15th century until the Interregnum.

role; rôle
A character in a dramatic work, portrayed on the stage by an actor.

roll
1. *roll 'em in the aisles:* To lay 'em in the aisles. Often as *rolling in the aisles,* laughing uncontrollably. 2. To CLEW.

roll ceiling
A cloth ceiling with a batten at the front and a batten at the rear so that it may be rolled for storage or transportation.

roll curtain; rolled curtain; roller curtain
A drop curtain which rolls itself around a batten as it is raised.

roll drop
A ROLL CURTAIN.

roll drop hook
A CURTAIN CLAMP.

roller
1. A caster wheel used under a wagon stage or under some other object. 2. A wooden batten around which a curtain can be rolled.

rolling cyclorama
A hanging cyclorama which can be rolled mechanically or electrically around a vertical batten.

roll out; roll-out
At the bottom of a scenic piece, a canvas flap through which an actor can roll horizontally to make a sudden appearance on-stage.

romance
A dramatic composition centered on an imaginative love story; also, a romantic play (see ROMANTIC DRAMA). Hence *costume romance*, DRAMATIC ROMANCE (which see), *historical romance*, etc.

romantic acting
An acting style marked by intensity in the depiction of passion, by a freer, less formal regard for gesture and delivery than that of classic acting.

romantic actor
1. An actor who has a part in ROMANTIC DRAMA (which see) or who specializes in such parts. 2. An actor whose manner is that of ROMANTIC ACTING (which see).

romantic drama
Drama which, typically, centers on a love story, idealizes life either plausibly or improbably, gives rein in style and content to emotion, fancy, mystery, charm, adventure, and more or less disregards formal dramatic principles. Hence *romanticism, romantic role, romantic setting*, etc.

rondel
Variant spelling of ROUNDEL.

room
A seating area in a gallery—Elizabethan. See GENTLEMAN'S ROOM, LORD'S ROOM, TWELVE-PENNY ROOM, TWO-PENNY ROOM.

rope
Short for ROPE LINE.

rope clamp
A ROPE LOCK.

rope house
A theatre using ropes which are hauled, rather than a COUNTER-WEIGHT SYSTEM.

rope line; short forms, **line, rope**
Any length of rope used for stage purposes.

rope line system; rope system
An arrangement for manipulating scenery by leading hauling ropes to a pin rail instead of to a counterweight carriage.

rope lock
A steel clamp, used to grip a line, as, an operating line at the lock rail.

Roscius
An actor. From the name of Quintus Roscius Gallus, a comic actor of ancient Rome (d. 62 B.C.). Also in the form *a Roscian*. Hence a *Roscian society*, etc.

rosine
A patented netting compound.

rostrum
A British term for a platform, dais, etc., commonly one which folds up. U.S.: See PARALLEL.

rough
A rough draft of a box-office statement, prepared by the manager of a touring company.

rough out
To make the preliminary preparations for a production, such as placing flats tentatively in position before painting them.

round

1. In the plural, the applause of spectators. Also, *a round of applause,* for a burst of applause in which several spectators join. 2. A circular place where miracle plays were sometimes performed. 3. See IN THE ROUND.

round actor

An actor who appears on the stage before the audience, in contradistinction to one seen in motion pictures, etc.

round batten

A wooden batten made up of two battens, semicircular in cross-section, fastened together on their flat sides.

roundel; rondel

A round glass color medium which may be clipped to a lighting unit.

round-plate dimmer

A PLATE DIMMER.

route sheet

A touring company's itinerary.

routine

An act or part of an act, such as dance steps, which an actor regularly performs—Especially, Vaudeville, Musical comedy. Also, to develop a routine.

row

1. A line of seats. 2. Short for GROUND ROW (which see); hence HORIZON ROW, SEA ROW, etc.

Royal Box

In British terminology, a box for the royal family.

royal circle

An alternative British term for a DRESS CIRCLE. U.S.: *first balcony,* MEZZANINE.

royalty
A payment made to an author (or other owner of the copyright) for the production or publication of a copyrighted dramatic piece, normally a fixed percentage of the profits. Hence *non-royalty play*, etc.

R.S.E.
Abbreviation of RIGHT SECOND ENTRANCE. See also R.

rubber legs
A person who does humorous contorted dances.

R.U.E.
Abbreviation of RIGHT UPPER ENTRANCE. See also R.

rules, (the)
In NEO-CLASSICAL DRAMA (which see), prescriptions derived from French and Italian critics, supposedly to conform to dramatic principles formulated by Aristotle—Especially, 17th and 18th centuries.

rumble box
A THUNDER BOX.

rumble cart
A thunder cart (see THUNDER BOX).

run
1. The period during which a dramatic production continues to be performed by an acting company; or the total number of consecutive performances. Also, (of a production) to remain in performance by a company, as, It *ran* for a year. 2. To slide something along the stage floor, as *run a flat*. 3. To operate a switchboard or a spotlight. 4. A ramp.

run away with the show
In acting, to excel, to stand out, to win greater applause than anyone else, especially when such success is unexpected.

306

rundhorizont
A cyclorama which is semicircular—A German word used in English. Sometimes italicized.

run down; run-down
A pause, when an actor forgets his lines.

runner
1. A slider. 2. Matting placed in the wings to deaden sound. 3. A groove in a color frame. 4. A ball sliding in a curtain track. 5. A CURTAIN TRACK.

running tab
A DRAW TAB.

run through; run-through
To rehearse, without pause for comment from the director or stage manager. Also, a rehearsal of this kind.

runway
A narrow projection of the stage, into the orchestra pit or into the aisle of an auditorium, on which a performer can walk— Especially Burlesque, Vaudeville, Revue.

S

sacred drama
Religious or liturgical dramas, collectively or individually.

saddle
1. Short for SADDLE BATTEN. 2. Short for SADDLE IRON. 3. Formerly, a payment by an actor to the theatre manager from the total receipts on his benefit night.

saddle (batten)
A batten used as a horizontal tie across the bottom of a door flat to give greater rigidity.

saddle iron; saddle-iron; short form, saddle
A term, used in the U.S. only, for a bar of steel or iron fastened as a tie across the bottom of a flat with a door or other opening to give greater rigidity; two pieces of steel or iron are welded to it to extend vertically at either side of the opening.

Sadler's Wells make-up
In British terminology, make-up improvised from handy but unlikely materials such as dust, chalk ("dip"), distemper from dressing-room walls, etc.—Especially, 19th century. Named for the London theatre, Sadler's Wells.

safety chain
A chain used as a secondary means of suspension for a piece of lighting equipment.

safety curtain
A term, chiefly British, for the FIREPROOF CURTAIN.

safety rope clamp
A ROPE LOCK.

Saint George play
The MUMMERS' PLAY (which see).

salary; short form (sometimes), **sal**
An actor's wages.

S and D
Abbreviation of SONG AND DANCE.

sand bag; sandbag
A canvas bag filled with sand, used on the end of a rope line to counterbalance hanging scenery.

sand cloth; sand-cloth
A ground cloth, painted to simulate a surface of sand or dirt.

sandwich batten
Two wood battens screwed together to hold the top or bottom edge of a drop curtain between them. Hence *sandwich-battening* (noun) for the process.

satire
Ridicule; a dramatic work emphasizing ridicule. Hence *satiric, satirical.*

saturable-core (or **saturated choke**) **dimmer**
A REACTANCE DIMMER (which see).

scaffold
1. A raised platform used as a stage. Called also *scaffold stage.* Hence also *scaffolding* (noun), etc. 2. A sitting-place for spectators, now a raised platform, formerly also a gallery. Hence *scaffolder,* etc.

scalper
A TICKET SPECULATOR (which see). Also as *ticket-scalper.* Hence *scalp, scalping.*

Scaramouch(e)
The role of a braggart coward; an actor playing such a role—Chiefly 17th century Harlequinade. Originally a character in the *commedia dell'arte* ("Scaramucchia"; French form, "Scaramouche").

scare wig
A FRIGHT WIG.

scenario
A detailed outline, a synopsis, of a dramatic composition.
Plural, *scenarios* or *scenari*. Hence *scenarist*, etc.

scene
1. A division of a dramatic work smaller than an act; any portion of a dramatic work taken by itself as a unit of action.
Hence *balcony scene*, MOB SCENE, *scene iii*, etc. 2. Scenery,
scenic hangings and pieces, scenic background, a stage setting.
Hence *behind the scenes*, EXTERIOR SCENE, *scene-builder, scene
design*, (formerly) *with no scenes*, etc. Also, to provide scenery
for; (in an obsolete sense) to display in scenes. 3. The location
in which a dramatic action is supposed to occur, as, The *scene*
is Rome. 4. Formerly, a (or the) drama; the stage; the theatre.
  (See also the combinations of SCENERY and SCENIC, with
which the combinations of *scene* are commonly interchangeable.)

scène à faire
A French expression used in English for an OBLIGATORY SCENE
(which see). Usually italicized.

scene bay; scenery bay
A term, chiefly British, for a SCENE DOCK, or a space between
packs of FLATS in a scene dock.

scene-board
A LOCALITY BOARD (which see)—Elizabethan.

scene change; scene-change
A changing of scenes, the replacement of one stage setting with
another. See SCENE SHIFT.

scene-chewer
See CHEW THE SCENERY.

scene cloth
A curtain, usually painted, as, a backdrop.

scene curtain
A curtain used to conceal changes of scenery.

scene designer; scene-designer
A person who designs stage settings.

scene division; scene-division
The separation of a dramatic composition into SCENES (sense 1).

scene dock; scene-dock; short form, dock
A place in a theatre, usually near the stage, where scenery is stored.

scene intermission; (British) scene interval
An intermission between scenes.

scene-keeper
A person in charge of scenery—Restoration.

scene-man; sceneman
Formerly, a shifter of scenery.

scene master
A MASTER SWITCH (which see) controlling several circuits.

scene of relief (or of relieve)
A RELIEVE SCENE (which see).

scene pack; short form, pack
A group of flats, whether "live" or "dead," especially when the flats are placed against a stage wall or in a scene dock.

scene paint
SCENIC COLOR (which see).

scene painter; scene-painter; short form, painter
A person who paints scenic pieces. Hence *scene-painting*.

scene picture
The STAGE PICTURE (which see).

scene plot; scene-plot
A list, a diagram, showing the scenery to be used in each scene of a production.

scene property; scenic property
A property (such as a rug) used as part of a stage setting.

scene rehearsal
A British term for a TECHNICAL REHEARSAL (which see).

scene-room
A room in a theatre for the storage of scenery. Now usually called a SCENE DOCK.

scenery
The elements of a stage setting, especially those made of wood and canvas. Also in the form *theatrical* (or *stage*) *scenery*. Hence SCENERY BAY, etc.

(See also the combinations of SCENE and SCENIC, with which the combinations of *scenery* are commonly interchangeable.)

scenery bay
A SCENE DOCK.

scenery dock
A SCENE DOCK.

scenery projector; short form, projector
A PROJECTION MACHINE.

scenery theatre
A SCENIC THEATRE (which see).

scenery wagon; short form, wagon
A low platform on wheels, casters, or rollers, used to support heavy scenery in a stage setting, so that it can be shifted

quickly. British: *truck, bogie,* BOAT TRUCK. See elso JACK-KNIFE
STAGE, SLIDING STAGE, WAGON STAGE.

scene shift; scene-shift; short form, **shift**
A movement of scenery by stagehands to change a stage setting.
British: *change of scene.* Hence *scene-shifting* (noun), SCENE
SHIFTER.

scene shifter; scene-shifter; sceneshifter
A term, chiefly British, for a stagehand whose duty it is to move
scenery; a GRIP (which see).

scene shop
A placc in a theatre where scenery is built or repaired.

scene sketch
A dramatic author's plan or outline for a scene, to show the
director what he has in mind for the stage movement, etc.

scene technician; short form, **technician**
A person who designs, makes, or handles stage scenery.

scenic
1. Of or pertaining to drama, theatrical production, the stage,
as, the *scenic representation* of plays. 2. Of or pertaining to
scenery, as, a *scenic artist* (a designer or decorator of scenery),
scenic design, a *scenic rock.*—Hence, for senses 1 and 2,
scenical, etc.
   (See also the combinations of SCENE and SCENERY, with
which the combinations of *scenic* are commonly interchangeable.)

scenic background; short form, **background**
The setting or scenic display before which actors perform.

scenic color
In the painting of scenery, a powder pigment which is used
with glue and water.

scenic effect machine
An EFFECT MACHINE (which see) used to create a visual effect, as, a sciopticon, a magic lantern, a Linnebach lantern.

scenic piece; short form, **piece**
A unit or element of scenery, especially one which is built up.

scenic theatre
A theatre which uses scenery, especially with a picture-frame stage.

scenic unit
A piece of scenery, such as a flat.

scenographer
A designer of scenery. Hence *scenography*, etc.

school
See DRAMA SCHOOL.

school drama
Plays, individually or collectively, produced at a school—Especially, Renaissance. Hence *school play*, etc.

Schwabe-Hasait lighting
An elaborate system of cyclorama lighting originating in Germany in the 1920s. Also as *Schwabe lantern*. Named for Max Hasait, a technical director, and the Schwabe brothers, partners in a German lighting firm.

sciopticon
A projection machine, a stereopticon, a development of the magic lantern, consisting of a strong spotlight (such as an arc lamp), a slide holder, a condensing lens, and an objective lens, used to produce effects, especially moving effects such as leaping flames and drifting clouds.

scissor cross
A crossing of the stage by two actors simultaneously in opposite directions.

score
The musical text for a musical dramatic work.

scout
See PLAY SCOUT, TALENT SCOUT. Also, to perform the functions of a scout, as, *scout for talent.*

scratch wig
A rough wig used by comic actors.

screen
1. A PROJECTION SCREEN (which see). 2. A folding partition used as a piece of scenery. Hence, a *screen setting.*

scrim
A thin open-weave linen (or other) fabric, used as a drop or as a section of a drop. It is coarser and less transparent than theatrical gauze, may be painted to make it seem opaque, and, when lighted from behind, gives an effect of dream, mist, haze, etc. It is used in draperies, and on the backs of pieces of profile board to strengthen them.—Also, to apply such a fabric to an opening in a drop or to a profile board. Hence, *scrim an opening, scrimming* (noun), a *scrim drop.* It is sometimes confused with THEATRICAL GAUZE and THEATRICAL NET.

script
The text of a dramatic entertainment (handwritten, typed, or printed). Also as *playscript.* Hence *script-reader* (see PLAY READER), etc.

scroll
In British terminology, a piece of cloth, on which a line of dialogue was lettered, carried onstage by an actor, as an evasion of the licensing laws—19th century.

scruto
A sheet of thin strips of wood, etc., mounted on a canvas backing, used as a curtain or trap cover in trickwork.

sculptural; sculptured
Said of a formal stage or setting which uses three-dimensional structures. See FORMAL.

searchlight technique
The use of spotlights to illuminate a portion of a comparatively dark acting area.

sea row
A GROUND ROW (which see) simulating a view of the sea.

season
The annual period when the theatre is most active, currently, in New York City, from September to June, but in Equity contracts fixed as the year commencing on June 1. Also as *theatrical season*. Hence *summer season*, etc.

season ticket
An admission ticket valid for an entire season at a subscription theatre.

seat
A place where a spectator may sit, now commonly a folding chair with arms, fixed in place and part of a row, or (in boxes) a separate chair; but formerly, and sometimes now, part of a bench, and formerly also a stage stool, etc. Also as *theatre-seat*. Hence *seating area, seating capacity, seating chart* (or *plan*), etc. Also, to escort a patron to his place; to occupy such a place; (of an auditorium, etc.) to contain seats (for spectators).

second
Short for SECOND MAN (or WOMAN).

secondary action (or **plot**)
A SUBORDINATE PLOT.

secondary suspension
In British terminology, an extra line or chain used as a safety measure on a hanging piece of stage equipment.

second balcony
An UPPER BALCONY. British: *second gallery, upper circle,* etc.

second boy
In British terminology, a young male actor in the most important role after the PRINCIPAL BOY (which see)—Pantomime (sense 2).

second business
A SECOND MAN (which see); a second woman.

second company
An acting company which is performing a dramatic piece on the road, or abroad, while the original company continues in the same piece.

second gallery
A term, chiefly British, for a SECOND BALCONY; an UPPER BALCONY.

second hand
A principal assistant, as, to the stage carpenter.

second lead
A principal role next in importance to the chief role.

second (man); (feminine) second woman
An actor who regularly plays the most important roles after the leads.

second night list
A list of persons, as for example drama critics, who are to receive free tickets for the second performance of a dramatic entertainment.

second price
HALF-PRICE (which see).

second production
A production by a SECOND COMPANY (which see).

second-run house

second-run house
A theatre where productions are revived or transferred rather than created.

second-string critic
A newspaper drama critic who substitutes for the regular critic.

second (woman)
Feminine form of SECOND MAN.

section
A lighting circuit in a series of circuits connected to footlights or other lights.

sectional
Made up of compartments, as *sectional footlights*.

secular drama
A play not religious in purpose; or religious but not liturgical; also collectively.

selective realism
A stage style which makes use of certain realistic elements but does not seek to simulate offstage reality as inclusively as does naturalism.

self release board
A direct control switchboard using dimmers which release themselves from their shafts at pre-set positions.

sell-out; sellout
A show so popular that all tickets have been sold, especially for some time to come; also as a *sell-out show*. Also a verb; hence, a *sold-out house*.

semi-arena theatre
A theatre in which the seats partly surround the stage.

Senecan tragedy
Plays, collectively or individually, modeled on the classical tragedies of the Roman dramatist Lucius Annaeus Seneca

(first century A.D.) in such respects as lofty rhetoric, the narration (rather than the simulation) of bloody events, and the absence of comic relief—Chiefly 16th and 17th centuries.

sennet
A trumpet call announcing a procession of persons of high degree—Elizabethan stage direction.

sensation scene
In British terminology, a representation of a striking view, such as some important large landmark—19th century.

sentimental drama
Dramas, collectively or individually, which are pathetic. Hence *sentimental comedy,* which favors pathos rather than laughter, earnest preaching rather than intrigue or other light subject-matter—Especially, 17th and 18th centuries. Hence also *sentimentalism,* etc.

sequel
A dramatic composition the plot of which is a continuation of the plot of another composition.

sequence
1. A series of scenes without a break in action. 2. The linking together of scenes in a pattern of continuity. 3. The spatial relationship of portions of the stage.

serial play
A play given in installments—19th century.

serious drama
A dramatic composition considered to be thoughtful, important, not mere entertainment or trivial pastime; also collectively. Hence *serious stage,* etc.

serious role
An acting part which is serious, in contradistinction to a comic role.

set

1. Short for (*stage* or *scenic*) SETTING. An arrangement of
scenery, properties, and lights to represent the locale in a dramatic performance. Also, to prepare such an arrangement, as
set a scene. 2. Said of scenic pieces which are constructed three-
dimensionally, as, a *set tree*. 3. To fix (by means of rehearsals)
the general patterns of lines and movements to be followed by
the actors.

(See also the combinations of SETTING, with which the combinations of *set* are commonly interchangeable.)

set back; set-back
A British term for a THICKNESS PIECE.

set line; (chiefly British) setting line
A line indicating the boundaries of a stage setting, or its parts,
to actors and crew. See also SIGHT LINE.

set of lines
A group of ropes or wires, usually three, used to suspend
pieces of scenery or lighting units.

set (of press matter)
A batch of publicity releases which an advance man is to dis-
tribute.

set piece; set-piece
A piece of scenery used in a set; that is to say, a two- or three-
dimensional unit of scenery, a profiled flat or a built piece,
which is not flied but stands independently within a stage setting, as, a (set) tree, rock, gate.

set property
A property which stands on the stage floor.

set scene
Formerly, a scene (that is, a setting) prepared behind another
scene which was then opened to reveal it.

set scenery
Scenery consisting of SET PIECES.

setting
The designing and staging of the locale and background of a dramatic presentation. Also as *stage setting*.

(See also the short form SET, with which, excepting the meaning given above, *setting* and its combinations are commonly interchangeable.)

setting line
A term, chiefly British, for a SET LINE (which see).

set unit
A SET PIECE.

set-up
The arranging of scenery, electrical equipment, and properties for a stage setting.

set waters
A simulation of a body of water, consisting of a series of ground rows, one behind another, so placed that a stage boat may move between them.

shadow
1. A shaded portion of the face, such as a hollow, or a portion to be shaded, as by lowlighting. Also, to shade with make-up. Hence *shadowing* (noun). See also EYE SHADOW. 2. The HEAVENS (sense 2)—Elizabethan.

shadow box
A metal hood containing spill shields, suspended from the first border to control light spill.

shadow projector
A LINNEBACH PROJECTOR.

shadow show

An entertainment, usually a pantomime, in which actors, puppets, or flat figures move between a light and a translucent screen, and are seen from the other side of the screen as shadows. Called also *shadow play, shadow pantomime, shadow theatre, shadowgraph.*

shaft and drum; drum and shaft

A system for moving a piece of scenery, or several pieces simultaneously, by means of a shaft (a wooden pole, around which lines from scenic pieces can be wound) and one or more drums (wooden cylinders of varying diameters, mounted on the pole, so that hauling lines can be wound around them), now outmoded by systems which move each piece of flied scenery independently. Sometimes used to operate a trap.

shallow

Said of an acting area, apron, setting, stage, etc., which is unusually narrow, from front to back.

shape

To control the beam from a lighting unit, as by a shutter, so that it covers suitably an area at which it is aimed. Hence *shaping* (noun).

share

1. In acting, to take some position on the stage equal in dramatic importance to the positions of other actors. Sometimes in the form *share a scene.* 2. A portion of the profits of an acting company, payable to a theatre owner or other persons. Also, to participate as a sharer. Hence *shareholder, sharing actor, sharing system,* etc. For the Elizabethan sense, see SHARER.

sharer

A member of a theatrical company who received a portion of the profits (a SHARE) from admissions and who, with his fellow sharers, was responsible for all expenses (and owner of all the company's possessions) except those involved in the theatre building itself—Elizabethan. Hence ACTOR-SHARER, *shareholder, sharing member,* etc. See (for later periods) SHARE.

sharing contract
An agreement specifying the business arrangements entered into between the producer of a touring show and the managers of the theatres to be visited by his company.

sharp-edged; sharp edge
Said of illumination which is sharply restricted to the area towards which it is directed. Hence *sharp-edged control.*

sheet
1. A box-office plan, on which can be indicated the seats for which theatre tickets have been sold. 2. A unit used in measuring the size of a theatrical advertising poster for billboards, referring to the paper size known as double crown (approximately 20 by 30 inches), as, a SIX-SHEET (for a poster consisting of six double-crown sheets).

shelf
A balcony. Hence, the *top shelf.*

she-tragedy
A love-and-honor tragedy in which the central figure is a woman—Late 17th and early 18th centuries.

shift
1. Short for SCENE SHIFT. Hence, a *shift routine,* etc. Also, to execute a scene shift. 2. An obsolete term for a dressing room.

shoe
Short for ROAD SHOE, TOGGLE SHOE.

shoe plot
A list of the shoes which the actors are to wear in a production.

shoe-string production; shoestring production
A stage production attempted with little if any capital. Hence *shoestringer.*

S-hook
A KEEPER HOOK (which see).

shop
1. A place where scenery or other theatrical equipment is made or put together. 2. In British usage, a theatrical engagement. Hence *seasonal shop*, etc.

short
Short for SHORT LINE.

short center (line)
In a set of four lines used to fly scenery, a line between a short line and a long center line.

short line; short form, **short**
In a set of lines used to fly scenery, the line nearest the pin rail.

show
1. A stage production. Also, to produce; to be exhibited as a production, as *now showing*. 2. A performance of a stage piece. 3. A dramatic work which is intended for or has achieved stage production.

show biz
Short for SHOW BUSINESS.

showboat
A term, used in the U.S. only, for a boat on which dramatic entertainments are performed, usually on a river, sometimes on a lake, infrequently on salt water. Hence *showboater, showboating* (noun).

show business; short forms, **show biz, business, bus.**
The professional theatre, usually in the broadest sense.

show-case; showcase
A production intended to display the talents of theatre people, usually amateurs, either for prospective employment (by guest producers and directors) or for publicity. Hence *showcase*

stage, show-case theatre, etc. Also, to act on trial in such a production.

showfolk
SHOW PEOPLE (which see).

show girl
A girl who appears in an ensemble, often displaying spectacular costumes, but who has no acting or chorus role—Chiefly Musical comedy.

show man ; showman
Anyone connected with a stage production; but especially a producer, actor, or author with a flair for success. Hence *showmanship.*

show must go on, (the)
A common theatrical expression alluding to the professional obligation to complete a performance despite any handicaps or interruptions.

show people
Professional theatrical people.

show-stopper
An actor, a part of a play, etc., so successful that the audience's applause momentarily delays the continuation of a performance. Hence *show-stopping.*

show town
A town or city where productions are presented, as, a good *show town.*

show-wise
Said of audiences which are theatrically sophisticated.

Shubert Alley
A short, narrow private street between 44th and 45th Streets, west of Times Square in New York City, where actors like to gather. Named for the family of theatre managers and pro-

ducers whose office is in the Sam S. Shubert Theatre, the stage door of which opens on the Alley.

shutter
1. Short for DOOR SHUTTER. 2. A device of metal, used in conjunction with a lighting unit, to limit the rays of light to any area desired. See also IRIS. 3. A TRAP. 4. A flat, usually one of a pair (in a series of pairs) sliding together in top and bottom grooves to form a stage setting and conceal other settings behind—17th century.

side
A sheet of paper, usually measuring about 6 by 9 inches, on which are typed (or less commonly written) the lines of a specific acting part with stage directions and cues—Usually in the plural.

side arm cloth
A curtain fastened so that it partly conceals the side of the stage.

side box; side-box
Formerly, a BOX (sense 1) at the side of the auditorium, to distinguish such boxes from those boxes then facing the stage. Also, to watch from such a box.

side-cloud
A cloud border, above a side shutter, suspended from an overhead groove along which it could be slid for scene-change—17th and 18th centuries.

side curtain
A curtain at the side of the stage.

side light; side-light; sidelight
A lighting unit placed at the side of the stage; especially, a TORMENTOR LIGHT. Hence *side lighting, side lighting unit.*

side-piece
Formerly, a WING FLAT.

326

side scene
1. Scenery near the side of the stage, as a wing flat or (formerly) a side shutter. 2. A scene played at the side of the stage.

side-show; sideshow
A minor entertainment which is incidental to a larger or main one—Circus, Carnival, etc.

side shutter; side-shutter; sideshutter
A SHUTTER (sense 4, which see) used at the side of the stage, a wing flat—17th century.

side space
The space to right or left of the acting area.

side stud type of mounting
A way of mounting a lighting unit by means of a fastening device on its side.

sidewalk actor
A person who likes to talk outside the theatre about how he thinks he would play a role.

side wall
1. A wall at the side of the stage. 2. A wall at the side of a stage setting.

sidewall slide
A counterweight track fastened vertically to the side wall of the theatre.

side wing; side-wing; sidewing
A WING FLAT.

sight comedian
A comic actor whose appearance and movement are funnier than his lines.

sight gag
A visual source of comedy derived from situation, business, or properties.

sight line; sight-line; sightline
An imaginary line from a seat in the auditorium to the stage, used in directing and scenic designing to determine how much a spectator, especially one in a remote or extreme seating area (sides, back, front), can see of a setting and the offstage space. Such lines, or portions of them, are sometimes shown on seating plans or stage drawings, or (in chalk or paint) on the stage floor. Sometimes considered to run from any spectator's eye to any point on the stage. Also called *line of sight*. See also DEAD-LINE, SET LINE.

sill iron
A bar of steel or iron, used as a tie across the bottom of a flat with a door or other opening to give greater rigidity. British: Also as *sill*.

sill rail
The bottom rail of a flat.

silo operator
A nickname for the manager of a summer theatre.

simultaneous setting
1. A MULTIPLE SETTING (which see). Called also *simultaneous scene*. 2. Said of the stage when the actors remain on it during a scene change or during the representation of a journey—An Elizabethan stage convention.

single
A flat 1 foot wide.

single bill
A theatre program consisting of but one dramatic piece.

sinking curtain
A curtain which can be rolled up at the level of the stage floor, or lowered through an opening in the stage floor so that the stage is revealed rather than concealed by its fall. See also REVERSE ROLLER CURTAIN.

sinkings
Formerly, descents through traps.

sinking stage
An ELEVATOR STAGE.

sit on one's hands
To give little or no applause; usually as *sitting on their hands*—
Chiefly Vaudeville.

situation
Short for DRAMATIC SITUATION.

situation play
See PLAY OF SITUATION.

six-sheet
1. To exaggerate, boast, lie. 2. Of an act (as in vaudeville), to
advertise it prominently.—In both senses, from the name of a
large size of theatrical advertising poster used on billboards
(see SHEET).

skate a flat
To slide a flat along the stage floor.

skeleton setting
A unit setting in which major structures remain in place
throughout the performance and minor elements are shifted
for changes in scene.

skeleton strip
A row of mounted receptacles into which lamp bulbs can be
screwed for the application of theatrical lamp dip.

sketch
1. A playlet in one scene. 2. A short scene—Revue, etc. 3. An
outline or preliminary text of all or part of a dramatic entertainment. 4. A drawing of a stage design.

skin

skin
1. A tarpaulin used to cover rolled-up drop curtains during shipment. 2. In the plural: Tights. Also as *skintight*.

skit
A short comic act or sketch, often one which is satirical—Vaudeville, Revue, etc. British: *turn*.

skull
An admission PASS.

sky batten
In British terminology, a strip light used to light a backdrop.

sky cloth
A British term for a SKY DROP.

sky dome; sky-dome
A CYCLORAMA, especially a half-dome.

sky drop
A back curtain painted to simulate the sky.

S.L.
Abbreviation of STAGE LEFT—A stage direction.

slap-stick; slapstick
A pair of lath paddles fastened together at one end, used by one comedian to belabor another noisily—Vaudeville, Circus. Hence, a rough, noisy comic entertainment. Also, said of entertainments or acting of this kind, as *slapstick comedy*.

sleeper
A show which is an unexpected success, as, for example, one which has previously had a poor out-of-town try-out.

sleeper-jump
A dressing room some distance from the stage—Chiefly Burlesque.

sleeve
A cylindrical louver used on a projector.

slice of life
A naturalistic play which attempts to capture the reality of life without artificial plotting—A translation of the French term *tranche de vie*.

slide
1. Short for GELATIN SLIDE. 2. A transparent plate, as of glass, used in a projection machine. 3. Short for SLIDER. 4. An alternative British term for a SLOAT (which see).

slide dimmer; slider dimmer
A dimmer in which a sliding piece makes contact through wire coils. British: Also, *wire (resistance) dimmer*.

slide holder
A frame on a projection machine into which a SLIDE (sense 2) can be fitted.

slider
In British terminology, a movable section of the stage floor, sliding in fillet grooves and covering a stage cut (*slider cut*)— Called also (*slider*) *filling*.

sliding scene
A scene (that is, a flat, etc.) which slides across the stage, in contradistinction to a DROP SCENE.

sliding stage
A stage, or more commonly a floor constructed in sections over the stage, which can be moved horizontally, as on rollers, so as to be replaced for a change in setting. Hence, a *sliding stage set*. See also WAGON STAGE, JACK-KNIFE (or SWINGING) STAGE.

sliding-trap; short form, slide
An alternative British term for a SLOAT (which see).

slip box
A British term for one of several boxes at the ends of the SLIPS (which see)—First half of 19th century.

slip connector
A STAGE CABLE CONNECTOR (which see).

slip counterweight
A counterweight grooved at the ends so that it can slide in a track.

slips
1. In British terminology, the ends of the upper tiers of seats— Late 18th and early 19th centuries. 2. Formerly, the WINGS (sense 2).

sloat; slote
In British terminology, a device consisting of grooved parallel rails (vertical or sloping) in which bearers or tongues, attached to a platform or a piece of scenery, slide, so that a winch or weights can draw lines to raise or lower an actor or scenery, as from below the stage level through a stage cut.

sloat box; sloat-box
1. A wooden CURTAIN TRACK. 2. A STAGE CUT (which see) into which a curtain can be rolled.

slow burn
In acting, a simulation of restrained, patient, slowly mounting exasperation which a comedian achieves by such means as tone of voice, gesture, or expression, sometimes preceding an angry outburst.

slow curtain
A gradual lowering of a curtain for artistic effect.

slow-motion wheel
A gearing device operated by a wheel, used to control a dimmer or group of dimmers in a very precise manner.

S.M.
Abbreviation of STAGE MANAGER.

small part
A minor role. Hence *small-part player* (or *man* or *woman*), an actor who commonly plays such a role. Hence also *small parts and understudies,* small-part actors who also understudy major roles.

small people
Formerly, small-part players (see SMALL PART), collectively.

small time, (the)
A circuit of theatres giving three or more performances daily —Vaudeville. By extention, that part of the theatre world which is not especially successful with the public; minor theatres, etc. Hence *small-time performer, etc.*

smart revue (or **review**)
See REVUE.

smash (**hit**)
A tremendously successful show. Hence *smash part,* etc.

smasheroo
An extraordinarily popular smash hit.

smell of (**the**) **grease paint,** (the)
The odor of GREASE PAINT (which see), typifying the glamor of the stage.

smoke box (or **case**)
A British term for a SMOKE POT.

smoke door
A door in the stage roof which is weighted to open, when a rope is cut, in the event of fire. See LANTERN LIGHT (British).

smoke pocket
One of two metal grooves, at the sides of the proscenium arch, in which the asbestos curtain slides.

smoke pot
A container used to hold the chemicals or other substances from which smoke is produced for certain optical effects. British: *smoke box* (or *case*).

snaffle-hook
A hook which fits into a screw-eye, used to fasten a light-weight drop to the permanent rigging.

snatch chain
A chain 3 feet long, used to fly equipment from a counterweight batten.

snatch line
A rope line used instead of a snatch chain.

snow
Free admission passes, collectively; also, persons admitted on these.

snow bag (or **box**)
British terms for a SNOW CRADLE (which see).

snow brown
To substitute an object (as, a property) for another object which is missing.

snow cradle
A device for creating a visual snow effect, consisting of a box-like frame or a pair of battens, bearing a piece of canvas or other fabric pierced with holes or slits, through which a material such as confetti can be sifted onto the stage. British: *snow bag, snow box, snow trough.*

snow trough
An alternative British term for a SNOW CRADLE.

soap
To cover a reflecting surface in a stage setting with soap as a means of eliminating glare from stage lighting.

social drama

Dramas, collectively or individually, dealing with man in his social environment, social problems, social life. Hence *social comedy, social dramatist,* etc. Sometimes synonymous with *bourgeois drama.* See also SOCIETY DRAMA. The term *social theatre* (or *stage*) equals LABOR THEATRE (which see).

society

See DRAMATIC SOCIETY, THEATRE SOCIETY.

society drama

A drama set in a fashionable, upper-class background. See SOCIAL DRAMA.

sock

1. Comedy, the comic drama, comic acting—A term derived from the Latin *soccus,* meaning the light, low, soft shoe worn in ancient Greek and Roman comic acting. 2. A tremendously successful show, performer, etc. Hence, a *sock hit.* Also as *socko, sokko.*

sock and buskin

Comedy and tragedy; the drama; the acting profession. See BUSKIN, SOCK.

socko; sokko

See SOCK (sense 2).

soft

See FALSE PROSCENIUM for the meaning of *soft false proscenium.*

soft-edged; soft edge

Said of illumination which is not sharply defined, which gradually diminishes towards the boundaries of the area towards which it is directed; also said of a lighting unit which throws such illumination, as, a *soft-edge spotlight.* Also, *soft-edging:* Treating a gelatin to give such illumination, as by piercing it or spotting it with grease.

sold out
Said of a theatre when no seats or places for standees are available at a performance. See also HOUSE FULL.

soliloquy
A speech, a monologue, usually fairly long, to convey a character's thoughts or other information to the audience, either while alone on the stage or in the presence of other characters who are supposed not to overhear him—A stage convention. Hence *soliloquize*, etc.

solo
To sing or dance alone; a song, dance, etc., performed alone—Chiefly Musical comedy and the like. Hence *solo dancer, soloist*.

song
A short, usually regular piece of music, presented vocally by one or more persons, frequently a part of the drama or of stage representation.

song and dance; song-and-dance;
   abbreviation, **S and D**
Pertaining to an entertainment combining singing and dancing, as, a *song-and-dance man*, a *song and dance play*—Chiefly Vaudeville, Musical comedy, and the like.

soubrette
A minor female role, such as that of a maid, in comedy; usually a saucy person devoted to the heroine and involved in intrigue.

sound
Short for SOUND EFFECT, SOUND EQUIPMENT.

sound-control booth
See BOOTH.

sound cue
A cue for the commencement of a sound effect. Hence, too, a *sound-cue sheet* (a list).

sound (effect)
See EFFECT.

sound (equipment)
The device or devices by means of which sound effects are produced.

sound horn
A piece of SOUND EQUIPMENT (which see) which reproduces sound electrically. It may be brought onstage by means of a *sound horn cradle* suspended from a track or a *sound horn truck* on wheels.

sound machine
Any piece of sound equipment.

sound plot
A sound-cue sheet (see SOUND CUE).

spacer
A piece of wood used on a flat to keep a pair of battens at the proper distance.

spacer frame
A wooden supporting frame used as an extra PARALLEL (which see).

space set
A stage setting for a SPACE STAGE.

space stage
A stage on which scenery is absent, or only vignetted, the actors appearing in a lighted portion against a dark background.

sparge-pipe
A RAIN PIPE (which see) or a DRENCHER PIPE (which see).

Sparks
A nickname, chiefly British, for an electrician.

speaking opening
See OPENING.

speaking part (or **role**)
An actor's role calling for participation in the dialogue.

spec
Short for TICKET SPECULATOR.

special
A spotlight used to emphasize a part of the stage where some important action occurs. Hence, more specifically, a *door special*, etc.

special effect
Any visual or acoustical effect (see EFFECT).

special effects board
In British terminology, a small switchboard sometimes used to take care of the electrical operation of special effects (see EFFECT).

special inner proscenium
A second false proscenium behind a FALSE PROSCENIUM (which see), used to reduce the proscenium opening still further.

specialist lead
A character actor who plays leading parts.

special performance
A performance at a time other than the regularly announced times.

specialty
Pertaining to the performance of specialized acts or turns (songs, dances, comic sketches), as, a *specialty act*, a *specialty artist* (or *actor*), etc.—Especially, Vaudeville.

specialty number
A song not intended to be fully integrated with the rest of the entertainment—Musical comedy.

338

specific lighting
Lighting which is thrown over a limited part of the stage.

spectacle
Elaborate stage display; a dramatic representation providing such display. Hence *spectacular*, etc.

spectator; (feminine) **spectatress** or **spectatrix**
A member of an audience, a person watching a performance.

spectatorial
1. Of or pertaining to a spectator. 2. Pertaining to spectacle.

spectatory
A term, now rare, for the following: An auditorium, a place for spectators; an audience in an auditorium.

speculator
Short for TICKET SPECULATOR.

speech
A unit of stage dialogue, all the LINES (sense 2) which an actor delivers in his turn up to the point where another actor speaks, the scene ends, or he goes out.

speech cue
A cue for the speaking of certain lines.

speech-prefix
The name of a character, preceding a speech in the text of a dramatic piece.

speech-tag
See TAG.

Spelvin, George
A fictitious name, dating from about 1886, traditionally used in theatre programs to conceal the identity of an actor who is doubling in a second role. Sometimes *George X. Spelvin* is given, when the character dies in the course of the performance. British equivalent: *Walter Plinge* (see PLINGE).

spherical reflector
A reflecting surface of metal or glass in the form of a portion of a ball.

spike
An indication (chalked, painted, or taped) on the stage floor of the proper position of furniture, scenery, or properties. Called also a *spike mark*. Also, to make such a mark. See also ON SPIKE.

spill
Collectively, rays of light, especially rays which are not useful in stage illumination. The area illuminated by such rays. Also, said of rays of light (especially superfluous rays) : To illuminate.

spill ring
One of several circular metal bands used in front of a lighting unit to control the spread of light.

spill shield; spill-shield
A cut-off hood used to prevent light spill, hung on a border light.

spine
In the Stanislavski method, the dominant trait in the character assumed by the actor.

spirit gum
A liquid glue (compounded of rosin, mastic, and alcohol, or similar substances) used to fasten false hair, such as a beard, to an actor's skin.

splay
See PROSCENIUM SPLAY.

splice plate; splice U-plate
See U-PLATE.

split stage
A stage used for two separate actions at once.

split week; split-week
A week played by a touring company partly in one town, partly in another.

spoken drama
Dramas, collectively or individually, in which lines are spoken, in contradistinction to mime or pantomime. Hence *spoken play*, etc.

spot
1. Short for SPOTLIGHT. Hence *spot it:* To focus a spotlight on part of the stage area. 2. An actor's place in the order of the acts billed—Vaudeville.

(See also the combinations of SPOTLIGHT, with which the combinations of *spot* are commonly interchangeable.)

spot batten; spot-batten; spot bar
In British terminology, a pipe batten (see BATTEN) used to carry spotlights, etc.; also, the lights on such a batten.

spotblock
A pulley block used for a special purpose, as for hanging a chandelier.

spot frost
A DIFFUSING MEDIUM (which see), the center of which is cut out or greased with vaseline or some other substance so that more light can pass through.

spot light; spot-light, spotlight; short form, **spot**
A lighting instrument used to provide sharp, intense illumination for a specific portion of the stage, by means of a high-powered carbon arc or incandescent lamp, a condensing lens, a focusing device, and usually a reflector. British: Also PROJECTOR LAMP, *spot lantern*, sometimes LIME LIGHT. Also, to turn a

341

spotlight on the stage (*spot* or *spotlight;* transitive verb). Hence *spot-lighting.*

(See also the compounds of SPOT, with which the compounds of *spotlight* are commonly interchangeable.)

spotlight booth
See BOOTH.

spotlight cradle
A horizontal pipe batten (see BATTEN) used to hold a spotlight.

spotlight strip
A row of spotlights, usually baby spots, suspended on a batten.

spotlight tower; short form, **tower**
A LIGHT TOWER (which see) used for spotlights.

spot line
A WORKING LINE of rope, used to hang a specific object at a given place. Such a line is said to be *spotted.*

spotting attachment
In British terminology, an extra lens used to sharpen the beam from a spotlight.

spread
The width of the beam emanating from a lighting unit.

spreader
A lateral brace between the battens on a ceiling frame.

spreader U-plate
See U-PLATE.

spread lens
A lens of fluted glass, used to broaden the beam of a lighting unit.

sprinkler
An automatic device which directs water upon the stage from above in the event of fire. Hence *sprinkler system,* etc. See also DRENCHER.

S.R.
Abbreviation of STAGE RIGHT—A stage direction.

S.R.O.
Abbreviation of STANDING ROOM ONLY. Hence, an *S.R.O. hit*, etc.

stability
In directing, the balancing of the positions of the actors in various parts of the acting area.

stack
A term, used in the U.S. only, for a SCENE PACK (which see). Also, to pack scenery.

stacking rack
A wood or metal rack in which flats can be stored.

stage
A platform or floor for dramatic performances; such platforms, collectively. Pertaining to, associated with, or used on a stage, as STAGE FRIGHT, a STAGE CARPENTER, a STAGE CREW. Simulated on a stage, as, a *stage meal*, a *stage sailor*. By extension, the acting and working spaces above and below the stage floor; a theatre; the theatre; the acted drama; the theatrical profession. Hence *stageland*, etc. Also, to produce a dramatic composition on the stage, to make the preparations (especially the scenic and acting preparations) for a dramatic representation. Hence *stageable*, etc.

stage action; stage-action
See ACTION (sense 1).

stage actor
An actor who performs on the stage, in contradistinction to a motion picture actor or the like.

stage area
A portion of the stage, one of the six or more sections into which the acting area is commonly divided: DOWN CENTER, UP

CENTER, DOWN RIGHT, UP RIGHT, DOWN LEFT, UP LEFT, and
sometimes also CENTER, LEFT CENTER, RIGHT CENTER, LEFT,
RIGHT, DOWN LEFT CENTER, DOWN RIGHT CENTER, UP LEFT CEN-
TER, UP RIGHT CENTER. See also ACTING AREA, STAGE POSITION.

stage art
DRAMATIC ART (which see).

stage audience
Members of the audience seated, not in the auditorium, but on
the stage, at the back or side—Elizabethan to 18th century.

stage box; stage-box
A box for spectators next to (and originally on) the stage.

stage brace; short form, **brace**
A length of wood (or iron), usually extensible, which is used
to support a standing flat (or other scenic piece). It stretches
diagonally downward from the back of the flat; a brace hook
at the top fastens into a brace cleat on the flat, and an eye at
the bottom receives a stage screw which fastens the brace to the
floor; but sometimes a braceweight is used instead of a screw.

stage business; short forms, **business, bus.**
An actor's motions and movements (also called PANTOMIME,
which see); more particularly, minor physical action either
called for by the script or introduced by the actor or the
director to bring lifelike completeness to a role (as in the
business of lighting a cigarette) or additional flavor to the
general action of a dramatic piece. Hence *knockabout business,*
etc.

stage cable; short form, **cable**
A flexible electrical conductor, consisting of one or more wires
or ribbons sheathed in rubber, fiber, or cotton, and covered
with heavy outer sheathing. British: *flexible cable, stage flex.*

344

stage cable connector; short forms, **cable connector, (stage) connector**
A two-piece fiber device with metal pins on one half and receiving sockets on the other, used to connect lengths of stage cable to each other or to lighting units. Often called *pin connector* or *slip connector*.

stage call
1. An ACT CALL (which see); an ACT WARNING (which see).
2. A stage conference of directors and actors.

stage career; short form, **career**
An actor's professional life, calling, occupation.

stage carpenter; short form, **carpenter**
1. A department head responsible not only for general carpentry but also for making, rigging, and handling scenery of all kinds, etc.; one of his assistants. 2. A PLAY DOCTOR (which see).

stage ceiling
The ceiling of a theatre over the grid.

stage children
Child actors.

stage-clamp
A metal device used to hold two flats together when a lash line is not strong enough to do so.

stage cloth; stage-cloth
A British term for a GROUND CLOTH (which see).

stage connector; stage-connector
A STAGE CABLE CONNECTOR (which see).

stage convention; short form, **convention**
Any well-understood means of making effective use of the peculiarities of theatrical conditions, such as a stage whisper, ensemble singing, spotlighting, the use of verse, mistaken identity.

stage-copy
A PROMPT COPY of a play—Elizabethan.

stage-cover; short form, cover
The HEAVENS (sense 2)—Elizabethan.

stage craft; stage-craft; stagecraft
Skill in (or the art of) composing for production, producing, or in any way participating in the production of, a dramatic piece. Hence *stage-crafter* (a technician). Sometimes, *theatre-craft*. See also NEW STAGECRAFT.

stage crew; short form, crew
The theatrical employees who build and shift scenery, handle properties, prepare lighting, and so forth; hence, specifically, such groups as the *paint crew*.

stage criticism
Dramatic criticism.

stage cut; short form, cut
In British terminology, an opening in the stage, especially a long narrow transverse section covered with movable flooring when not in use, serving as a trap, or as a passage for a bridge, curtain, etc., rising above the stage floor. U.S.: *stage elevator* (see ELEVATOR).

stage decoration; stage-decoration; short form, decoration
The decoration, the artistic preparation of the stage for dramatic representation, the scenic setting of the stage. Variously equivalent to décor or scenic (or stage or theatrical) art or design.

stage dip
THEATRICAL LAMP DIP (which see).

stage direction; stage-direction
1. In a script, an indication of the expected stage action or other production arrangements. 2. The preparation for the stage rep-

resentation of a dramatic composition; the work of the stage director. Hence *stage directing*.

stage director; short form, **director**
A person to whom the producer assigns the responsibility for the integration of an entire production, from the basic interpretation of the text through all the acting and technical phases up to the time of first performance, when the stage manager takes over. Formerly, a person who exercised the functions of the present-day STAGE MANAGER. British: PRODUCER. (In current British usage, the *stage director* is a person who combines the work of the persons who in American usage are called the producer and the stage manager.)

stage door
1. An outside door at the back or side of a theatre for actors and other theatre people or for the passage of scenery. 2. A door used on the stage.

stage door Johnny; stage-door Johnny
A man who waits at a stage door to meet actresses.

stage door keeper; stage door-keeper;
    stage-door keeper
A term, chiefly British, for a STAGE DOORMAN (which see).

stage doorman; short form, doorman
A custodian who is responsible for permitting only authorized persons to pass through the stage door. British: *stage door keeper, hall-keeper*.

stage dressing room
A QUICK CHANGE ROOM (which see).

stage effect; stage-effect; short form, effect
1. The quality of being striking or effective on the stage; a striking bit of stage representation; sometimes with the connotation of meretricious effort. 2. See EFFECT.

stage electrical circuit; short form, **(electrical) circuit**
A distinct portion of the electrical system used on the stage, consisting typically of a lighting unit or group of lighting units, a dimmer, a switch, a fuse, and the wiring connecting these to each other and to a switchboard.

stage English
A "standard" form of the English language used conventionally for stage purposes, free of peculiarities of place, and in pronunciation generally resembling the educated usage of southern England.

stage entrance
An access to the stage from the area behind it.

stage exit
An egress from the stage to the area behind it.

stage fall
In acting, a purposeful drop or tumble to the stage floor, in such a way as to avoid injury.

stage flex
A British term for a STAGE CABLE.

stage floor; stage-floor
The surface of a stage, commonly made of wood, on which players perform.

stage-folk
Collectively, actors.

stage fright; stage-fright
An actor's nervousness before or during his stage appearance. Hence *stage-frighten* (transitive verb).

stage furniture
The furnishings of the stage, other than properties.

stage grouping; (stage) group
The STAGE PICTURE (which see).

348

stage hand; stagehand
A person who sets the stage, changes scenery, and performs other duties, usually as a member of the stage carpenter's crew. British: Often, SCENE SHIFTER.

stage history; stage-history
The history, or a history, of the stage, of the theatre. Hence *stage historian.*

stage house; stage-house; stagehouse
1. The stage floor and all the space above it up to the grid; the walls enclosing such an area. 2. In an obsolete sense: A theatre.

stage jubilee
The celebration of an acting career which has lasted fifty years.

stage-keeper
A person charged with the general custody of the stage, including sweeping—17th century.

stage left; short form, **left;** abbreviation, **L.**
Left stage, or LEFT OF STAGE (which see).

stage level
The level or elevation of the stage, relative to that which lies below or above the stage floor.

stage machinery; short form, **machinery**
Collectively, the mechanical devices used on the stage. Hence also *stage machinist.*

stage main
1. A MASTER SWITCH (sense 1). 2. A cable carrying current from a source of supply to the stage switchboard.

stage manager; stage-manager; abbreviation, **S.M.**
The head of the production staff, who assists the stage director, during rehearsals, in technical matters such as lighting, costumes, settings, prompting, etc., and who, once the production opens, takes complete charge of the stage, the actors (but not

the acting), and the crews. (In current British usage, the *stage manager* is a person with similar duties who is responsible to the theatre manager and takes charge once the producer, in the British sense, has prepared the production for performance.) Hence *stage management, stage managership,* etc.

stage manager's desk
Usually, a shelf backstage and close to the proscenium, upon which the stage manager may lay his copy of the script and other small items, and above which his signaling equipment is located.

stage movement; short form, **movement**
The movement of an actor across the stage, rather than his action while executing a body movement or a piece of stage business.

stage name
A name assumed by an actor for professional purposes.

stage nursery; short form, **nursery**
A center for the training of actors, with or without a stage (*nursery theatre*) where plays could be produced—Chiefly Restoration.

stage peg
A STAGE SCREW (which see).

stage picture; stage-picture
The view of the stage presented to the audience at any given moment, with the actors in their positions relative to one another; also frequently meant to include the arrangement of the lighting, the scenery, and so forth at such a moment.

stage play; stage-play; stageplay
A play for the stage, an acting play; a play for theatrical (rather than motion picture, television, or other non-theatrical) production. Hence *stage-player, stage playing.*

350

stage plug
An electrical plug, consisting of a fiber block and two exposed copper bars with binding posts, used to connect a stage cable to a stage pocket or to a plugging box.

stage pocket; short form, pocket
One of several metal boxes set into the stage floor outside the acting area, containing receptacles into which stage cables can be plugged to connect lighting units with the stage electrical system. British: *dip*. Sometimes such a pocket placed in the stage wall (a *wall pocket*).

stage position; short form, position
The place where an actor stands at any given moment, conceived in terms of the division of the stage into arbitrary areas. See STAGE AREA.

stage presence; short form, presence
An actor's bearing in his role, his ability to hold an audience.

stage property; stage-property
A property which remains on the stage throughout a scene, especially an indication of locality such as a piece of furniture or a rug; also, equipment used for EFFECTS (which see), with the exception of lighting equipment; any PROPERTY (which see).

stager
An actor. The term is rare, except as OLD STAGER (which see).

stage rehearsal
A rehearsal held on the stage, rather than in a rehearsal room or elsewhere.

stage right; short form, right; abbreviation, R.
1. Right stage, or RIGHT OF STAGE (which see). 2. The privilege, usually reserved by copyright, of staging a dramatic composition—Usually plural.

351

stage roof
The roof of a theatre, over the grid.

stage-room
Space enough on the stage for stage action.

stagery
Display or portrayal on the stage.

stage screw
A large metal hand screw, with a grip or handle, used for fixing a stage brace or a foot iron to the stage floor to brace scenery.

stage seat
A seat for a spectator on the stage—A modern term for an Elizabethan and Restoration practice.

stage setting
See SET.

stage society
In British terminology, an organization which produces plays privately, usually for artistic and non-commercial reasons, sometimes to evade the licensing laws.

stage space
The space between the stage floor and the roof.

stage speech
STAGE ENGLISH (which see).

stage staff
The technical and other people involved in the work of the stage: The business manager, the designers, the crews, the technical director, but not the actors.

stage step
A portable stage stair unit—usually in the plural, and designated a *one-step*, a *two-step*, etc., according to the number of steps or treads in the unit. British: *tread*.

352

stage stool
A stool used as a spectator's seat on the stage—18th century and earlier.

stage stride
See STAGE WALK.

stage struck; stage-struck
Fascinated by the stage; especially, ardently desirous of becoming an actor.

stage switchboard
See SWITCHBOARD.

stage technician; short form, **technician**
A person engaged in the technical work of stage production, as an electrician, a SCENE TECHNICIAN, etc.

stage technique
1. STAGECRAFT. 2. Skill in the art of acting.

stage trick; short form, **trick**
A means for effecting some illusion to surprise the audience, as by means of traps or scenic devices.

stage upholstery
An obsolete term for the furnishings used in a stage setting.

stage version
1. An acting version (see ACTING EDITION). 2. A DRAMATIC VERSION (which see).

stage wagon
A SCENERY WAGON (which see).

stage wait; short form, **wait**
A delay which is unintentional.

stage walk; stage stride
In acting, a series of steps, used to convey in the narrow confines of the stage an impression of a longer walk which would be possible offstage.

stage whisper
In acting, a loud whisper, a softly-spoken utterance, audible to the audience but imagined to go unheard by certain characters—A stage convention.

staging
1. The bringing of a dramatic composition to the stage. 2. A technique or style in stagecraft; also collectively. 3. The setting of a dramatic representation.

stagy; stagey
Theatrical, usually in a derogatory sense.

staircase cut
A STAGE CUT (which see) for a flight of stairs.

stair run
A staircase for stage use, consisting of a PARALLEL (which see) with a flight of stairs.

stall
In British terminology, a seat, commonly with arm rests, in a theatre auditorium; this is now the usual designation of the reserved seats between the stage and the pit, which command the highest prices in the house after the boxes. (The American equivalent is commonly *orchestra seat*, but orchestra seats extend into the area which in British usage is called the PIT). Hence, in the plural, the spectators in such seats. See also BALCONY STALL, DRESS STALL, ORCHESTRA STALL (sometimes also U.S.), PIT STALL.

stand
1. An engagement of an acting company for a given number of performances, or for a specified period, as, a ONE NIGHT STAND, a *week stand*. Also, the visit itself; the town or theatre in which the performances are given. 2. A theatrical poster, as, a *24-sheet stand*. 3. Short for LIGHT STAND.

standard
1. A light stand. 2. In British terminology, a lighting unit used on a light stand; called also *standard flood, standard lamp,* etc.

standard drama
Plays, usually collectively, and especially of earlier periods, which are outstanding in popularity or worth and are therefore often revived over the years. Hence *standard comedy,* etc.

stand-by
1. A direction given by the stage manager to actors to be ready for a curtain call, or (after an act call) to be ready for their entrances on cue; or given to stage crews so that they will be ready to perform their functions. (Also as two words.) 2. A well-known actor who is not a member of the cast but is engaged to remain on call so that if necessary he can take the place of a principal. (Also as one word.)

stand-by table; standby table
A PROPERTY TABLE (which see).

standee
A member of the audience who has bought a ticket for standing room rather than for a seat.

standing floodlight
A floodlight on a light stand.

standing room
Space for a spectator standing rather than sitting.

standing room only; abbreviation, S.R.O.
A call or a sign warning ticket-buyers that all the seats have been sold and that only standees can be admitted.

standing-room section
A part of the theatre, usually at the back of the auditorium, where STANDEES can be accommodated.

standing unit
A flat, or a similar piece, considered as belonging to unit scenery.

stand in line
To wait in line at a box-office window in order to buy tickets. British: *queue up.*

Stanislavski method
A set of theories and techniques dealing with the problems of acting, and advocating a naturalistic, sincere acting style (opposed to the conventions and declamation of theatricalism) which has been highly influential in the modern theatre. For example, the actor seeks to enrich his interpretation, to find the "inner reality" of his part, by trying to feel as the character he is portraying feels. Named for its formulator, known professionally as Stanislavski (real name: Konstantin Sergeyevich Alexeyev; 1863–1938), Russian actor and author, co-founder and stage director of the Moscow Art Theatre. Sometimes called a "system"; "Stanislavsky" and variant forms of his other names are sometimes used.

star
The leading actor or actress in a company or in a given production, whose name usually precedes the title of the dramatic composition in the billing; especially, an actor or actress who has attained pre-eminence in the theatrical world. Pertaining to a star or stars, as *star billing, stardom, star dressing room* (or *star room*), *star entrance* (see ENTRANCE, sense 2), *star part, star play* (or *vehicle;* see STARRING VEHICLE), etc. To hold or to have held the rank of star; to give or be given the role of a star. Hence *starring* (participle, featuring a star), *star turn.*

star cloth
A hanging pierced with holes through which small electric lights shine, used to achieve a star effect (see EFFECT).

starring vehicle
A dramatic piece especially rich in opportunity for a star actor. Called also *star play, star vehicle*.

star room; star-room
Short for *star dressing room* (see STAR).

star system
The practice of giving special emphasis to a star, in order to attract the public. Sometimes as *starring system*.

star theatre
A theatre, now often a summer theatre, making constant use of the STAR SYSTEM (which see).

star trap
A trap in the stage, commonly circular, with a star-shaped lid consisting of six wooden triangles hinged radially to the circumference, through which an actor standing on a counter-weighted platform can make sudden appearances and disappearances.

state theatre
In the U.S., a theatre subsidized by one of the states; in other parts of the world, a national theatre.

static play
1. A play in which there is no marked change in characters or situation. 2. A play devoted to dialogue with little stage movement.

station
A halting-place for a wagon stage on which a scene in a mystery play was acted—Medieval.

stationary setting
A PERMANENT SETTING (which see).

stay

A strip of wood or metal, used for additional bracing on the frames of two flats or other scenic pieces which have been fastened together.

stay in character

In acting, to continue in a role without resuming one's normal personality, as when interrupted by members of the audience or when taking a curtain call.

steal

1. An actor's seizure of the attention of the audience when he has no right to it, as by unfairly moving upstage center so that he commands the best position, forcing other actors to turn their backs to the spectators. Also, to commit a steal, as *steal the limelight, steal a scene.* 2. To move from one position to another on the stage, inconspicuously—Sometimes, a stage direction. 3. To FAKE (sense 2). 4. In directing, the placement of actors so that their faces can be better seen, in positions somewhat unlike those which they would occupy in a situation offstage. Also, to place actors in this way.

steal a bow

To take a bow or an encore without sufficient demand from the spectators.

steal the show

To act so well that one is acclaimed out of proportion to the expected potentialities in one's role.

steam barrel

In British terminology, a steel or iron pipe (British: *barrel*) closed at one end and perforated with small holes on the under side through which steam can escape to give the appearance of fog or mist.

358

steam curtain
A rare means of curtaining off the stage from the view of the audience, during scene-changes, especially in outdoor theatres, by permitting steam to escape from perforated pipes.

steerer
A ticket speculator's representative, who sends those who cannot get tickets at a box office to the speculator.

Stem, (the)
Short for BIG STEM, MAIN STEM.

stencil
A piece of cardboard or other material through which a design is cut, used like a slide in a projection machine to produce such effects as lightning, moon, or stars. This device is now rare or obsolete.

step
1. A STAGE STEP (which see). 2. An electrical contact button.

step dance; step-dance
A dance, such as a clog or tap dance, emphasizing steps rather than ballet or similar movements. Hence *step dancer, step dancing.*

step lens; stepped lens
A glass lens with ridges. Sometimes hyphenated.

step on someone's laughs
To speak up so that the audience does not have time to laugh at another actor's jokes.

step on the laughs
To tell a series of jokes rapidly without pausing for an audience's laughter.

stepped lens; stepped-lens
A STEP LENS.

stereopticon
A SCIOPTICON.

stichomythia; stychomythia; stichomythy
A form of dialogue, used occasionally in highly emotional scenes in which two actors alternately deliver single lines (or short speeches)—A Greek word (meaning "speech in lines") used in English. Hence, too, *stichomythic*. Called also *cut-and-parry* (or *cut-and-thrust* and *cat-and-mouse*) *dialogue*.

stick
In acting, to forget one's lines or business, to pause.

sticks, (the)
The ROAD (which see); the towns outside of a large theatre center; a tank town circuit. British: (the) *provinces*.

stiffener
A wood batten, used to strengthen the back of a piece of scenery.

stile; style
A strip of wood used as one of the two vertical outside pieces in the frame of a flat, or as door or window trim.

still music
Incidental background music, played on recorders or similar instruments to help convey a mood—Elizabethan.

stock
1. Short for STOCK COMPANY. Also, collectively, the theatres where stock companies play. Hence *stock actor, stock rights, summer stock*, etc. 2. Repertory. Hence *stock actor, stock rights*, etc. 3. Typical, frequently used, or recurring, as a *stock character, stock costumes*, a *stock drama*, a *stock setting, stock situations*, etc.

stock company; stock-company
An acting company having its own theatre (or a traveling company with a circuit of theatres) and a series of plays to be produced in turn, or in repertory; often the actors are typed.

stock debt
In British terminology, the amount of money owed on accumulated bills by the management of a theatre—18th century.

stock dramatist; stock-dramatist
In British terminology, a writer regularly employed by a theatre manager to furnish dramatic pieces to order—19th century.

stomp
Variant spelling of STUMP.

stooge
A STRAIGHT MAN, a feeder (see FEED), an actor who heckles a comedian or is the target of his jests.

stool
1. In British terminology, a small seat which a theatre patron may leave marked with his name in a queue, so that he may go away and return to secure admission when the pit or gallery opens, without losing his turn. 2. A theatre seat without arms or back, a type now uncommon.

stool-holder
A spectator who occupied a seat on the stage—18th century and before.

stop block
A piece of wood used for the same purpose as a STOP CLEAT.

stop chain
A chain between the grid and the top of a fly curtain, used as a safety device to allow the curtain to fall only to the stage floor.

stop clause
A condition inserted into a theatre owner's contract with a producer, so that the arrangements can be terminated if the gross receipts are poor.

stop cleat
A metal cleat, used on flats to make it easier to fasten them at right angles to one another, or used on doors and windows to keep them from swinging backward.

stopper line
A rope line used for fastening a hauling line to the lock rail.

stop the show
In acting, to win such vigorous applause that the performance is momentarily halted.

story
The narrative element in a dramatic piece, from which the plot is developed; sometimes, the plot itself.

story line
The narrative thread in a dramatic piece, in contradistinction to its other characteristics.

story play
A play strong on story rather than on idea.

straight
1. Normal, natural, not eccentric, requiring no special emphasis on characterization in make-up, speech, etc., as, *straight make-up, play it straight.* Also, sincere and earnest, without travesty or burlesque. 2. Pertaining to legitimate drama, rather than to vaudeville, musical comedy, etc., as, a *straight actor,* a *straight part*—both expressions can also be used in sense 1—a *straight play*, etc.

straight line
A line of dialogue spoken by a stooge, which a comedian plays upon for a laugh.

straight man
An actor who has a straight role (see STRAIGHT, sense 1) rather than a character part, as (especially in vaudeville) a stooge.

strap
A piece of plywood used as a corner brace.

strap arm
A metal arm, used on a pipe batten to hold the yoke on which a spotlight is hung.

straw-hat; strawhat
A summer theatre. Hence, pertaining to a summer theatre or to such theaters collectively, as, the *straw-hat circuit*, a *straw-hat theatre*. The initial letters are sometimes capitalized.

stray light
SPILL (which see).

stretcher (batten)
A TOGGLE RAIL.

strike
1. A removing of scenery to clear the stage. Also, to dismantle, remove, and store scenery used in a stage setting, as *strike the set*. A command given by the stage manager to the stage crew to clear the stage of scenery. 2. To bring together and then separate the electrodes of an arc lamp. 3. In a sense now rare: To turn down a light.

striker
A GRIP, a SCENE SHIFTER.

stringer
A plank or board supporting a stair tread, a platform top, etc. Hence *cross stringer, side stringer*, etc.

strip
1. Short for STRIP LIGHT. 2. To apply a STRIPPER (which see) to the crack between two flats. 3. See STRIP-TEASE.

strip (light)

Any short row of lamps used to illuminate the stage; commonly, a row of low-powered lamps mounted in a trough with a reflecting hood, and often also with color frames and a hook at one end, used for diffused lighting, as behind a wall, door, or window, or just behind the proscenium arch. Hence PROSCENIUM STRIP, etc.

stripper

1. A piece of fabric glued over a crack between two hinged flats, and painted. 2. A strip-teaser (see STRIP-TEASE).

strip-tease

An act in which a girl dancer gradually takes off her clothing—Burlesque, Revue. Hence *strip* (verb), *strip-teaser* (or STRIPPER).

strolling player

An itinerant actor. Formerly called also a *stroll* or *stroller*. Hence *strolling company*, etc.

strong

Said of a part, a curtain fall, dialogue, body movement, a stage position, etc., which is, or is deemed to be, relatively important and emphatic, and thus capable of drawing the attention of the audience.

structural scene

A REHEARSAL SCENE (which see).

structure

Short for DRAMATIC STRUCTURE.

strut

A STAGE BRACE.

stub

1. The portion of a theatre ticket which is collected by a ticket-taker. Also as TICKET STUB. 2. A lining stump (see STUMP).

364

stub-receptacle
A ticket-taker's box.

stud contact dimmer
A RESISTANCE DIMMER in which the resistance wire is tapped and brought to contact buttons or studs.

student drama
Collectively, plays produced by students.

studio
1. A theatre workroom, as, a place for scene-making. 2. Short for STUDIO THEATRE.

studio production
1. A try-out of a stage production, with little preparation in the way of casting, rehearsing, lighting, or setting. 2. A production in a laboratory theatre.

studio (theatre)
A theatre for the training of actors and technicians and for experimentation and research; a laboratory theatre.

study
1. To memorize, or to work at memorizing, dialogue (for an acting part). Hence *studying* (noun). A person who does so, as, a *good study*, a *slow study*. See also QUICK STUDY. 2. The inner or alcove stage—Elizabethan.

stump
In make-up, a stubby pointed roll of paper used in lining. Also as (*artist's*) *paper stump, lining stump*, etc.

style
1. A theory or practice in staging, acting, etc., as, the *arena style*, an *illusionistic style*, a *naturalistic style*. 2. Variant spelling of STILE.

stylization

A theory and practice in stagecraft, attempting to express the meaning and mood of a dramatic piece through some pattern of forms in one or more of the aspects of production (speech, movement, setting, costume, etc.). Stylization is formalistic, presentational, non-illusionistic, theatrical, rather than realistic or naturalistic, but the distinction is one of emphasis rather than of hard-and-fast antithesis. Thus dominant characteristics may be exaggerated; or an abstract or conventional simulation may be introduced, as, a framework instead of a solid-looking structure to suggest a house. Also *stylistic, stylize, stylized realism*, etc.

sub-master (control); submaster control

A device for a stage switchboard, used to control groups of circuits, and in turn controlled by a master control.

subordinate plot; short form, sub-plot, subplot

A minor plot, a plot less important than the principal plot of a dramatic piece, an underplot.

subscription

The purchase of theatre tickets for a series of performances, usually for a season, by arrangement in advance, as part of a system whereby a theatrical organization is assured of sufficient financial support. Hence, *subscribe, subscriber, subscription audience, subscription theatre*, etc.

suburban theatre

A theatre in the environs of a city, usually New York or London.

subway circuit

Collectively, the theatres on the outskirts of New York City, especially in Brooklyn or the Bronx, available for alternating engagements—Especially, Vaudeville.

succès d'estime
A dramatic piece which is a recognized achievement artistically, but which does not succeed with the public; also, the reception of such a piece—A French expression (meaning "success of esteem") used in English.

summer house
See SUMMER THEATRE.

summer stock
STOCK (which see) as a summer affair, although nowadays it has frequently become associated with package arrangements. Hence *summer stock theatre, summer stock company.*

summer theatre; summer house
A theatre or acting company producing plays in the summer only. [Formerly, according to British practice, in London, a *summer theatre* (or *summer house*) might obtain a license to produce legitimate drama when the patent theatres (WINTER THEATRES) were closed—Late 18th and early 19th centuries. Hence *summer manager,* etc.]

sunburner
A combination gas-light and air cleanser in an auditorium—19th century.

Sunday theatre club
In British terminology, a STAGE SOCIETY (which see) offering its productions on Sundays.

sun spot; sunspot
A strong spotlight used to simulate sunlight.

supe
Short for SUPERNUMERARY. Also, to serve as a supernumerary.

super
Short for SUPERNUMERARY.

super master; super-master
A person in charge of supernumeraries. Called also *head of the supers.*

supernumerary; short forms, **supe, super**
An extra, a walk-on, sometimes a person who is not regularly employed as an actor.

supper room; supper-room
In British terminology, a place where patrons could watch music-hall shows while eating supper, a kind of cabaret—19th century.

supper-turn
A turn played in a continuous-performance theatre during the dinner hour—Vaudeville.

support
An actor who plays opposite a star; collectively, the actors performing with a star. Also, to act with a star; in the passive voice, *be supported by*, to have a star role in a cast including other actors whose names are given. Hence *supporting actor, supporting cast, supporting role.*

sure fire; sure-fire
Certain to succeed, as, a *sure-fire act.*

surf
In British terminology, an actor, or sometimes any person of the theatre, who takes other work during the day.

surrealism
In the theatre, since the 1920s, a neo-romantic, anti-naturalistic dramatic or stage style, deliberately fantastic and distorting, using images supposed to come from the unconscious (that is, subconscious) mind. Hence *surrealist*, etc.

suspended
Said of a character in a dramatic piece who for a while has no lines to speak.

suspense
Short for DRAMATIC SUSPENSE.

suspension arm
A metal device, sometimes used instead of a yoke for the support of a spotlight.

swab
To apply a solution of glue to a canvas scenery patch.

swag
A term, chiefly British, for a festooned, looped-up curtain or other hanging cloth. Also, to loop up. Hence *swag border, swag curtain, swagged,* etc.

swallow
A British term for memory. Also, to memorize, and especially to do so easily.

swifter
A taut steel line, along which persons or objects can slide.

swinging flat
A flat which is hinged to swing around an upright.

swinging stage; swing stage
A JACK-KNIFE STAGE.

swing joint
A flat circular metal device by means of which a lighting unit can be fastened to a stand so that the unit may be turned.

swing stage
A JACK-KNIFE STAGE.

switchboard, switch-board; short form, board
A panel on which are mounted all the controls for the electrical equipment needed on the stage or in the auditorium, usually but not necessarily located on the stage. The complete term is *stage (lighting) switchboard.* Hence *switchboard operator.*

369

sword dance
A dramatic entertainment, consisting of dialogue, sword dancing, and instrumental music; from it the Saint George play developed—Medieval.

symbolic
Figurative, as, a *symbolic play*, a *symbolic setting*.

symbolism
In playwriting and stagecraft, an attempt to bring out the aesthetic meaning of a dramatic piece, by working through feeling, atmosphere, impression, suggestion, rather than through strict realism, although realism can borrow aspects of symbolism. Scenically, romantic and fanciful freedom is evident at every turn; the actor is more important than anything else, but all the elements of production are carefully synthesized; the emotional possibilities in stage lighting become important, and a single scenic detail can symbolize an entire setting. Hence *symbolist*, etc.

symmetricals
Padded TIGHTS (which see) worn by actors, acrobats, etc.

symphonic drama
A kind of pageant, historical in content, with much spectacle and music.

Syndicate, (the)
The Theatrical Syndicate, also called *the Trust* or *the Theatre* (or *Theatrical*) *Trust*, a commercial trust (1896–1916), which achieved a virtual monopoly of booking contracts in first-class theatres throughout the United States, and operated abroad as well.

synthesis
A theatrical concept which stresses the combination of the separate elements of stage production into an artistic whole.

System, (the) (*Stanislavski*)
See STANISLAVSKI METHOD.

T

tab
1. A small, often narrow, masking drop; often short for TAB BACKING. 2. Short for TABLEAU CURTAIN. 3. Short for TABLOID.

tab (backing)
A drop behind a tableau curtain. Seldom used on the legitimate stage.

tab hook
A hook with a spring, used to hang a curtain such as a DRAW TAB.

tableau
A picture presented by a group of motionless and silent actors, usual at the end of a performance or act. Plural, either *tableaus* or *tableaux*.

tableau curtain; short form, **tab curtain** or **tab(s)**
1. A curtain either behind an act curtain or used in place of one, which rises, usually in festoons, or divides and is drawn across the stage. 2. A tableau held by actors as the act curtain rises after the end of an act or play for the spectators' applause.

tableau vivant
A French expression ("living picture") used in English for a TABLEAU. Plural, *tableaux vivants*. Often italicized.

table stage
A REVOLVING STAGE, a turntable stage (see TURNTABLE).

tabloid; short form, **tab**
1. A CONDENSATION (which see). Also as *tabloid play*. 2. A short musical comedy or the like. Also as *musical tab, tab show*.

tabs
Short for TABLEAU CURTAIN—But usually TAB.

371

tack-up

tack-up
A heavy poster card about 20 by 24 inches, used in theatrical advertising to announce a production.

tag
The end, the last line or lines, of an episode, scene, act, or dramatic piece, pointing up what has gone before, or serving as a cue, or providing an effective exit for an actor; in a modern play, commonly the CURTAIN LINE (sense 2). Pertaining to a tag, as, a *speech-tag*, a *tag line*.

tail
A British term for the following: 1. A short masking border, hung from the pin rail rather than flied. 2. A LEG DROP (British: both *leg drop* and *tail*). 3. A PIGTAIL (which see).

take
In acting, to do that which will obtain the attention of the audience, especially by moving into a dominant position (usually upstage center). Thus *take (a) scene; take (the) stage.*

take a Brodie
See DO A BRODIE.

take a call (or **bow**)
To come forward, or come onstage, or remain on the stage, to acknowledge applause, usually at the end of a performance or an act, and after the closed curtain has again been raised (or drawn). Actors bow and actresses curtsy, or they give some other sign of appreciation; but when the whole company takes a call, such gestures are usually omitted.

take an encore
To perform an encore.

Take a strain on your center
A command given to a flyman, to haul on a center line to relieve a sag in the middle of a piece of scenery.

372

take in

To move scenery into a theatre; to move scenery into position, as by lowering it from the flies. Also, the moving in, or lowering, of scenery. British: *get in*.

Take it away

A command, given to a curtain operator, to open the curtain.

take out

To move scenery out of a theatre; to remove scenery from position, as by raising it into the flies. Also, the moving out, or raising, of scenery. British: GET OUT.

take the corner

A British term for the following: 1. In acting, to move toward either front corner of the stage. 2. To replace the prompter or the stage director.

take three bends and an encore

To bow three times and repeat part of a performance, when the audience has applauded heartily.

take up a cue

To respond to a cue.

take-up block

In the counterweight system, a pulley block sliding in the track, so that its weight prevents any slackening in a line passing through it.

Take your tie

A command given to a flyman, to fasten lines when scenery is satisfactorily in position.

talent scout (or agent)

A representative of a producer, etc., who watches productions in order to report on likely actors who are not yet well known.

talky play
A play which emphasizes dialogue at the expense of stage movement.

tall grass
Collectively, remote one-night stands.

tank spectacle
An AQUATIC DRAMA (which see).

tank town; tank-town; short form, tank (usually in the plural)
A small town, remote from the big theatrical centers.

tapped transformer dimmer
A British term for an AUTO-TRANSFORMER DIMMER.

tarras
An upper-stage acting area, in front of the CHAMBER—Elizabethan. Variously spelled, and sometimes modernized as *terrace*.

T-bar track
A counterweight track, in cross-section shaped like a T, fastened vertically to a wall.

team
A pair or more of actors playing together; especially when they do so regularly.

tea party
In British terminology, a morning performance to circumvent the licensing laws—18th century.

teapot style
A style of acting marked by measured formality, practiced in speech by the delivery of a rising and falling chant, and in gesture by the sweep of an extended hand downward in curving motions while the other hand rested on the hip—19th century.

tear-jerker; tearjerker
A play, or an actor, attempting through obvious appeals to sentiment to reduce an audience to tears.

teaser
1. A short horizontal curtain (border) or flat, neutral in color, used to mask the flies and to frame the top of the inner stage opening at any desired height just behind the front curtain and just in front of the TORMENTORS. British: Usually *proscenium border*. 2. An advertisement inviting attention to a play the name of which is withheld.

teaser curtain
A teaser which is a curtain rather than a flat piece.

teaser drapery
A curtain partially covering the top of the inner proscenium, made of the same color as the act curtain.

teaser position
The BRIDGE POSITION (which see).

teaser thickness
The THICKNESS PIECE (which see) in a BOX TEASER (which see).

technical
Pertaining to the arts and skills of stage production other than acting, such as the preparation and handling or operation of scenery, lighting, etc. Hence *technical department*, etc.

technical director
The person working under the stage manager who has charge of all the technical aspects of a production, such as the construction of scenery and the operation of equipment, both before and during a run.

technical rehearsal
A rehearsal of scenes at which the technical personnel practice all their operations, usually in conjunction with the actors'

technician

rehearsal of business, movement, and cues. British: *scene rehearsal.*

technician
Short for STAGE TECHNICIAN.

technique
A general method, or a specific application of a general method, in any aspect of the theatre arts, as, *acting technique, dramatic technique, stage technique, theatrical technique.*

telegraph
In acting, to give the audience a signal, such as a glance or gesture, to convey the information that one is about to say or do something. Hence *telegraphing* (noun).

telescope
To speed up one's acting so that one's speech or business overlaps that of another actor. Hence *telescoping* (noun).

template
A workbench on which the frames of flats are assembled.

tempo
PACE (which see).

Ten minutes!
An ACT CALL.

tennis court (or tennis-court) theatre
A tennis court (for court tennis) used for the production of plays; later, one converted into a theatre—16th and 17th centuries.

ten percenter; ten-percenter
A nickname for an agent who charges ten per cent.

tension
Short for DRAMATIC TENSION.

376

tension idler
A TAKE-UP BLOCK (which see).

tension pulley
A block on the stage floor, used to keep a hauling line taut.

tent show; tent-show
A show produced in a tent.

tent theatre
A theatre under canvas, commonly a circus tent; also collectively. Hence *musical tent theatre* (for musical shows).

ten-twent'-thirt'; ten-twenty-thirty
A sensational melodrama, stereotyped in form, with an admission scale of 10, 20, and 30 cents—Late 19th and early 20th centuries.

terrace
See TARRAS.

testa
The HEAVENS (sense 2)—Elizabethan.

tetralogy
A group of four plays dealing progressively with a single general dramatic action. Hence *tetralogic, tetralogue.*

text
A published playscript.

Thalia
The Muse of comedy—Greek mythology.

theatre
See THEATRE, the more common spelling in the theatrical profession.

theaterian
An obsolete term for an actor.

theatral
Of or pertaining to a theatre (particularly to the acting area),
or to the theatre in general.

theatre; theater
A building housing a stage for dramatic performances; such
buildings, collectively. A substitute for such a building, as, a
floating theatre, a tent theatre, an outdoor amphitheatre. See
STAGE. Of, pertaining to, or used in a theatre. By extension,
a stage; the stage; dramatic pieces or productions, collectively;
the dramatic art; the audience; an acting company. Said of a
dramatic piece or performance or of some portion thereof, in
regard to its stage effectiveness, as, That bit of business is
good (or *bad*) *theatre.* Hence *theatrecraft, theatredom, theatre-
less, theatrelike, theatreward(s), theatrewise, theatro-,* etc.

Spelling: The ending *-re* is more often used in the professional
theatre, *-er* in general American English. In England, *-er* was
more often used until the 18th century, when *-re,* which is now
the only British form, began to prevail.

theatre architect
An architect who designs theatres. Hence *theatre architecture.*

theatre art
DRAMATIC ART (which see).

theatre building
A theatre, a building housing a stage.

theatre club
A British term for a STAGE SOCIETY (which see).

theatre critic
A DRAMATIC CRITIC (which see).

theatre family
A THEATRICAL FAMILY (which see).

theatre folk; theatre-folk
The people of the theatrical world.

theatre-goer; theatregoer
A PLAY-GOER (which see). Also *theatregoing* (noun and adjective).

theatre group
An amateur acting company.

theatre history
The history, or a history, of the theatre, of the stage. Hence *theatre historian*.

theatre in the round (or **-in-the-round**)
A theatre using the arena style of production; also collectively.

théâtre intime
A French expression used in English for an INTIMATE THEATRE. Usually italicized.

theatre-keeper
A STAGE-KEEPER (which see).

theatre laboratory
A DRAMA WORKSHOP (which see). See also LABORATORY THEATRE.

theatre manager
A person who manages a theatre.

theatre musician
A musician who plays music in a theatre.

theatre owner; short form, owner
A person to whom a theatre building belongs.

theatre party
1. A special performance, such as a benefit. 2. Collectively, persons who buy a block of (or all) tickets for a performance, usually so that they may sit together; any group of persons who attend the theatre together.

379

theatre people
People connected with the theatre.

theatre plant
A theatre building and its equipment, particularly in regard to its facilities for production.

theatre proprietor; short form, **proprietor**
A term, chiefly British, for a THEATRE OWNER.

Theatre Regulation Act
See THEATRES ACT.

Theatre Royal
In British terminology, a theatre authorized under royal charter or patent, with various advantages, as, formerly (1660–1837), monopoly and subsidy.

Theatres Act
The common name for an Act of Parliament (Statutes 6 and 7 of Victoria, c. 68), 1843, controlling the production of stage entertainments and the use of buildings as theatres through licenses (in London, except for Drury Lane and Covent Garden, and in places of royal residence, issued by the Lord Chamberlain; elsewhere, issued by local authorities). This Act is still in force. It followed the LICENSING ACT (which see). Called also *Act for Regulating Theatres, Theatre Regulation Act.*

theatre school
A DRAMA SCHOOL.

theatre society
A body of persons interested in the theatre.

theatre theatrical, (the)
In dramatic composition and production, emphasis on the theatre for the theatre's sake, on theatricality, on theatricalism.

theatre ticket; short form, **ticket**
A spectator's admission slip, usually made of cardboard and consisting of two portions, the stub and the coupon (or check).

theatre treasurer; short form, **treasurer**
1. A theatre official in charge of the finances of a theatre or of a production. 2. A box-office treasurer.

theatre workshop; short form, **workshop**
A DRAMA WORKSHOP (which see).

theatric
1. Theatrical; suited for stage performance. So also *theatricable*. 2. See THEATRICS.

theatrical
1. Connected with or pertaining to the theatre, especially acting, often with the favorable connotation of suitability or competence, or with the unfavorable connotation of affectation or extravagance. Hence *theatrically, theatricalness*. See DRAMATIC, STAGY, THEATRICALISM, THEATRICALITY. 2. Pertaining to THEATRICALISM (which see). 3. See THEATRICALS.

theatrical agent
An AGENT (which see), especially one who combines such functions as those of a PLAY AGENT and TALENT SCOUT.

theatrical architect
An architect who designs theatres. Hence *theatrical architecture*.

theatrical art
DRAMATIC ART (which see) in the general sense, collectively, in the singular or the plural.

theatrical attorney
An attorney who specializes in matters dealing with theatre law, such as the preparation of contracts.

theatrical boarding house
A boarding house catering especially to theatre people. The type is now rare.

theatrical bobbinet(te) ; short form, **bobbinet(te)**
THEATRICAL GAUZE (which see).

theatrical career; short form, **career**
An actor's professional life, calling, occupation.

theatrical club
1. A subscription theatre organization. See SUBSCRIPTION and STAGE SOCIETY. 2. A social group of theatre people.

theatrical coach
A person who trains actors.

theatrical cold cream
A special cold cream used in theatrical make-up.

theatrical convention
A STAGE CONVENTION.

theatrical critic
A DRAMA CRITIC (which see). Hence *theatrical criticism*.

theatrical decoration
STAGE DECORATION (which see).

theatrical face powder
A powder used for stage make-up, having special adhesive characteristics.

theatrical family
A family which counts several members who have appeared on the stage.

theatrical gauze; short form, **gauze**
A thin open-weave linen fabric, semi-transparent (but more transparent than scrim), used as a drop. When lighted from behind, it gives an effect of dream, mist, haze, etc. It is also

called *theatrical bobbinet,* and is sometimes confused with
SCRIM and THEATRICAL NET.

theatrical hardware; short form, **hardware**
Collectively, small pieces of stage equipment made of metal,
such as brace cleats and hanger irons.

theatrical history
The history of the theatre, of the stage.

theatricalism
1. A personal feature, quality, or peculiarity usual on or suited
to the stage. 2. A concept in production emphasizing the importance of the imaginative use of the conventions, artifices,
and exaggerations of the stage, and opposed to realism, naturalism, and illusionism. Hence *theatricalist* (noun and adjective).
See also THEATRE THEATRICAL, THEATRICAL, THEATRICALITY.

theatricality
That which is theatrical. See THEATRICAL, THEATRICALISM.

theatricalize
To dramatize, prepare for, perform in, or attend the theatre.
Hence *theatricalization.*

theatrical lamp dip; short forms, **lamp dip, dip**
A special lacquer dye for stage lamps. British: Also, *dope.*

theatrical lawyer
A THEATRICAL ATTORNEY (which see).

theatrical net; short form, **net**
An open-weave fabric, used as a hanging on which cut-out foliage can be mounted, or to reinforce cut-out foliage borders. It
is sometimes confused with THEATRICAL GAUZE and SCRIM.

theatrical paste
A flour paste which, mixed with glue and water, is used in
covering flats and in making papier mâché.

theatrical people
People connected with the theatre.

theatrical rooming house
A THEATRICAL BOARDING HOUSE (which see).

theatricals
1. DRAMATICS (sense 1). 2. Actors—The term rarely occurs in the singular.

theatrical speech
STAGE ENGLISH (which see).

theatrical supply company (or **house**)
A business firm which furnishes supplies and equipment for the stage.

theatrical technique
Stage technique, STAGE CRAFT (which see).

theatrical world, (the)
The world or domain of the theatre, of show business; the body of people principally concerned with the stage.

theatrician
A person specializing in dramatic production.

theatricism
THEATRICALISM (which see).

theatricize
1. To make theatrical. 2. To perform.

theatrics
The art and skills of stage production.

theatrize
To THEATRICIZE (which see).

theatrophone
A telephonic device, formerly sometimes used in theatres to permit members of the audience (those hard of hearing or

placed in seats where there was an acoustical difficulty) to listen to the sounds of a stage performance. Hence *theatrophonic*.

theatry
An obsolete term for THEATRE.

theayter
A misspelling and mispronunciation of THEATRE, used humorously.

theme
1. The principle topic or thesis of a dramatic piece. Hence *thematic* (adjective). 2. An actor's improvisation in verse on a subject provided by a member of the audience, as a form of stage entertainment following a dramatic performance—Elizabethan.

theme song
A tune repeated as a motif—Chiefly Musical comedy.

thesis play (or **drama**)
A DRAMA OF IDEAS (which see, for comment on related types of play). Hence also *thesis playwright*.

thespian
Pertaining to acting, to the drama, as, the *thespian art*. Hence, an actor; also in the forms *child of Thespis, thesp,* etc. Derived from the name of Thespis, a Greek tragic poet of the sixth century B.C., who is said to have first introduced an actor into dramatic representations (which until then had been performed only by a chorus with a leader).

thickness
Short for THICKNESS PIECE; but sometimes, a painted imitation of this. Of the nature of or equipped with a thickness piece, as, a *thickness door*.

thickness piece; short form, **thickness**
A narrow board, flat, or other piece of rigid material, placed at right angles to a piece of scenery so as to give an appearance of depth, thickness, and solidity to an opening or a wall.

thimble
A grooved metal ring, commonly tear-shaped, used in the theatre
on a ring or eye to keep a loop of rope or wire (an eye splice)
from chafing.

thinking part; thinking-part
A role without lines.

third company
A company which is performing on the road or abroad in a
play that is simultaneously being performed by two other companies.

third day
A benefit (the third) performance for a dramatist—Restoration.

three
See IN THREE.

three-a-day
A theatre holding three performances each day—Vaudeville.

three-fold
A scenic unit made up of three flats hinged together.

three-quarter position
An actor's body position, when he faces one of the back corners
of the stage, or is turned only a quarter from a position with
his back to the audience.

three-sheet
1. To exaggerate, boast, lie. 2. To stand in the lobby, after one
has acted in a performance, to converse with the departing
spectators. 3. Of an act, to have the leading part—Chiefly
Vaudeville.

In all senses, from the name of a fairly large size of theatrical
advertising poster used on billboards, etc. (see SHEET).

threesome (scene)
A scene for three actors.

three-step
A stage stair unit with three steps. British: *three-tread*.

three-tread
A British term for a THREE-STEP (which see).

thriller
A play which provides the excitement of suspense, danger, violent action, or the like, as, a mystery play or a melodrama.

throw
The effective distance to which light beams can be projected, as, a *long throw*.

throw a (or the) line
To prompt, as *Throw me the line*.

throw away
1. To underemphasize or underplay lines or business, either deliberately (in order to pass rapidly over a momentary situation offering little opportunity to an actor, or to bring out other lines or business by contrast) or aimlessly (from weakness in technique). Thus, *throw away one's lines, throw it away*. Hence, a *throw-away line*, etc. 2. As one word, or hyphenated: A piece of printed matter advertising a production, sometimes offering a reduction in ticket price.

throw line; throwline
A British term for a LASH LINE.

thrust out
To push a heavy property on (or forward onto) the stage—Elizabethan stage direction.

thunder-barrel
A THUNDER CRASH (which see).

thunder box
A device used to obtain a thunder effect, either a box containing channels along which run iron balls (called also *rabbit hutch, rumble box, thunder roller, thunder run*) or a weighted wagon with unbalanced wheels which is pushed across the back of the stage (called also *rumble cart, thunder cart*).

thunder cart
See THUNDER BOX.

thunder crash
A device used to obtain a thunder effect, as, a suspended barrel from which stones are dropped onto iron sheets.

thunder drum
A drum, or drum-like device, used to obtain a thunder effect. See also THUNDER BOX.

thunder roller
See THUNDER BOX.

thunder run
See THUNDER BOX.

thunder sheet; thunder curtain
A device used to obtain a thunder effect, a suspended sheet of metal (commonly iron) which is shaken by a handle or struck with a drumstick.

thunder tank
A device used to obtain a thunder effect, a suspended galvanized iron tank which is struck with a drumstick.

thyratron dimmer
A remote-control dimmer of the electronic type, employing a heavy-duty grid-controlled thyratron tube as the dimming element.

388

ticket
1. Short for THEATRE TICKET and such more specific terms as *box ticket*. Hence *ticket-buyer, ticket-holder*, etc. 2. An obsolete term for a printed advertisement of a play; a bill or handbill.

ticket agency
A business office, independent of a theatre, where a playgoer may buy tickets upon payment of an extra fee. Hence *ticket agent* (clerk, or agency operator). British: Usually *booking office, library*.

ticket box
Short for TICKET-TAKER'S BOX.

ticket broker; short form, broker
A ticket agent (see TICKET AGENCY).

ticket checker; short form, checker
An alternative British term for a TICKET TAKER.

ticket collector
A TICKET TAKER.

ticket gouger
A SCALPER.

ticket hustling
Illegal speculation in tickets.

ticket night
Formerly, an arrangement whereby theatrical people on a given night could receive half of the proceeds from tickets they could sell.

ticket office
An office where theatre tickets are sold.

ticket rack; short form, rack
A board with slots, in a box office, where tickets are kept until they are sold.

ticket-scalper
See TICKET SPECULATOR, SCALPER.

ticket seller; ticket-seller; ticketseller
A person who sells tickets to spectators, usually the box-office treasurer.

ticket speculator; short forms, **speculator, spec**
A person who buys theatre tickets at the box office in order to re-sell them at a profit. Called also SCALPER.

ticket stub; ticket-stub; short form, **stub**
The portion of a theatre ticket detached and retained by a ticket-taker.

ticket taker; ticket-taker
A person who collects tickets of admission from spectators. British: *check taker, (ticket) checker.*

ticket-taker's box; short forms, **ticket box, box**
A container into which ticket stubs are dropped by a ticket-taker as the spectators enter the theatre. See PAY BOX (British).

ticket window
A box-office window. British: WICKET.

tie cord
A cord used as a TIE LINE (which see).

tie-in (system)
An illegal requirement by a ticket broker that a patron, in order to get tickets for one performance, must also buy tickets for another performance.

tie line
A cord or rope used to fasten a curtain to a batten.

tie off
1. To make fast a line. But sometimes *tie off* implies a more temporary fastening than MAKE FAST. Also, to close the lock of

a counterweight unit in order to make fast the lines. 2. Hyphenated: A knot used in tying lash lines.

tie-off cleat
A small metal cleat, screwed into the stile at the top of a flat, used as a tying-place for a lash line.

tie-off hook
A TIE-OFF SCREW.

tie-off pin
A pin of wood or metal on a pin rail, used as a tying-place for fly lines.

tie-off rail
The lower of the two rows of pins comprising a PIN RAIL (which see), used for the permanent fastening of a line during a performance. Called also *trim rail*.

tie-off screw
A screw used instead of a tie-off cleat.

tier
1. One of several theatre galleries. 2. One of several rows of theatre seats or boxes, especially when these rise behind or above one another.—In both senses, to arrange or to be arranged in this manner.

tights
A tight-fitting garment, usually covering the legs and lower part of the body, sometimes worn by actors (as in a costume play placed in a period when such garments were commonly worn), dancers, etc. Less often called a *skintight*, or *skins*. See FLESHINGS (FLESHING TIGHTS), SYMMETRICALS.

tilting fork; short form, fork
A YOKE (which see).

time
1. In the plural: The dates of a touring company's engagements. 2. A specification in a dramatic composition, program, etc., of

time book

the supposed time of the action at the beginning of a scene or act. 3. See BIG TIME, SMALL TIME.

time book

A British term for a TIME SHEET.

time cue

A cue of some duration, rather than merely momentary.

time sheet

A stage manager's report of the exact time taken for scenes, acts, and intermissions, with comments on the spectators' response and any unusual events. British: Also as *time book*.

timing

1. PACE. 2. RHYTHM.

tin beard

A beard made of crepe hair, improperly smoothed into an actor's make-up.

tin hat

A FUNNEL (which see).

Tin Pan Alley

A name for an area in New York City, applied first to 28th Street near Broadway, currently to the vicinity of Broadway and 50th Street, where the publishers and composers of popular music center their activities. A name for similar areas in other cities. Hence the song writing and selling business in general.

tip-jack

A triangular jack on rollers, used to shift scenery, especially in large units.

tire

An archaic term for attire. Hence several terms, variously spelled (thus, *tyring*), peculiar to or commonly used in connection with the stage, pertaining to dress and wardrobe, in the

Elizabethan and Restoration theatre: *tiremaid* (or *tiring maid*), *tireman*, *tirewoman* (or *tiring woman*), *tiring*, etc. See TIRING-HOUSE, TIRING-ROOM.

tired business man; tired businessman
A proverbial type of theatregoer, supposed to relish light entertainment rather than heavy.

tiring house; tiring-house; attiring-house; tirehouse
A portion of the theatre backstage used as a place for dressing and storage, for a green room, etc., and sometimes for an inner stage—Elizabethan and Restoration.

tiring-room; attiring-room; tireroom
A dressing room, or other place for dressing—Elizabethan and Restoration.

title
1. The name of a dramatic composition. 2. Short for TITLE BOARD.

title board; title-board; titleboard; short form, title
A placard displayed on the stage to announce the title of a play; sometimes, a LOCALITY BOARD (which see)—Elizabethan.

title role; title-role
The role of the character from whose name a dramatic composition takes its title. Called also *title character, title-part*.

Toby
1. A comic character type, a boisterous, blundering yokel as the protagonist. Hence *Toby play* (or *show*), a repertory favorite.
2. Punch's dog, in the Punch and Judy shows.

toggle
Short for TOGGLE IRON, TOGGLE RAIL.

toggle bar
A TOGGLE RAIL.

toggle (iron)
A metal device, such as a socket, used to fasten a toggle rail to a stile.

toggle (rail)
A wooden batten used horizontally at the middle of a flat to strengthen it.

toggle shoe; short form, **shoe**
A TOGGLE IRON.

Tom show; Tomshow
A production of *Uncle Tom's Cabin* by a touring company; also, the company itself—19th century. Thus also *Tom company*, a *Tommer* (actor in a Tom show), *Tomming the tanks*.

tonal lighting
Lighting which blends into a single soft color the illumination provided by various colored lamps.

Tony
A nickname for one of the several awards given annually by the American Theatre Wing for outstanding contributions to the theatre. Named for Antoinette Perry, the American actress, manager, and producer (d. 1946). Plural, *Tonys*.

toomler
A comedian on the BORSCHT CIRCUIT (which see) who keeps up a continual tumult for the entertainment of hotel guests.

tooth enamel
A liquid used either to conceal or to whiten an actor's teeth.

top
1. To BUILD (sense 1), to speak louder, faster, more intensely, at a higher pitch. Usually as *top it*. Also *topping* (noun). 2. The highest price asked for seats (excluding the box seats) at a given performance, as, a *$4.40 top, top prices*. 3. Short for PARALLEL TOP.

394

top banana
The comedian with the top billing on the program—Burlesque.

top billing
Star billing (see STAR).

top cues
To TOP (which see) after another actor has spoken.

top drop
Formerly, a border.

top lighting
The illumination of the upper part of a scene.

top liner; topliner
A British term for a headliner (see under HEADLINE).

top of the bill, (to be)
In British terminology, to be a headliner (see HEADLINE)—Music hall.

topping the bill
A British term for headlining (see under HEADLINE).

top prices
See TOP (sense 2).

tormentor; (infrequently) **tormenter**
One of a pair of narrow curtains or flats, neutral in color, just behind the front curtain and teaser, used to frame the sides of the inner proscenium opening at any desired width and to mask the off-stage space at the sides; formerly, a sliding extension of the proscenium wing.

tormentor batten
A pipe batten (see BATTEN), rising vertically from the stage floor behind a tormentor, used as a mounting for tormentor lights.

395

tormentor drapery
A curtain, of the same color as the act curtain, partially covering the side of the inner proscenium.

tormentor entrance
A space which may be used for an entrance, between a tormentor and the proscenium arch.

tormentor flipper
A FLIPPER (sense 1) used with a tormentor.

tormentor follower
A curtain or flat used as an adjustable supplementary tormentor.

tormentor leg
A tormentor in the form of a LEG DROP.

tormentor light
A light, usually a spotlight or a strip light, mounted on a tormentor batten for side lighting.

tormentor tower; short form, **tower**
A light tower used for tormentor lights.

tormentor wing
A wing flat used as a tormentor, or the off-stage space behind a tormentor.

toupee tape
A double-faced adhesive tape, used to attach false hair in making up.

tour
A trip made by a theatrical company to give a series of performances in different towns. See the ROAD. Also, to make or cause to make such a trip. Hence, *on tour*, a *tour staff*, a *touring company*, *tour with* (a play, a company).

tower
Short for LIGHT TOWER, SPOTLIGHT TOWER, TORMENTOR TOWER. Hence said of lighting units mounted on a light tower, as, a *tower flood*.

town
A British term for London, as in *town production, town staff,* etc.

town theatre
A community theatre.

toy theatre
A miniature stage for use as a child's plaything, such as one utilizing the JUVENILE DRAMA (which see). Hence *toy stage, toy-theatre play,* etc.

T-plate
A flat T-shaped piece of metal pierced with holes, which is screwed into a TOGGLE to hold it to a STILE.

track
Short for counterweight track (see COUNTERWEIGHT SYSTEM) or CURTAIN TRACK.

track bracket
Short for CURTAIN TRACK BRACKET.

tracker line (or wire)
A wire used for the remote mechanical control of a dimmer or other piece of apparatus.

tracker wire board
A stage switchboard using tracker wires for the control of dimmers.

tragedian
1. A person who acts in tragic roles. Feminine form, *tragedienne*. 2. A writer of tragedies.

tragedienne
Feminine form of TRAGEDIAN.

tragedy
A play which, typically, is serious, solemn, sorrowful, and ends disastrously, usually fatally, for the central figure; also collectively. By extension, the composition or acting of such plays, and the art of doing so. Hence *tragedist, tragedy of revenge,* etc.

tragic
Of, pertaining to, appropriate to, or containing the elements of tragedy. Hence also *tragic actor, tragic author, tragical,* etc. Humorously, applied incongruously to light forms of entertainment, as, a *tragic extravaganza*—Chiefly 19th century.

tragic carpet
A ground cloth of green baize upon which actors in tragedy could lie in "death" to keep their costumes clean—17th to 19th centuries.

tragic error
A fatal mistake made by the principal figure in a tragedy—From the doctrine of *hamartia* (see TRAGIC FLAW).

tragic flaw
A trait of character in the principal figure of a tragedy which leads to his doom; the outward error proceeding from such a trait—From the doctrine of *hamartia* ("defect of character," "false step," "mistake," "error," etc.) in Aristotle's *Poetics.*

tragic history
A tragedy, especially a historical tragedy.

tragic irony
DRAMATIC IRONY, applied to tragedy.

Tragic Muse
Melpomene; the spirit of tragedy.

tragi-comedy; tragicomedy
A play combining some of the features of both tragedy and comedy; especially, a play which is serious and leads to the expectation of catastrophe, but which ends happily or at least not fatally. Hence also *tragicomedian, tragicomic,* etc. See also DRAMATIC ROMANCE.

trailer (wing)
A wing, narrow and suspended from a track, which trails a curtain behind it when it is pulled onstage.

trailing tab
A TABLEAU CURTAIN which is suspended from a curtain track.

train call
A notice, to actors in a touring company, of the time of a coming train journey.

trampolin(e)
A framework supporting a net, canvas, or webbing upon which a performer may safely jump or fall from a height; also, a mat with springs for the same purpose—Chiefly Ballet and Vaudeville. British spelling also *tramplin.*

tranche de vie, (une)
A French term used in English for a SLICE OF LIFE (which see). Often italicized.

transformation (scene)
A portion of an entertainment in which the entire setting is changed as if by magic, in view of the audience, through the use of flaps, SCRIM, lighting effects, etc.; especially, such a scene in PANTOMIME (which see, sense 2), during which the characters of the opening undergo a "transformation" into those of the harlequinade.

transitional scene
A scene of no particular dramatic importance in itself, but serving to connect two important scenes.

translucency
A drop curtain through which light can shine, usually dye-painted and with the rear partially opaque.

transparency
A transparent curtain, commonly one of linen which is illuminated from behind so that a painted scene appears to change as the light increases.

Transpontine melodrama
In British terminology, sensational melodramas, collectively; originally those produced in London theatres on the south side of the Thames—19th century. Hence *Transpontine hero*, etc.

trap
An opening for the passage of actors, objects, etc., commonly in the stage floor or in a piece of scenery, concealed by a cover (such as a flap). Also in the form *trap door*. Hence, a STAR TRAP, *trap-cellar*, (*-dock, -room*), *trap work*, a *trapped area*, a *trapped stage*, etc.

trap light
In British terminology, a footlight which could be raised or lowered through a trap in the stage floor—Chiefly 18th century.

trappe anglaise
A French expression used in England for an ENGLISH TRAP (which see)—19th century. Usually italicized.

traveler
1. A draw or TRAILING TAB, a DRAW CURTAIN. British: Usually *traverse curtain*. Hence *front traveler*, etc. 2. A CURTAIN TRACK (which see). 3. A TRAILER WING (which see). 4. A device by means of which a performer can simulate aerial flight, such as a kind of cart (on tracks above the stage) from which hang wires to be attached to the body.

traveler curtain
A TRAVELER (sense 1).

400

traveler track
A CURTAIN TRACK.

traveling company
A touring company. Called also a *traveling theatre*.

traveling cyclorama
An ARM CYCLORAMA (which see).

traveling stage
A stage which can be moved from one position to another within a theatre or, as in the Elizabethan period, from one outdoor location to another.

traveller
See TRAVELER.

traverse
1. Short for TRAVERSE CURTAIN. 2. The recess revealed by the drawing aside of a traverse curtain—Restoration.

traverse (curtain)
A draw curtain, especially one of a pair. U.S.: Usually TRAVELER.

travesty
A dramatic composition which burlesques or parodies another work. Also, to burlesque or parody.

tread
See STAGE STEP.

tread the boards
To act on stage. See BOARD.

treadmill
Short for TREADMILL STAGE.

treadmill (stage)
An endless belt on which actors and scenery may appear to be moving while remaining in view of the audience.

treasurer
Short for *box-office treasurer* (see BOX OFFICE), COMPANY
TREASURER, THEATRE TREASURER.

tree
A LIGHT TOWER with branch-like arms.

tree tab
A TAB (sense 1) shaped like a tree top, to go with a painted
tree trunk.

trestle stage
A stage mounted on a trestle.

triangle play
A play dealing with the love entanglements of two men and one
woman, or two women and one man.

triangular movement
Stage movement in which three or more actors assume positions
corresponding to the points of a triangle.

tributary theatre
Collectively or individually, the professional and amateur theatres outside New York City, or at least outside the Broadway
theatre district. This expression is used in recognition of the
enriching flow of dramatic compositions, actors, techniques,
and ideas from such theatres into the principal theatre center.

trick
A device, such as a trap, a transparency, a piece of scenery
which can be suddenly altered, used to create an illusion or
deception. Hence *trick change, trick scene,* etc. See also TRANS-
FORMATION SCENE.

trick line
A cord or line, especially a black string, used for the removal
of an object (as, a property) from the stage undetected by the
audience, or for the movement of scenery in quick-change
effects.

trigger
A handle beneath the stage floor used to control the movement of a SLIDER.

trilogy
A group of three plays dealing progressively with a single general dramatic action. Hence *trilogic*, *trilogist*, etc.

trim
1. The adjustment of scenery so that it is hung in its proper position, as, the *trim* of a piece, or *in* (*on*) *trim* (British: *on the dead*). Also, to adjust scenery in its proper position. British: to *dead*. 2. Decorative woodwork. Hence, *facing trim*, etc. Also, to add such woodwork to a setting. 3. Collectively, small pieces of furniture not intended for any important use.

trim block
A TRIMMING CLAMP.

trim chain
Short for BATTEN TRIMMING CHAIN.

trim clamp
Short for TRIMMING CLAMP.

trimmer
A TRIMMING CLAMP.

trimming
TRIM (especially in sense 1).

trimming chain
Short for BATTEN TRIMMING CHAIN.

trimming clamp; short form, **trim clamp**
A metal device, used to attach rope lines to a counterweight arbor or to sandbags, so that scenery can be held in trim.

trim prop
1. A property, such as a picture, which does not rest on the stage floor. 2. TRIM (sense 3).

403

trim rail
The lower of the two rows of pins comprising a PIN RAIL (which see), used for tying off lines when scenery has been trimmed. Called also *tie-off rail.*

trip
1. A rope line used to trim a piece of scenery. Also, to trim scenery with such a line. 2. To clew a cloth.

tripe
In British terminology, a length of stage cable running from a light batten to a stage pocket.

triple bill
A theatre program consisting of three separate dramatic pieces.

trope
A recitative or dialogue interpolated into the Mass, as, to celebrate some special festival—Medieval.

trough
A long container, now usually of metal, in which lamps are set. Hence *footlight trough,* etc.

troupe
An acting company, especially a touring company. Also, to tour; to take productions on a tour, as, to *troupe* Shakespeare.

trouper
An actor; an actor who is touring; a seasoned veteran of the hardships of many tours.

truck
A term, chiefly British, for the following: 1. A SCENERY WAGON. 2. A cyclorama floodlight on casters.

trunnion
One of the two pivots on which a yoke or tilting fork turns.

try back
A rehearsal direction, calling for the actors to repeat part of their performance.

try it (out) on the dog
To try out a theatrical piece, usually outside of the city where it will eventually be given its principal production. Hence *doghouse, dog show, dog town.*

try out; try-out; tryout
1. A trial public performance of a production (usually in an out-of-town theatre; sometimes repeated there or elsewhere) before the major opening. To give such a performance; to open or continue as a trial production. Hence *try-out theatre, try-out tour, try-out town,* etc. 2. An AUDITION (sense 1). 3. Any theatrical experimentation, especially during a rehearsal.

tube dimmer
A dimmer which is controlled by a gas-filled electronic tube. British: *valve dimmer.*

tucket
A trumpet call, usually announcing the arrival of a person of high degree—Elizabethan stage direction.

Tudor drama
The English drama of the Tudor period (1485–1603), covering the reigns of Henry VII, Henry VIII, Edward VI, Mary, and Elizabeth I.

tumble
In British terminology, to clew a cloth, to raise a drop (or a hinged flat) by pulling on lines attached to top and bottom so that the piece folds in two or three sections. See also TUMBLER BATTEN.

tumbler batten; short form, **tumbler**
In British terminology, a batten, used inside canvas scenery which is rolled up, to hold the canvas stiff and straight, or used hinged between two flats as part of a three-fold.

turkey

A show which fails deservedly. Formerly, said of actors (*turkey actors*) who got up weak Thanksgiving productions which the indulgent public patronized as an annual tradition—U.S. only.

turn

A term, chiefly British, for an ACT—Vaudeville.

turnaway, (the)

Collectively, persons who cannot be sold tickets because the house is full. Hence *turnaway money*.

turn in

To CLOSE IN (sense 2).

turning point

A crisis.

turn out

In acting, to OPEN UP (which see).

turn over

To examine a pack of flats.

turntable

A revolving circular platform, usually part of a revolving stage, and either forming part of the stage floor or resting on the stage floor by means of casters.

turret

An upper part of the TIRING HOUSE, above the CHAMBER and TARRAS, used as a music gallery, as a place for the creation of sound effects, and as an acting area—Elizabethan.

twelve-penny room (or box)

A gentleman's room, a room or box in a gallery next the stage —Elizabethan.

two-a-day

A theatre offering only two performances daily, and hence belonging to the big-time circuit (see BIG TIME)—Vaudeville.

two-faced door
A door on the stage, two sides of which are visible to the audience.

two-fer; twofer
1. Short for TWO FOR ONE. 2. An electrical device in which one plug is coupled to two receptacles.

two-fold; twofold
A pair of flats booked (hinged) to fold together face to face, and therefore able to stand without support. British: *book flat*. Hence also *two-fold wing*.

two for one; two-for-one; short form, twofer
Two tickets offered to the public at the price of one, or a card authorizing such a transaction, used to obtain audiences in a slack period or during a poor run.

two-leaf ceiling
A BOOK CEILING.

two-line gag
A gag set up in two parts, cue and response.

two on the aisle
Two seats together (one of them on the aisle) such as are preferred by play reviewers.

twopence coloured
See PENNY PLAIN, TWOPENCE COLOURED.

twopenny gaff
See GAFF.

two-penny gallery
See PENNY GALLERY.

two-penny room
A room or box in the galleries, in contradistinction to the two-penny gallery (see PENNY GALLERY)—Elizabethan.

407

twosome (scene)
A scene for two actors.

two-step
A stage stair unit with two steps. British: *two-tread*.

two-tread
A British term for a TWO-STEP (which see).

two weeks under, one week out
A stop clause in a theatre lease, giving a theatre owner the right to require a producer to close or move a show within one week if the weekly gross receipts drop below a certain figure.

tyer
A canvas strip used to tie up rolled drops which are not in use.

type
1. An actor suited to one kind of role. Also, to cast an actor, especially more than once, in one kind of role for which he seems particularly apt. Hence *type casting, typing,* etc. 2. A role with certain characteristics, recurring in drama.

type-cast
To TYPE (which see). Hence *typecasting, type casting.*

typing
Type casting (see TYPE).

U

U.C.; UC
Abbreviation of UP CENTER.

U.L.; UL
Abbreviation of UP LEFT.

U.L.C.; ULC
Abbreviation of UP LEFT CENTER.

underact
To UNDERPLAY (which see). Hence *underacting* (noun), etc.

underaction
1. A minor portion of the dramatic action (see ACTION, sense 2). 2. ACTION (sense 1) which is weak; the result of underacting (see UNDERACT).

underline
A brief notice of the name and opening date of the next attraction at a theatre, printed at the bottom of an advertisement of the current production.

underplay
To underact, to play weakly, to underemphasize lines or business. Hence, as nouns, *underplaying* or *underplay*.

underplot
A SUBORDINATE PLOT.

under-rouge
WET ROUGE.

understage space
A theatre cellar (see CELLAR).

understudy
To learn the role of another actor so that if necessary one may take his place. Also, an actor (almost always a member of the

cast) who so prepares himself. Hence *understudying* (noun), *understudy rehearsal* (or *call*), etc. See also WALKING UNDERSTUDY.

understudy list
A roster of understudies, posted by the stage manager on the call board.

undertaker
A person who produces or manages a stage production.

unemphatic
1. Said of stage business, a property, etc., which is not essential to the dramatic action, though possibly of considerable incidental value; for example, in characterization. 2. Said of an ending or curtain which is marked by some deliberately casual or anti-climactic piece of business or CURTAIN LINE (sense 2), for greater realism.

unhappy ending
In a play, a conclusion which is unfavorable for the characters with whom the spectator (or reader) is especially sympathetic.

union
1. Said of a counterweight system (and of its parts: grid, set of lines, etc.) in which the lines are fastened permanently to a batten at one end and to the counterweight arbor at the other end, so that the movement of a weight shifts the scenery up and down without the necessity of handling the individual lines. 2. A labor union, as, the *International Alliance of Theatrical Stage Employees.* Called also *stage* (or *theatrical*) *union.*

unit
1. A piece of scenery, with its component parts if any, which is inserted into a flat, as, a *fireplace unit.* 2. A piece of scenery which forms part of a UNIT SETTING (which see), as, a *unit flat.* 3. A piece of lighting equipment, consisting not only of a lamp (or lamps) but also of other devices such as a reflector and shield.

410

unit frame
A UNIT SETTING.

unit scenery
Scenery used in a unit setting.

unit setting
A stage setting which consists of units of scenery capable of re-arrangement in various combinations for different scenes, though some sections may remain in place through more than one scene and various units may be introduced or taken off.

unity
Short for DRAMATIC UNITY.

unity of action
A principle of dramatic structure, one of the three unities sup-posed by Renaissance and neo-classic critics and dramatists to have been formulated (as indeed, within certain limits, this one was) by Aristotle. Aristotle wrote that tragedy should consist of an imitation of an action that is complete, and whole, and of a certain magnitude, with a beginning, a middle, and an end, and with a logical causal relationship between the parts. This was taken by some to mean that no serious drama could con-tain both tragic and comic elements or a subplot; less strictly interpreted, the principle has survived as an influential theory.

unity of place
A principle of dramatic structure. See UNITY OF ACTION. The supposed Aristotelian doctrine, limiting the action to one local-ity, in reality was an unwarranted inference from Aristotle's unity of action.

unity of time
A principle of dramatic structure. See UNITY OF ACTION. The supposed Aristotelian doctrine, variously interpreted as limiting a tragic action to 24 or 12 hours or to the duration of the performance itself, was in reality drawn from Aristotle's not-

quite-accurate observation that the tragedy of his own time confined itself approximately to a single revolution of the sun.

university play
A play produced at a university, especially at Cambridge or Oxford during the Renaissance. See ACADEMIC DRAMA.

university theatre
A theatre in, and usually maintained by, a university; also, such theatres, collectively.

university wit
One of a group of playwrights, most of whom had been students at Cambridge or Oxford, who contributed energetically to the development of the drama—Elizabethan.

unlicensed theatre
In British terminology, a theatre not authorized to produce legitimate drama—Prior to 1843.

unpractical
Said of a piece of scenery or a property which is apparently but not actually solid, functionable, or workable.

Unreason, Abbot of
See MISRULE.

up
1. *be up* (*in one's part*) : In acting, to know one's part well. 2. *be up:* In acting, to forget one's lines or business. 3. Short for UP STAGE. 4. See FULL UP. 5. See BRING UP THE LIGHTS.

up center; abbreviation, **U.C.** or **UC**
A stage position or area, center, upstage—Sometimes, a stage direction.

upholstery drama
In British terminology, individually or collectively, plays realistically "upholstered" as to dress and furniture, but unrealistically melodramatic as to plot—19th century.

412

U-plate
A flat piece of steel, bent at the ends in the shape of the letter U and pierced with holes for bolts, screws, and lines; a *spreader U-plate* keeps counterweight tracks apart, a *splice U-plate* ties one length of track to another, and a *spreader and splice U-plate* combines both functions.

up left; abbreviation, **U.L.** or **UL**
A stage position or area, left (the audience's right), upstage—Sometimes, a stage direction.

up left center; abbreviation, **U.L.C.** or **ULC**
A stage position, upstage of left center position—Sometimes, a stage direction.

upper balcony
The topmost seating area in an auditorium. British: Usually UPPER CIRCLE.

upper circle
A term, now chiefly British, for a seating area, usually the topmost, above the DRESS CIRCLE. U.S.: UPPER BALCONY, when the topmost such area is meant.

upper gallery
A term, chiefly British, for a balcony seating area, usually the topmost.

upper stage
Now commonly understood to have been the CHAMBER and the TARRAS, and sometimes also other space above the stage level (such as balcony windows)—Elizabethan, although not an Elizabethan term.

up right; abbreviation, **U.R.** or **UR**
A stage position or area, right (the audience's left), upstage—Sometimes, a stage direction.

up right center; abbreviation, **U.R.C.** or **URC**
A stage position, upstage of right center position—Sometimes, a stage direction.

up stage; up-stage; upstage
1. The entire back half of the stage. Hence also *upstage wall*, etc. 2. Any part of the stage considered as a position, in relation to something or someone farther front. 3. A transitive verb: To move upstage of another actor so that he cannot face the audience while speaking. Hence *upstaging* (noun). 4. Said of an actor who is haughty and self-centered.

U.R.; UR
Abbreviation of UP RIGHT.

U.R.C.; URC
Abbreviation of UP RIGHT CENTER.

usher
A person who leads spectators to their seats and distributes programs. Hence also *head usher, usherette*. British: Also as *attendant*. Also, to serve in such a capacity.

U.T.C. company
Short for *Uncle Tom's Cabin* company. See TOM SHOW.

utility
1. Short for UTILITY ACTOR (which see). 2. Said of stage hardware which is of general usefulness, as, a *utility clew*.

utility (actor)
An actor in STOCK (which see) who is available for a wide variety of minor roles and backstage tasks; a small-part player (see under SMALL PART). Called also a GENERAL UTILITY or a *utility man*. Hence *utility role*, etc.

utility character
A character in a dramatic piece who is useful but not essential in the development of the plot.

utility property
A property which is used as part of the scenic setting, as, household furnishings.

utility truck
A dolly, a wheeled platform or cart used to move scenery or other stage equipment.

V

valance; valence
A border or similar drapery which is hung above the front curtain to conceal the flies or above a window curtain to conceal a pole.

valve dimmer
A British term for a TUBE DIMMER.

vamp
1. To improvise, especially to substitute some makeshift for a scenic piece, a property, etc., in order to save time or money, or in an emergency. Hence *vamped up* (as of scenery made up from old scenic pieces). 2. A short introductory bit of instrumental music, often repeated more than once, before a song or dance, etc.—Especially, Vaudeville. 3. Short for VAMPIRE. Hence, to play the role of a vamp or vampire. 4. Short for VAMPIRE TRAP (or door).

vampire; short form, **vamp**
The character of a seductive person, especially of an amorous woman who debases her lover; an actress playing such a role. Hence *vampire* (or *vamp*) *part*, etc.

vampire trap; vampire-trap; short form, **vamp (trap)**
A trap with two spring flaps or leaves, in the stage or in a scenic piece; sometimes, a star trap. Called also *vampire door*. Named for a 19th century play, *The Vampire*.

variable transformer dimmer; variable load dimmer
An AUTO-TRANSFORMER DIMMER.

variety
1. A British term for vaudeville. Hence also *variety show*, etc. "Variety," which originally (in the 1880s) was a common term in America, has recently come back into American usage. 2. The

416

name of a periodical (1905–), currently "the ACTOR'S BIBLE" (which see). The initial letter is capitalized.

vaudeville
A stage entertainment consisting of varied acts, usually unrelated, usually brief, such as skits, songs, dances, and acrobatic feats; also collectively. Hence *vaudeville theatre, vaudevillian, vaudevillist*, etc. British: MUSIC HALL, VARIETY, and sometimes *vaudeville*.

vehicle
A dramatic composition considered with a view to its acting potentialities, as, a *starring vehicle*.

velarium
A British term for a ceiling cloth, hung loosely.

ventilator
1. In British terminology, a dramatic work or a performance so bad that the audience leaves. 2. An aperture above the gridiron, used to air and light the backstage space.

veritism
In the Stanislavski method, a guiding principle in stage production: The replacement of exaggeration and other falseness with sincerity.

verse drama
Dramas, collectively or singly, which are poetic. Hence *verse play*, etc.

version
An adaptation, a script which has been altered from its original form. Hence *acting version, condensed version, musical version*, etc.

vestibule
A British term for a theatre lobby (see LOBBY).

vice, (the)
A stock comic character (originally, probably not comic), a buffoon, a trouble-maker, sometimes personifying a particular vice—Medieval and Renaissance (in mysteries, but especially in moralities and interludes); later surviving under various names (as Fool, Clown, Matthew Merrygreek, etc.).

vignette
A glimpse, a portion of a view, a stage setting using selected realistic details to suggest to the spectator's imagination more objects than are actually shown (as, a corner of a room on a stage otherwise bare) or a large space (as, a view of a room beyond the main acting space). Also, to create such a setting, as on a space stage. Hence *vignette setting*, etc.

villain; (feminine) **villainess**
An ANTAGONIST (which see), an evil figure.

vis comica
The comic spirit or force—A Latin expression used in English. Often italicized.

vision
See LINE OF VISION.

vision cloth
A curtain used for a vision effect, with a gauze inset behind which an actor will be seen when light is thrown on him.

visual effect; visual-effect
See EFFECT.

vocal
A song—Musical comedy. Hence *vocalist, vocalize.*

void
See EMPHASIZED VOID.

vomitory
A rare term for a passage for spectators, opening from a bank of theatre seats.

W

wagon
Short for SCENERY WAGON.

wagon stage; (British) waggon
1. A stage using one or more SCENERY WAGONS (which see), sometimes with guide tracks, for quick shifting of scenes. Hence also a *wagon stage set.* See also JACK-KNIFE STAGE, SLIDING STAGE. 2. A stage built on a cart for outdoor performances; a PAGEANT (sense 2)—Medieval.

wait
1. Short for STAGE WAIT. 2. An intermission between acts.

walk a flat
In scene-shifting, to carry a flat upright. Followed by *up* or *down,* to raise a flat to, or lower it from, a vertical position by hand.

walk-around
1. A stage procession or march, or the music for it. 2. A kind of dance, or the music for it—Minstrel shows.

walker-on
An actor in a walk-on part (see WALK ON); an actor who plays such parts more or less regularly.

walking gentleman; (feminine) walking lady
An actor in a minor part, as, a bit actor or super. Collectively, *walking ladies and gentlemen.*

walking part
See WALK ON.

walking surface
The top of any practical structure (see PRACTICABLE) capable of bearing an actor's weight.

walking understudy; walk-on and understudy
An understudy in a walk-on part.

walk on; walk-on
An actor in a part without lines, an extra, a super; sometimes a bit actor, with a few lines to speak; the role itself, as, a *walk-on* (or *walking*) *part,* (to) *play walk-ons.* Also as WALKER-ON. To serve as an extra, or sometimes a bit, actor. Hence *walking on* (noun).

walk the boards
To act, to perform. See BOARD.

walk through
1. To rehearse not only by reading lines but also by adding physical movement. Also, the first rehearsal of this kind. 2. To act, to recite one's lines, perfunctorily. 3. Hyphenated: A part without lines, a walk-on part.

wall pocket
See STAGE POCKET.

Walter Plinge
See PLINGE.

wardrobe
Stage costumes (and articles associated with them) assembled for use in stage productions, or stored in the theatre; also, a room for their storage and repair. Hence *wardrobe master* (or *mistress*), formerly *wardrobe keeper.*

warehouse
See GO TO CAIN'S (WAREHOUSE).

warn
To give a signal (a *warning* or a *warning cue*) by bell, light, or voice to caution an actor or crew member to stand by for a coming cue.

wart
A DUTCHMAN (sense 1).

watch the gate
To see that the ticket-takers are carrying out their task, that the spectators are entering in good order, that the ticket sales are filling the theatre; it is the responsibility of the company manager to do so.

water curtain
1. A pipe pierced with holes, across the top of the proscenium arch just behind the asbestos curtain, from which water can be sprayed in the event of fire. 2. A pipe pierced with holes, crossing the stage near the footlights, sometimes used in outdoor theatres to provide a curtain of spray behind which scene-changes can be made.

water-joint; waterjoint
A plumbing joint sealed with water, connecting a pipe or rubber tube from a gas lighting unit to an outlet in the stage floor—19th century.

weak
Said of dialogue, body movement, a stage position, etc., which is deliberately unobtrusive, seemingly unemphatic, but which may actually be emphatic and important.

week-stand house
A ONE-WEEK HOUSE.

week-to-week notice
A CLOSING NOTICE (which see), stating that the current production will close at the end of the week unless its run should be extended by a subsequent notice. Also, a *week-to-week basis*.

well
A subcellar, used for machinery to work traps, etc. See also ORCHESTRA WELL.

well firmed
In British terminology, said of an acting part: Thoroughly memorized.

well-made play
A play marked by emphasis on plot, careful exposition, and the logical and economical development of situation and incident; the type was brought to a high level of dramatic craftsmanship by French dramatists in the 19th century (as the PIÈCE BIEN FAITE); it enjoyed a long vogue in translation and imitation in other countries, but the contrivances used, though technically excellent, often seemed slick and unconvincing, inadequate for the ideas attempted, and became subject to ridicule.

West End
The principal theatre district in London. Hence, collectively, the commercial theatres of that city. U.S. equivalent: *Broadway*.

wet rouge
A sticky rouge for coloring lips or cheeks.

wet white
Liquid white (see LIQUID MAKE-UP).

wheel
Formerly, in U.S. terminology, a circuit of theatres, or the syndicate controlling a circuit—Burlesque.

wheeze
A joke, gag, device, especially an old, creaky one.

whitening; whiting; white
1. Powdered chalk, used in scene-painting. 2. A make-up preparation (see CLOWN WHITE and LIQUID MAKE-UP). 3. See OPEN WHITE, a lighting term. 4. See GREAT WHITE WAY.

whodunit
A MYSTERY PLAY (sense 2).

wicket
A British term (rarely U.S.) for a ticket window, especially one in a BOX OFFICE.

wig
An artificial head-covering of hair (made of human hair or a substitute, or both intermixed, and often mounted on a network or other base) used as part of a stage costume. Also as *theatrical wig*. Hence also WIG MAKER, etc.

wigband
A cloth strip which holds a wig to the forehead.

wig line
The edge of a wig where it meets the face.

wig maker; wig-maker; wigmaker
A theatrical technician who prepares wigs.

wig-paste
A substance used to fasten a wigband in place and conceal the wig line; loosely, grease paint.

wig plot
A PLOT (sense 2) which indicates the use of wigs.

Wild West show
An entertainment dealing, not necessarily realistically, with the rough Western frontier period in the United States.

wind machine
An effect device to simulate the sound of wind, consisting of a wooden cylinder which turns against a piece of canvas or silk.

window
See BOX OFFICE, GHOST.

window flat
A flat with an opening for a window unit.

window opening
A window through which spectators can see, and which therefore requires a backing or other scenery.

window stage; window-stage
A playing space at a gallery window (see UPPER STAGE), over the platform stage—Elizabethan.

wing
1. Short for WING FLAT. 2. Usually in the plural: The offstage space at the side of the acting area.

wing and backcloth setting (or scene)
A stage setting using a drop at the back, borders at the top, and wings at the sides.

wing a part
In acting, to fasten the sides (pages) of a script to a wing flat or other part of a wall for quick reference during a performance. See also WING IT.

wing (flat)
A flat, usually one of four, usually a two-fold, and usually painted, which conceals the off-stage space at the side of the acting area and helps decorate the stage setting; often such a flat slides in a groove. Hence *wood wing*, etc.

wing flood
A floodlight designed for and used in the wings.

wing it
To act without having learned one's lines, relying on prompting or a quick glance at one's part before coming onstage. See also WING A PART.

wing-ladder
Formerly, in British terminology, a perpendicular strip of lights in the wings.

wing man
A stagehand responsible for the handling of the wing flats.

wing piece
A WING FLAT.

wing setting; winged setting; short form, **wing set**
A stage setting framed by wing flats, a backdrop, and borders.

winter theatre
A theatre or acting company producing plays in the winter (that is, normally from fall through spring) only. For a special British sense, see SUMMER THEATRE.

wire resistance
A British term for a RHEOSTAT.

wire (resistance) dimmer
A British term for a SLIDE DIMMER.

wire rope (or **cable**); short form, **wire**
A strong rope made of wire, used in the counterweight system. Hence *wire rope clip* (U-shaped), *wire guide.*

with
A preposition used in programs and advertisements, immediately below the title of a production, to identify a featured actor.

within
Behind the portion of the stage visible to the audience, behind the scenes, backstage—A stage direction.

wood border
A FOLIAGE BORDER.

wood wing; wood-wing
A flat or two-fold at the side of the stage, painted and cut to simulate a tree. Called also *tree wing.*

word
See GIVE THE WORD.

word rehearsal
A rehearsal for spoken lines rather than for body movement.

work a show
To carry on the operations necessary to stage production, during a performance, such as the changing of scenery and the management of lighting equipment.

workers' theatre
LABOR THEATRE (which see). Hence *workers' play*, etc.

working area
The stage area outside the acting area, available for stagehands' work.

working border
A BORDER (sense 1) which is moved up or down during performances.

working flies
A FLY GALLERY, when used for working rope lines.

working light
A WORK LIGHT.

working line
A LINE (sense 1) which is adjusted during a performance.

working manuscript
A prompt copy (see PROMPT BOOK).

working rail
The upper of the two rows of pins comprising a PIN RAIL (which see), used for the temporary tying of lines. Called also *fly rail*.

working rope
A WORKING LINE (which see).

working script
A WORKING MANUSCRIPT (which see).

working side
The PROMPT SIDE.

working title
A title for a dramatic work adopted temporarily, prior to staging, until a better title can be found.

work light; working light
A light used to provide illumination for rehearsing, scene-shifting, or other work onstage or backstage, rather than for the stage setting during performances.

workshop
1. Short for DRAMA WORKSHOP (also called *theatre workshop*).
2. A place backstage where equipment such as scenery and properties is made, repaired, painted, etc.

workshop flex
In British terminology, a cable for stage electrical use, which is not so heavy as the usual cable.

work upstage
To move gradually upstage (of another actor).

wow
1. To make an audience applaud loudly. 2. A very popular show.

X

X
Symbol used for CROSS (which see). Hence also XDR (CROSS *down right*), XUL (CROSS *upper left*), etc.

X-ray border light; short forms, X-ray light, X-ray
A first border light, one of the border lights farthest down-stage, equipped with a compartment, a reflector, and a color frame, and used to provide general illumination for the stage.

Y

yard
The PIT (sense 3)—Elizabethan.

yellow card
A request from a U.S. touring company, asking a local labor union in a town on the circuit to furnish stagehands.

yoke
A bracket used to hold a lighting unit to a batten, commonly U-shaped, sometimes universal in movement.